# I CAN TAKE YOUR PAIN AWAY

## A DOCTOR'S STORY

**Dr Sergey Sergeevich Konovalov**

with Elena Bogatyreva

◊

**Special English Edition**

translated and edited by Helen Rappaport

CREATION™

PUBLISHING

Special English edition first published in Great Britain by Creation
Publishing Limited, 2004

Creation Publishing Limited
PO Box 43291
LONDON E14 3XP
UK

www.creationpublishing.co.uk

ISBN 0-9547187-0-4

British Library Cataloguing in Publication Data
A CIP record for this title is available from the British Library

Whilst every effort has been taken to ensure that all information
contained in this book is correct at the time of publication, this book is
intended only as a guide and should not replace consultation with or
treatment by your doctor or any other healthcare professional.

The stories of recovery from ill health described in this book are genuine,
based on the accounts of real patients. Nevertheless, neither the author or
the publisher gives any guarantee or makes any representation that your
use or application of techniques in this book will be equally successful or
that they will be suitable to your individual medical needs. For this
reason the author and publisher disclaim any liability arising from the
use or application of the techniques and exercises contained in this book.

Text: Dr Sergey S. Konovalov and Elena Bogatyreva
English translation: Helen Rappaport
Illustrator: Tony Wilkins
Printed and bound in Great Britain by Short Run Press Limited, Exeter

# CONTENTS

# DEDICATION
# TO ALL MY PATIENTS EVERYWHERE
*By Dr Sergey Konovalov*


I dedicate this book to my patients, to every single one of the thousands and thousands who have come to me with their problems, their sufferings, in a distressed state and, sometimes, in despair, but yet still with a glimmer of hope in their hearts and minds. I dedicate this book to you, my dear friends. To those of you who have put your trust in me and who have had faith. Today we can say that we have won through. We have conquered not only sickness, but also ignorance; we have overcome the crude perception we had of ourselves and of the world around us. Today we are beginning to understand the true value of life and the true value of good health, but the most important revelation of all, and it is one we have reached together, is that of self-discovery: our own uniqueness and individuality in the midst of other unique and individual people, in a unique and individual world.

I dedicate this book to you, my dear patients, because you and only you have given and continue to give me the strength to keep going forward towards new discoveries and achievements. I honour you, dear patients, and thank God that he has united us in your hour of need. And may he protect you, your families and the good that you do.

*Dr Sergey Sergeevich Konovalov*
*17 February 1999*
*St Petersburg*

# FOREWORD
# TO THE FIRST ENGLISH EDITION
*By the Translator, Helen Rappaport*

Over the last twenty years or more, there has been an explosion of interest here in the West in alternatives to conventional medical treatment. Much of this has been a natural progression made by people who feel burdened and pressured by the modern world we live in, who, having come to reject the intrusive methods of modern-day medicine and drugs, have sought out different ways of coping with their physical illnesses and problems. The growing availability of holistic therapies such as acupuncture, shiatsu, reiki healing, yoga, meditation, and so on, has in turn spawned the publication of a plethora of books on self-help, healing and alternative medicine, all of them offering a wide range of remedies and treatments, and some making extravagant claims about quick and easy roads to recovery.

One might imagine therefore that we already have more than enough such books to choose from, so why should we stop and read yet another? Because this book is written by a Russian and offers a unique perspective that till now has never been available in English. Any Russian-speaker will confirm that it has a distinctive Russian voice – a compelling, sometimes messianic one that is quite unlike any other book you will ever read on alternative medicine. Translating Dr Sergey Konovalov's book (which was written in conjunction with Elena Bogatyreva, who is the narrator of much of the original text) I was struck by its many specifically Russian qualities, notably its spirituality and depth of feeling; the passionate conviction with which Dr Konovalov conveys his ideas; and the intensely moving testimony of some of the patients who tell their own uplifting stories in it. The capacity for faith and the ability to survive the worst kind of adversity has always struck me as being a peculiarly Russian trait – such stoicism is there in the novels of Tolstoy and Dostoevsky, in the devotion of the Russian Orthodox to their faith – a religious devotion that 73 years of communism never succeeded in breaking – and in an overriding and intense union that many Russians feel with nature and their Russian homeland. Many of these qualities resonate throughout the text, giving the book its uniquely Russian tone.

I have thus set out to preserve the linguistic and stylistic idiosyncrasies of the Russian original as much as possible, because they are so intrinsic to Dr Konovalov as both man and doctor, to his own personal belief systems and the spiritual and philosophical background that is the basis of all his work and thinking. But in translating the book I also had to ensure that it was accessible to readers in the West who knew nothing of Russian history, or the structure of the present-day Russian medical system, or the way people live and struggle in a country still trying to come to terms with the legacy of communism. This has necessitated some judicious editing or expansion of the text in certain places, as well as some reorganization of the structure of the original, in order particularly to present a cohesive overview of how Dr Konovalov came to the point he is at today, after many years in medical practice.

Life in Russia today is still hard for the vast majority of Dr Konovalov's patients; the former Soviet Union, of which Russia is part, lost more people than any other country as a result of over a century of war, revolution, famine and political oppression, under a communist system where life was one continuous struggle to earn enough to buy the everyday things which we in the West have for so long taken for granted. Suffering has been ingrained into the Russian psyche over many centuries of despotic rule, yet in learning to survive it the Russians have developed an astonishing capacity to endure. This book is in many ways a celebration of that ability to survive – of the joy experienced by ordinary Russians when, thanks to Dr Konovalov's therapies, guidance and dedicated support, they finally recover their health, in many cases being brought back from the brink of terminal illness. The joy of elderly people, long neglected by an overburdened and inefficient medical system, who have their lives finally restored to them after years of unendurable pain, is particularly moving.

The case histories that make up the core of this extraordinary book are not just a testament to the triumph of the human spirit over adversity, illness and pain, but also to the dedication of a truly extraordinary, almost self-effacing man, who has dedicated his life to ordinary people, giving them back not just their physical health but also a reason to go on living. In October 2003, I had the great pleasure of meeting both Dr and Mrs Konovalov when they were over in England visiting their son Yaroslav. One could not wish to meet a more charming and unassuming couple. Dr Konovalov is not one to trumpet himself, or his work, or the spectacular successes he has achieved with thousands of patients in Russia, yet despite a dogged refusal to self-advertise or in any way commercialise the work of his Humanitarian Rehabilitation Centre in St Petersburg, his name has become familiar to millions of Russians, who, over the last fourteen years, have been spreading the word among other, expatriate Russians now living in America, Britain, Israel and Europe.

This special revised and edited edition of *I Can Take Your Pain Away* is one in a series of books produced in Russia over the last ten years under the collective title of 'Books That Heal', which have now sold in excess of 5 million copies there in the last five years alone. It was translated and edited in consultation and collaboration with Dr Yaroslav Konovalov, to whom I owe my special thanks for his kindness, patience and generosity. I would also like to thank the publishing and design team of Creation Publishing's UK division for their constructive criticism and the design of the book jacket, logo and the company's publicity material.

Oxfordshire, England
January 2004

# FOREWORD
# TO THE SPECIAL, 2002 RUSSIAN EDITION

*By Elena Bogatyreva*

This book is dedicated, first and foremost, to those readers who are already well-acquainted with the work of the famous Russian doctor, Sergey Konovalov; to those who will not part with their copies of his books and who, reading and re-reading them, have only one complaint – that the paperback editions will not last for ever. It is for those who have already written more than one letter to the publishers saying that paperback copies are of no use, that it's not fair bringing them out because, after being read for a fifth time (!) the pages are falling apart. Indeed people don't read them five times, or even ten. They read them over and over again. And this is because the things that the pages of the 'Books That Heal' teach them are so extraordinary, that it is difficult to take in everything in one reading. People want to go back over familiar pages again and again, because not only do they open up new realms of knowledge, they also help people cope with illness, with their problems, and find a way forward. It helps them discover health and happiness, to visualize a whole new attitude to living, as well as to the life of the planet and the universe.

Those who have never visited Dr Konovalov's centre in St Petersburg read and re-read his books, in order to relive, vicariously, the extraordinary atmosphere of his treatment sessions, an atmosphere which is so movingly revealed on the pages of the questionnaires filled in by his patients. Regular patients (although it might be more accurate to call them followers, as their health has now been restored), many of whom have been seeing the doctor for more than ten years now, also re-read his books, in order not to lose touch with the path to harmony and a healthy life that has been opened up for them.

Patients from Kaliningrad, [near St Petersburg], and as far away as Sakhalin Island [in the Far East of the Russian Federation], today take part in link-up treatment sessions. The doctor's books are now being translated abroad. His work is now being talked about in Europe and in America, where growing numbers of Russian expatriates are spreading the word about him, and this is leading to an increasing demand for his books to be made available in English. For this reason, and in response to the wishes of our Russian readers, that is, the millions of Dr Konovalov's patients who already join in link-up sessions and write to him, this book is being republished in hardback. [Note: the English editions of the books will be in paperback. Editor]. We hope that copies will therefore last longer and be read as many times as desired without incurring any wear and tear.

The book that you hold in front of you contains material drawn from other previously published books by Dr Konovalov. The text has been augmented with a great many new examples of recovery sent in by the doctor's patients. In addition, you will also find included stories of recovery from patients who have been treated via link-up sessions, which will be fully explained in the book. This is not a book to be read in a day. Thousands of people write to us about how they would like to pass it on to their children and grandchildren. The knowledge imparted on its pages will be put to use by future generations.

The triumphant progress across Russia of the information-energy doctrine of Sergey Konovalov, is already an established fact. This is endorsed by the millions of sales of his books and the tens of thousands of letters received monthly both by the publishing house and the doctor himself. In fact, Sergey Sergeevich predicted that this would happen when the 'Prime-Evroznak' publishing house brought out the first of his books. He predicted it when the books had only just appeared on the shelves, at a time when people hardly knew what they were all about. 'Be prepared', he said, 'there will be a demand for millions of copies.'

We have done our utmost to ensure that the subject matter of this book is as well-structured, consistent and accessible for general consumption as possible, irrespective of a person's education and experience. The task has however been was made more complex by the phenomenon that is Sergey Sergeevich Konovalov – a man whose work cannot be neatly slotted into familiar systems of logic or our own preconceptions about life.

With this in mind, we have strived to convey the atmosphere that prevails at Dr Konovalov's centre, during his treatment sessions and all around him. As a result, you have before you a book which has been prepared with an awareness of its ongoing mission, a book which promises to play an enormous role in the destiny of many nations. It is a book that will find its rightful place in the worldwide, golden library of mankind.

# CHAPTER 1

# AN INTRODUCTION TO THE MIRACLE OF HEALING:

## TESTIMONIALS FROM FELLOW DOCTORS, SCIENTISTS AND EDUCATIONISTS

### The Miracle that is Both the Future of Medicine and of Mankind

From the moment he first appeared on earth, man has looked upon everything that is beyond the realms of his own human capabilities as a gift. Everything that is beyond the realms of a gift he has called genius. As for anything that does not fall within his own understanding – this he calls a miracle.

And so, if one had to summarize, this book is about the genius of a doctor who draws back the curtain of the unknown for people, and reveals to them what is known as the miracle of healing. All the many things that he has already achieved have become part of the history of the development of human civilization. It is impossible to predict what more awaits him, because it all falls beyond the bounds of human understanding and belongs in the realms of what we might call the supernatural.

Dr Konovalov's method, which returns people to a full and active life, is nothing short of a miracle. His knowledge is the basis for very many of today's theories on the recovery of health. Whatever one might say about Dr Sergey Konovalov, as his colleague I [Elena Bogatryeva] am only repeating other people's words, because it is impossible to have a narrow view of the man and his work. So, instead of repeating myself, and bearing in mind that the reader is more inclined to trust the opinion of experts, I will quote from a selections of letters sent to Dr Konovalov by fellow doctors and scientists, which will serve as testimony to his extraordinary gifts and his unique work.

## 'Here is the Book that Will Help You Embark on a New Life'

*'The most complex of life's arts are the art of teaching, the art of healing and the art of judging people.'* SOCRATES

Man is a combination of two worlds: one of infinite complexity and the other of infinite wisdom. Leo Tolstoy once wrote that 'an immortal soul requires an immortal deed – the continuous perfecting of itself and of the world'.

There is hardly a serious scientist today who rejects the existence of an omnipotent source of knowledge in the universe. But only exceptional people, endowed with God-given gifts, and who have been 'initiated', know the hidden paths that lead to the innermost structures of the cosmic 'information bank'. This 'database' preserves information on every phase in the development of every creature in the universe. Each natural, living organism goes through several, clearly defined stages of development – the life cycles of birth, growth and the attainment of maturity, followed by a prolonged period of decline. The main objective of modern man is to strive for self-knowledge and self-fulfilment, and to make use of the knowledge which comes to him from the depths of the universe, transmitted to mankind by those who have already been initiated.

Nature has endowed man with the ability for self-renewal and regeneration, which on many occasions has protected him from illness, from physical death and given him a new lease of life. However, with the passing of thousands of years, man has, in the course of his own physical development, almost totally failed to exploit his organism's capabilities.

Specialists and medical scientists have observed that at certain stages of his development, man has particular need of spiritual and physical improvement and other, additional, adjustments to the world around him. This relates in particular to the ages of 55 to 60. It is precisely at this time that we experience those classic feelings about the hopelessness and futility of life and when all sorts of physical ailments first begin to appear. At this critical period, it is essential that a person adjusts physically and psychologically, having recognized the natural, inner crisis they are going through and the need to progress to a new cycle of spiritual development. But people shouldn't have to go through all this when they are about to retire and about to collect their pension! Between the ages of 55 and 60, a person who is physically active, as well as intellectually and spiritually enriched, acquires a new surge of life-affirming energy. During this period, the creative, active part of a person's way of life comes to the fore, as he or she gains faith in themselves and in the existence of the healing energy of the universe.

It is a well-known fact that a weak person looks for an easy route to recovery, whilst a strong and brave one strives, of his or her own accord, to win for themselves a second chance. They need only good advice in order to be able to do this. For the wise, those who have accepted the faith, there is only one path – upwards along the spirals of knowledge – until ultimately they are born anew. This kind of internal, physical and spiritual renewal is facilitated by the treatment programmes and series known as the 'Books that Heal', devised by their great exponent, the physician and experienced professional, Dr Sergey Sergeevich Konovalov, a man renowned throughout Russia and abroad.

Not long ago, the twelfth anniversary of Dr Konovalov's spiritual-healing practice was triumphantly celebrated in St Petersburg, an occasion upon which noted Russian specialists and medical scientists acknowledged the supreme scientific significance of Dr Konovalov's information-energy doctrine and the effectiveness of his methods of treatment (see the testimonials that follow).

As doctor, scientist and a member of the International Academy of Ecology, Man and Nature Protection Sciences, Sergey Konovalov enlists his extraordinary natural talents and his medical knowledge in improving the well-being of human beings everywhere. One might say that the great Homer had doctors in mind when he remarked: 'One skilful salve is worth a hundred warriors.'

The Konovalov way to health is not one of passively waiting for a miracle cure, but rather a determined and dogged battle with their illness on the part of patients, as they travel the road to self-perfection and, with it, the acquisition of faith. In the words of Dr Konovalov: 'You must go forward with courage, without dwelling on the seriousness of your disease. Believe in yourself and in the strength that I will bring to you. Let us join forces in helping you break the shackles of your disease. And may your faith and your new-found knowledge help you in this.'

Dr Konovalov's 'Books That Heal' are written in an accessible and flowing style. They demand serious thought and are crammed with real-life, genuine testimonials from patients to their dramatic recovery from the most serious of diseases, some of them terminal.

The characteristic features of Dr Konovalov's books are their optimism, their faith in the possibility of recovery and their respect for humanity. The present book is no exception. ... It demonstrates that Dr Konovalov, as both teacher and healer, travels the road to recovery together with his patients, taking up and sharing with them both their suffering and their joy.

People who have not – due to various circumstances – had the opportunity of attending Dr Konovalov's treatment sessions in St Petersburg should understand that they nevertheless have a unique chance to rid themselves of their illnesses by reading his self-help books on healing. This can, of course, only be achieved through a concerted effort on the part of the individual to achieve self-perfection and with a firm belief in their own organism and in the doctor who has revealed the secrets of the universe to mankind.

Take up the book which will help you to begin a new life. Be healthy and happy!'

*24 March 2001*

*Dr V. S. Luchkevich*
*Vice-President of the International Academy of Ecology, Man and Nature Protection Sciences*
*Head of the Department of Public Health and Public Health Services, St Petersburg State Academy of Medicine*

## 'Perhaps if We Try Not to Avoid Confronting Important Issues They Will, in the Fullness of Time, be Explained'

'Medicine has progressed along a centuries-old path of development. Mankind has reached the greatest heights in technological innovation and the computerization of medical diagnostics and treatment. We have come to grips with genetic engineering and have pushed forward the boundaries of our knowledge about the human organism. But here lies the paradox. For thousands of years people have been suffering from illnesses that were first described by the great healers long before the modern era. And in the search to find new ways of curing them, we are once more returning to the works of Hippocrates. Unfortunately, the application of progressive technologies and the unjustified prescription of the most powerful, up-to-date drugs have led to a situation where the treatment of one illness has given rise to a great number of other complications. A significant number of people today lose their lives primarily as the result of chronic disease, and medicine has now accepted the concept of the 'incurable' disease.

To go against the ways of nature leads to conflict, the destruction of the equilibrium and disharmony. Every one of us, even the most eminent academic, from time to time feels the need to be at one with nature, to be healed by the power of the earth, water and the sun. Man's intellect recoils from the tempestuous power of the elements. A sense of our own powerlessness brings us back to reality, to the question of man's development as an integral part of life on earth.

The question of the origin of life on our planet is an eternal one. A system of logical reasoning and explanation of how this came about has already been established and the phenomenon had been given an exhaustive grounding in fact. So what more is there to know? ...

What we need is for scientists to acquire the ability to think like philosophers.

How can the wisdom and expertise of the ancient healers – their knowledge of the healing effect on the human organism of natural remedies – be applied and combined with the latest achievements in medical science?

We are attempting today to do this through the use of natural remedies. Meanwhile, the author of this book, the celebrated physician, Dr Sergey Sergeevich Konovalov, has been achieving extraordinary results through the power of his own unique gifts. In order for medical specialists to reach a fuller understanding and evaluation of his work, it is essential that, first and foremost, they attend his healing sessions. It is impossible not to sense, behind the calm exterior of these proceedings, the colossal effort, the tension and concentration of mind of a man who is both physician and healer. Indeed, his centre is full of patients suffering from the most acute diseases which traditional methods of treatment have failed to eradicate. In order to fully and comprehensively evaluate the results of his work one must spend time in the centre's computerized archives, working through tens of thousands of case histories.

What seemed a miracle to us one hundred years ago, now, today, seems utterly mundane. Today we see the evidence: Dr Konovalov gives significant help to hundreds and thousands of sick people with "incurable" diseases, across a whole range of cases where the gloomiest of diagnoses have been given.'

*Dr V. Kh. Khavinson*
*Director of the St Petersburg Institute of Bio-regulation and Gerontology*
*Vice-President of the Gerontology Society of the Russian Academy of Sciences*

*17 August 1999, St Petersburg*

## 'The Scientific Community Can No Longer Ignore Dr Konovalov's Work'

'First and foremost, I must state that Dr Sergey Konovalov has helped me overcome a serious illness of considerable duration and has significantly improved the state of my health.

But, more importantly, I must, in this instance, stress how essential it is that the attention of the wider scientific community is drawn to his method of healing, the results of which appear to be truly miraculous.

It is becoming more and more apparent to scientists and biologists that they will never be able to grasp the full extent of the amazing complexity of the human organism unless they are prepared to venture beyond the realms of their own current levels of knowledge and conventional attitudes.

This great gift, with which Dr Konovalov has been endowed by superior powers, and which cannot be either understood or explained by us at the present time, contains within it depths of knowledge and physical potential which humanity will need time to comprehend.

Humanity can only reach an understanding of this gift by constantly striving for perfection. And indeed, the faith that Dr Konovalov's patients have in their own recovery is part and parcel of the spiritual perfection which they achieve during the healing sessions. It has been said "To each according to his faith", which is why Dr Konovalov's abilities, as they have been revealed to me, seem to be truly messianic. They do not conform to any accepted thinking on "alternative medicine".

The successful treatment of thousands of people who believe in the doctor and in his teachings, brings one to the conclusion that Sergey Sergeevich Konovalov is a valuable national asset.'

*Professor Vitaly Morachevsky,*
*Doctor of Physical and Mathematical Sciences, St Petersburg State University*
*Member of the Russian Ecological Academy*

*16 November 1994*

## 'The Facts that Keep on Surprising Us'

'Please accept the sincere appreciation of the St Petersburg Teachers Training College for the noble work that you and your colleagues are doing for people.

We never cease to be amazed by the details reported in questionnaires or passed on by your patients during healing sessions. We are aware that this is no illusion, no outpouring of infectious mass emotion, but rather a serious, vital process whereby the patient is healed. We do indeed experience the influence upon us of the healing power of the living cosmos, which is so skilfully transmitted to us by the doctor.

Our physical recovery and the renewal of our mental equilibrium are accompanied by the enhancement of our professional, creative powers. And this in turn provides educationists, teachers and practitioners such as us with the prospect of achieving a wholeness of the person that is becoming ever more attainable. At the same time, we have become aware of many general problems in therapeutic and educational practice: the restoration of the teacher's and student's health, how to overcome setbacks in our psychological development or our individual feelings of inferiority in our day-to-day living.

So may the healing arts long continue to reign at your centre. We would also like to hope that, in the future, the development of scientific and creative contacts will be possible in the search for basic approaches to the process of the regeneration of the whole person and of the world around them.'

## 'The Intelligent Person has no Right to Fall Sick'

'As geologists of St Petersburg's State University, we heartily congratulate you and all your wonderful staff on your jubilee. For people like us, used to working with time-periods of hundreds of thousands, millions, and even billions of years, this tenth anniversary is but a moment in time, but we work with inanimate material. Many of us, by virtue of our upbringing and education, adhere to materialistic views about life on earth, but, at the same time, if we were to equate our understanding of God with that of Nature, then all divergence of opinion disappears. You, Sergey Sergeevich, work your unrepeatable miracles with that most valuable of things on earth – with life itself. You not only heal the physical bodies of a great many and different patients, but also bring our souls to perfection and sometimes even put us on the path towards goodness, and a more positive way of thinking.

Many years ago, Vladimir Soloukhin published an article: "Can an intelligent person get the flu?", in which he posited the idea that an observance of the basic rules of hygiene would protect people against illness. And now that you have come on the scene and taught thousands of your patients how to get well, we can, Sergey Sergeevich, paraphrase the words of Soloukhin: the intelligent person need fall ill neither with influenza, nor with chronic – and that includes the most serious of – illnesses; or, at the least, he should not have to put up with them. You remind us of the wise man who saves the hungry, not by giving them fish, but by teaching them how to catch them.

In particular, we value your amazing intelligence, and the tact and wisdom with which you approach us; how you are able, with literally a couple of words, to inspire in us new feelings of hope and optimism, and teach us to chose the correct path towards recovery even in the most complicated of situations that life places us in. We all thank our lucky stars that we have discovered your healing sessions and we wish you and your staff prosperity, new achievements in your work and every happiness.'

18

# CHAPTER 2

# THE THERAPEUTIC EFFECTS OF THIS BOOK:

## PATIENTS TELL THEIR OWN STORIES

### A Selection of Case Histories

It is hard to believe it, but Dr Konovalov is real. Everything that he does is beyond our comprehension, yet, on the other hand, much of it is totally grounded in reality. His analyses and medical conclusions testify to the recovery of his patients. Their letters and testimonies are sent in their thousands, giving voice to their gratitude, love and admiration for the doctor and for the way in which he has not just saved them from life-threatening diseases but changed their lives – forever. Here are just a few of them.

*From case history 1015727 (born 21 August 1939)*
'I am one of your patients and have been attending the fifth programme of treatment sessions.* I am registered as disabled (category 2). I want to share with you my joy at what my consultant gastro-enterologist has told me. I visited her surgery and she asked me what was the matter. "Doctor," I said, "I'd like you to look at my liver; I've got cirrhosis." She examined me and was extremely surprised. She told me that she had been a doctor all her working life and had never made a mistake in diagnosis. She was amazed when she read through the notes she herself had made the year before. "There's no sign of cirrhosis now." She arranged for me to have an ultrasound examination and other tests. After that I went to see her again. And she asked: "Who treated you and what did they use?" I said that I had been treated by Dr Konovalov. She was pleased and said with a smile that she had

heard many good things about you. As I left, she said: "Keep on going to Dr Konovalov. He has done wonders for you." And I wept with happiness. I'm not good with words, and can't find the right ones with which to thank you.

Thank you so much, dear Sergey Sergeevich. I am very grateful to you and I am so glad that I had faith in you from the start.'

*12.12.99. St Petersburg*
(* Note: each treatment programme consists of ten sessions)

### From case history 1015917 (born 12 September 1949)

'I am attending my 4th treatment programme ... I came to you with a problem with my spine, which is S-shaped, in the third stage of scoliosis and second stage of osteochondrosis. I also have osteoporosis. I was offered an operation at the Institute of Orthopaedics and Traumatology. In addition, they recommended I wear a surgical corset. I turned down the operation and on 25th January 1999 I had my first consultation with you. I sat there in my wheelchair, choked with tears and emotion.

The treatment I went through was painful. My leg was aching and I couldn't sit comfortably. During the main part of the treatment session I was unable to sleep, just sat there with my eyes closed. And on top of this, during the second series of treatment sessions, I had lumbago from my spine, down to my spleen, and then in the left leg and the knee. Later on, the pain in my left leg became much worse, and it hurt whether I was lying down or sitting. For the first three treatment programmes I wore a surgical corset, and could bring very little water with me because it was so difficult. I had to sort out everything in my handbag, every object weighed something, and I could barely make it to the clinic. I could hardly walk with the acute pain in my left leg, let alone carry anything.

Apart from the problems with my spine, I have also been diagnosed with other complaints, but these pale into insignificance compared to how difficult it had become for me to walk. I'd take a few steps, stop for a minute in order to change the position of my back, and then move on.

You can just imagine my joy, when now, during my fourth treatment programme, I am already walking without the corset and can carry half a litre of water around with me! I am very grateful to you, I am in your debt, thank you so much for your hard work. I feel as though, little by little, the pain is going away. It's easier for me to walk. And coming to the treatment sessions makes me feel good.

I come and visit you as though it were a day out, like visiting a loved one, a close friend who is always there waiting for me. With love and gratitude.'

*7.07.99 St Petersburg*
*(In October 2001 she felt well and was no longer wearing the corset)*

### From case history 1011620 (born 3 April 1920)

'Thank for curing not only our ailments but also for healing our souls. During the time I've been attending your treatment sessions my personality has completely changed. I used to be hypersensitive. Even a child could upset me. But now I pay no attention to such things. I've stopped going on at my son and my grandchildren, and I now get on well with them. I was afraid of everything before, and self-conscious too. It was a real problem even for me to go to the Housing Department. But now I feel confident, like a real human being – like how I felt before I was ill. This has been of far greater service than merely taking my pain away.

During the summer I had a stomach ulcer, but when I recently had an endoscopy they could no longer detect it. I'd had bad blood tests (very low haemoglobin), but the latest tests came back with good results. The acute pains in my heart, liver and kidneys have disappeared. No protein was found in my urine tests. More importantly, I don't have any throbbing or pain in my head, oesophagus or bowels. My bowels work without the terrible pains (I used to have spastic colitis). The stones in my gall bladder had dissolved. Last year, I fell over and damaged my patella. The surgeon said I would never walk again. I would have to take painkillers and would only be able to sit down with the aid of crutches. That was on the 3rd of June, but by August I was already going mushroom-picking in the woods with just a stick. And yet more joy – the latest tests showed my blood sugar level is normal. My hair is growing well, it's thick and shiny and a good, dark colour. I had been having fits after my operation (for a brain tumour), but since attending your treatment sessions I haven't had a single attack. I live alone and can prepare my food, wash and tidy up for myself. I love preparing and cooking meals for people, I love having guests. I like doing the washing. I sleep for an hour or two during the day. I don't watch the television. I read and listen to records. I love classical music, operatic arias and romances. I go to the theatre, to exhibitions.

In six months' time I will be 80 years old. And I am living life to the full. Thank you for everything, doctor.'

*October 1999, St Petersburg*
*(In October 2001 her condition was stable)*

### From case history 1009885 (born 1950)

'This is my fortieth treatment programme. I am extremely happy and I want to share this with you. I've had an examination at the Institute of Oncology. The doctor took so long examining my breasts that I started worrying and asked "What is it?" She replied "I can't find any sign of the fibroadenoma in your right breast which was detected during your examination last year." "It must have gone away", I replied. She gave me a strange look, but nevertheless noted down that the previous symptoms could not be found. This made me enormously happy – it was proof that the body can fight back and heal itself.

I rushed home, in order to tell my husband the good news as soon as possible, but then I suddenly remembered I shouldn't really do this. But all the specialists' examinations had made me so happy. The gynaecologist says everything is fine. My blood is normal. Thank you so much, Sergey Sergeevich, for everything. However, there's still my benefit assessment on the 15th October. Please could you help me in this difficult situation. I very much hope I won't be deprived of financial support from the state at this complex and difficult time.

*October 1999, St Petersburg*
*(In October 2001 condition stable. Continues to attend treatment sessions)*

### From case history 1009004 (born 1944)

'I have attended 27 treatment programmes with you since 6 September 1994, with a break only during the summer. I'd like to report back to you on my last nine treatment programmes since March 1998. With yours and God's help, I have made great progress; after the first, I had rejected all the medication prescribed for me by the Cardiology Institute, without which, so my consultant there had told me, I wouldn't last a month. Little by little, the attacks of stenocardia stopped tormenting me. I was no longer short of breath. My pulse, which was usually 120–140 beats per minute, is now normal. I had been diagnosed with chronic diffuse glomerulonephritis, and had lost seven kilos [15 lbs] by the summer of 1999 (going from 73 to 66 kilos; [160 lbs to 145 lbs]). But after the two most recent courses of treatment it has returned to normal. After the one in October I noticed I was getting thinner, although my stomach, which had become distended after my gynaecological operations, stayed the same. I wasn't entirely happy with the results and in my mind I appealed to you: "Dear Sergey Sergeevich, could you somehow get red of this stomach of mine too?" Of course, I said it as a joke, but the effect was striking – my stomach began to shrink and even my navel, which had long since been hidden in rolls of fat, was just about visible. As a result, I now weigh 60 kilos and am 160 metres tall.

The attacks associated with my carotid stenosis, and which were accompanied by severe headaches, loss of speech, and brief periods of unconsciousness, have long since stopped. But the persistent swelling on the left side of my neck, which got worse whenever I was under stress or unduly emotional, still hadn't gone. Then two days ago I noticed that it had vanished. During this time I had not once been bothered by my reactive arthritis and my joints hadn't bothered me in bad weather either. I haven't been troubled with osteochondrosis for five years now, or haemorrhoids either. My bowel movements are practically normal (constipation is rare and no longer lasts for 7–10 days, as before). Insomnia, which plagued me for years (I never got to sleep before four or five in the morning) has gone, with rare exceptions and then only with good reason. My fibroadenomatosis has also disappeared.

And there's a change too in my dependency on nicotine. Without the least effort, I can get up in the morning without thinking about having a cigarette, although I've still got the bad habit of smoking one after breakfast.

Dear Sergey Sergeevich, I cannot find the words to express the feelings I have for you – the gratitude, respect, and appreciation. I am very thankful that you are here, that you have chosen this path in life, for your unceasing labours, for your love, and for giving us not only hope, but also the confidence that we will be healthy both in body and in mind.

I forgot to say that all these successes have been achieved against the backdrop of a life that has been far from easy. I have many family difficulties and problems, worries about my granddaughter, my daughter and my son-in-law. They are all tired and so I take a great deal upon myself. I often don't get enough sleep, I have to prepare tests for my students and the following day go through the answers with them.'

*December 1999, St Petersburg*
*(In October 2001 she felt well. Her treatment sessions continue)*


### From case history 1012331 (born 1945)

'I have been attending treatment sessions since March of 1996: this is my 23rd series. I came to you with four fundamental problems, which had caused me constant pain:
1. Loss of energy – I felt better immediately after the first session
2. Radiculitis – this hasn't bothered me for two years now
3. The pain in my knees has gone; the pain in my arms – I now only have a slight pain in the fingers of my right hand and my right shoulder
4. Bleeding fissures on the soles of my feet – four or five on each foot simultaneously.

This summer everything was fine. In the autumn they once more started to appear, but after the third session of this series new fissures did not appear, and I hope will not recur.

The 3rd of December was a very happy day for me. We had a medical at work. I specially wanted to see the eye specialist, as I had felt that my eyes were better, they had stopped hurting, although I wasn't a hundred per cent sure, because I hadn't had them checked. And now I'm happy because I've got rid of one more complaint. The blood pressure in my eyes is normal: 18 in the left eye and 19 in the right. For the last 20 years it had been 25. My grandmother had glaucoma and both her eyes were operated on.

Many thanks indeed for everything that you are doing for us. God bless you. With sincere gratitude.'

*7 December 1999, St Petersburg*
*(In October 2001 she was still visiting the clinics. A very good course of recovery)*

*From case history 1016605 (born 1970)*

'I am on my 7th treatment programme. I came to you first in March 2000 with the following diagnoses: three myomas of the uterus, pituitary adenoma, hormone disturbance and (worst of all) sterility.

I came to you after my faith in conventional medicine had completely collapsed, after the doctors, at a loss to know what to do, had quietly turned their backs on me. Some of them suggested surgery as the only hope of a cure. Others advised I should continue with a programme of in-vitro fertilization, although I'd already had three unsuccessful attempts at it.

When I came to you, I somehow immediately had a feeling of confidence that, no matter what, everything would be fine. Your treatment sessions gave me a sense of peace and I have stopped rushing around, forever in a hurry.

My greatest wish has come true! It happened during my second treatment programme. I cannot express in words the joy and happiness I felt when I found out that I was pregnant.

The pregnancy (now 38 weeks) has generally been going well. During the 4th and 5th treatment programmes my myoma of the uterus gradually got better. My general health improved. My bowels are now like clockwork.

Dear doctor, I wanted to say a huge thank you to you for all that you have done for me, for having given the spark to a new life on this earth.

I have no doubts that I shall give birth to a fine, healthy baby. Indeed, the fact that it is growing in my womb has only been possible thanks to your treatment. All that I can say to you is thank you, and offer you my deepest respect. Dear Sergey Sergeevich, wish me well for the forthcoming birth.'

*26 March 2001 St Petersburg*
*(On 6 April 2001 she gave birth to a girl. All is well)*

*From case history 1017945 (born 1951)*

'I am just completing my 8th treatment programme, without noticing how time has passed and that it is already my second year. At the first treatment session of my 1st series I was absolutely amazed. My pain receded; I was shaking all over, my arms and legs were trembling and I felt cold.

I attended four treatment programmes during 2000. I didn't pay any attention to the diagnostic periods. Since October 2000 I had been aching all over, there was pain everywhere. I have been saved by your healing booklets* and by the healing water**. The diagnostic period lasted from three to six days. But I kept in mind your words: 'Have patience, my dear.' Then I had a dramatic weight gain. You said that it was renal insufficiency. But what was noticeable was that my toes straightened out, the bonelets reduced, my knees stopped twisting, and the backaches receded. My radiculitis no longer bothers me. For this last year and a half, I haven't had bronchitis, or wind. I have daily bowel movements and my stomach doesn't bother me. In the past, whenever I got up in the morning I couldn't so much as pass a glassful of urine from the whole of the night, but now it's as it should be. I'd had a prolapse of the back wall of my womb – but that has now righted itself. My right kidney had dropped, but now everything's fine. I've forgotten all about my angina.

I am keener than ever to come to your clinic, to your place where wishes are fulfilled, where there is music and tranquillity. I don't feel this in church, where the atmosphere is completely different. Take care of yourself. We need you so much. God grant you strength and the patience to continue helping each and every one of us.'

*18 June 2002 St Petersburg*
(* the term 'healing booklet' is frequently used by Russian patients to describe the healing leaflets devised by Dr Konovalov as part of the self-help programme that patients can follow at home; **'healing water' is similarly used by patients to refer to the specially energized water that is also part of the self-help programme.)

### From case history 1018808 (born 1 January 1932)

'I am now taking part in my 7th treatment programme. I am very happy to tell you that practically all my aches and pains (more than 90 per cent) have gone. First of all, I can walk normally and sometimes even run, and yet before I was treated by you I could only walk by holding on to the wall. This was the main reason I came to your clinic, even though I had many other ailments. My right arm is fine now, yet before I could hardly lift it. The osteochondrosis of my spine doesn't bother me any more, my left hip joint doesn't trouble me, and my liver and pancreas are fine. I don't have any wind. I can bend and unbend the fingers on my right hand, the growths on my left arm have disappeared. My bladder has settled down and I no longer have to keep running to the toilet. I don't get cramp in my feet at night. My memory has improved. But the most wonderful thing that has happened is with my right leg. I broke it fifty years ago. After they took off the plaster-cast it remained swollen and I was left in constant pain. I had long since become reconciled to this and tried not to pay it any attention. And then, just recently, I noticed that there was no swelling and pain any more. This is something that had plagued me constantly for fifty years and now it has completely disappeared. What a miracle!

Dear Sergey Sergeevich, during the whole time I've been treated at your centre I haven't taken a single tablet, yet previously I couldn't go for a single day without them. That too is a miracle! Thank you very much for everything. With the deepest respect and admiration, and my sincerest affection.'

*February 2002, St Petersburg*

'I suffer from the following diseases: dropping of both kidneys, chronic pyelonephritis, salt deposits in my bladder and ureter, stomach ulcer, chronic gastritis with high acidity levels, chronic enteritis, colitis, stage II endometriosis of the lining of the womb, yeast colpitis, streptococcal infection, chronic tonsillitis, stomatitis, herpes, osteochondrosis of the spine, intercostal neuralgia, neuralgia of the facial and trifacial nerves, neuralgia of the vagus …. All of these became much worse after the death of my mother. Terrible pain; I couldn't eat anything (lost weight and became nothing but skin and bones). But I had to go on living, to bring up my children who themselves weren't very well and had health problems. The doctors in the clinic bemoaned the fact (in my opinion people shouldn't talk like that in front of patients) that my children might end up without a mother, rather than offering their support. And then, when things were as bad as they could be, I found out about you, doctor. I was given, or rather, received your first book as a gift. At first I didn't believe it and didn't even bother to read it. But a few days later I felt really awful when I was out in the car, so bad that I didn't know what to do with myself. I thought I ought to go to the hospital. We turned round and went back home. I was literally praying and begging to God and the blessed Virgin Mary to help me, save me. To my amazement, by the time we got home, the pain had receded. I went into the building, but not sooner had I entered the door of our apartment than I felt as though someone or something was urging me: "Take the book and read it; it will be your salvation." There and then I went and looked for the book, found it and straight away began reading. I couldn't tear myself away from it. I read it in one go and more than once. I felt a sense of relief, of calm and was filled with hope. Aunt Nadya, a relative of Andrey's, gave it to me. We rang her up and asked her to get a subscription for a treatment programme. And she, to my enormous gratitude, made me a present of a subscription to your healing sessions. It has been a most precious gift. Nadezhda Fedorovna is a regular patient of yours. And so, in July 1999 I first came to see you and I shall keep coming until I am fully recovered. By the 2nd treatment programme I had already recovered my appetite and I can now eat everything and my weight is normal (I've gained 5 kilos).'

*20 October 1999, St Petersburg*

## The Testimony of a Medical Practitioner

'I am writing to tell you about the recovery of four patients after receiving external treatment and reading the case histories in your book. In all cases, the patients achieved complete recovery from their clinical symptoms. I would like to draw particular attention to the rapid reduction in inflammation effected by the healing leaflet: leukocytosis 15.8 dropped to 9.3 and bronchial obstruction was reduced.

1. A patient with a duodenal ulcer, exacerbated by leukocytosis of 15.8, of uncertain causation. Two days after first consulting the healing booklet the leukocytosis was 9.3. Before the booklet was used the leukocytosis had ranged between 15.8, 14.2 and 14.8.
2. Severe, double pneumonia, confirmed by X-ray, accompanied by a high fever and obstructive syndrome had progressed to clinical recovery by the ninth day. The obstructive syndrome had completely disappeared. Rasping breath, with shallow, dry and micro-vesicular wheezing had changed to vesicular breathing and the temperature was normal.

3. Acute respiratory disease, complicated by bronchitis with a discharge of rich purulent sputum, brought on by exudative pleurisy of the tuberculous aetiology, was transformed into a full clinical recovery, the improvement of the patient's condition, the normalization of the temperature, and the cessation of coughing and the discharge of sputum.

4. An acute case of chronic obstructive bronchitis and first signs of bronchial asthma. After external treatment and the use of the case histories in the healing booklet, the patient made a complete clinical recovery. After external treatment, the spirogram did not detect any fault in the bronchial airway or any expiratory constriction of the respiratory tract.

The experiment took place on Sundays between 21.00 and 21.30. (the healing leaflet was recharged at each session).

Dear Sergey Sergeevich, thank you very much for everything: for healing, for hope, for the sheer fact that you are here, among us. We are in great need of you.'

*Dr Larisa Vasilievna Spiridonova*

# CHAPTER 3

# THE GIFT OF HEALING

The modern-day reader has, in recent times, been exposed to a huge number of stories about miraculous healers, and to incredible, almost fantastical tales about things that have happened to this or that person as the result of their encounters with UFOs, alien civilizations, the sixth dimension of outer space, and so on. At first, such stories capture our attention, but in the end they inevitably disappoint us. Those looking for gimmicks in the work of Dr Konovalov will be disappointed. He is no showman, and his work is not a spectacle. All there is to see during one of his healing sessions with patients at the Humanitarian Rehabilitation Centre in St Petersburg is a man, alone on stage, whose only tools are his unique and calming presence, his soothing voice and his own beautiful, specially composed music.

And so, my task [i.e. Elena Bogatyreva's – the original co-author; Ed.] in this book is to tell you about the work of Dr Konovalov in as full and detailed way I can, to explain the path he has chosen in life, beginning with his early life in Ukraine and his army service and describing his progression over the course of the last thirty years from doctor to healer, and how it came about that he received the special knowledge to be able to follow this path.

Basing what I say primarily on the doctor's own experience of healing, that is, on practical results, I shall reveal, step by step, both the kind of person Dr Konovalov is, as well as explain his amazing theories, supported by concrete results and patients' testimonies. The reader must understand that we are dealing here with an exceptional phenomenon for which there is no precedent either in present-day medicine or in our current scientific understanding of the universe. This book contains nothing superfluous, not a single page which can be skipped without something significant being missed. Every detail is important, because it is this kaleidoscope of detail that makes up the path which Dr Konovalov follows, along which we too must travel to be initiated into the process of healing. Yet, on the other hand, writing about this is also extraordinarily easy, because the volume of information passed on to me by Dr Konovalov is limitless; what is more, I have at my disposal thousands of testimonies to the recovery of thousands of patients.

## The Necessary Path Along Which Every Step is Painful

It is mankind's destiny that from time to time people such as Dr Konovalov should appear on earth – people who can take our pain upon themselves, and our spiritual burdens too. Books have been written about some of these people and seem nothing short of fantastical. Other healers have been canonized in sacred texts down through the ages, whilst yet more have since sunk into oblivion. But the saddest thing of all is that not a single one of them was able to escape either stoning by the mob, or persecution and words of abuse. These amazing people were aware, from the very outset, of the thorny path that lay ahead. And yet they sought no other.

Why can't they live as others do and content themselves with doing small acts of kindness to the needy and unfortunate? If they are so gifted then why not seek out a career in some prestigious field of science? Why should they choose a path where every step is painful and reject all the benefits and respect offered them as professional scientists? What motivates them? Providence? A superior power? God?

And when will the human race begin to look upon such people as a gift to them? Could it possibly happen now, today? Has the time perhaps at last come for us to recognize a miracle in the midst of our rational world? To recognize it, wonder at it and then, after encountering it, set out to be better, purer and happier in ourselves? Perhaps we should be more disposed to acknowledging the existence of such wonders instead of repeating the pattern of centuries by rejecting such things out of hand, as heresy.

Whichever way things turn out, whatever fate has in store, whatever you may decide for yourself, this miracle definitely already exists. Which means that we have been given the chance – through Doctor Konovalov – either to embark on a new life or to stay the way we are, which in turn means that we must go on living with all our illnesses, each one of us alone, and isolated in all our misfortune.

## The 'Books That Heal' are the Future of Mankind

The series of books conceived by Dr Konovalov [of which there will be 16 in print in Russia by the spring of 2004] describe his life's path, his gifts, his lectures and healing sessions. They describe the causes of illness, the concept of the sensitive-body system, the origins of the universe and many, many other things.

Dr Konovalov was and remains a scientist, a researcher and a medical practitioner. For this reason, he feels there is no need to swamp the reader with a mass of knowledge that they will not be able to take in, even if it is of the greatest interest. One must learn how to make proper use of any kind of knowledge and I ask the reader to be patient. This book tells you everything. It is a book which life itself has written and will continue to write, as Dr Konovalov will now relate:

*My Dear Reader*

*I have been writing this book over the course of many, many years. I don't know whether it will ever be published\*... In my hours of relaxation away from my everyday work I express myself in music or like this, sitting at my typewriter. Over the last few years I have put together most of the pages of this manuscript. But I haven't managed to sort them into a proper order. And there's a reason for this: my work has no end, there is no limit to it. I actively seek it – it is precious, wonderful and never-ending.*

*Every time I sit down in front of my typewriter, I find it hard, very hard, to bring myself to write about things that are of no interest to me in terms of personal knowledge. I've long since left this behind and it's all been laid down in my practice. I am moving ahead: my interest is there, ahead of me, and I don't want to stop, let alone look back. I don't need to do so anyway, because what awaits me is a real-life patient who is expecting my help. And it's essential they get it right now, because tomorrow may be too late. Patients come to me as a last resort and it is my duty to help them.*

*Nevertheless, this book is still relevant, because it is about you, it is for you and dedicated to you ...*

*I ask God to give his blessing to this book, because I know only too well that tomorrow I will have no more time to think about it, because, from first thing in the morning till late in the evening, my battle against the illnesses with which people come to me will once more be renewed.*

*How can I tell you about everything that I know today? How can I possibly find room for all I know within the meagre sentences and lines of a book?*

[* This observation was made before the first book came out]

## Doctor Konovalov's Great Gift

The bulk of the practical material in this book has been written or conveyed to me by Dr Konovalov. It is a great responsibility to present that material in a way that best conveys its full implications to the reader. But the responsibility is not an onerous one; on the contrary I find it extraordinarily inspiring. The first healing session I attended filled me with a sense of exaltation, as though I were being bathed in a whole ocean of energy. I have a large family and a great deal of work, and as a result suffer from chronic insomnia. But I've got used to it. I was still half asleep when I walked to the first healing session early one morning. Yet I came home feeling as though I had just spent a month in a health resort. And that was only my first impression. A week later, I had come to understand that Dr Konovalov's great gift in winning over even the most hardened and unhappy of hearts is to be found, not in his skills at transmitting healing energy, but in a genuine and unconditional love for humanity that is far beyond words. After three weeks I gave up any attempt to find a logical explanation for what precisely makes this extraordinary man tick. I am now convinced that it is impossible ever to 'know' him. He is like a precious jewel with a limitless number of facets, which means that every time you see him, you find something different in him, notice something new, something that previously had been unfamiliar. Maybe this happens because we ourselves are changing with him. It's impossible to pigeonhole the doctor, fit him into any convenient category; he cannot be comprehended, nor described in terms of some kind of phenomenon. At his healing sessions, when he opens up his soul to those gathered there, it is clear that everyone can sense the breath of the universe.

*From case history 1001098 (born 1963)*
'Thank you for my 14th treatment programme. You had a profound effect on me. Despite the fact that this was not the first time we had heard the music in the treatment centre, nevertheless you have injected something new into every single one of your counselling and therapy sessions. With your emotive music, you stimulate our emotions and make us more and more sensitive to things. The session was a complete outpouring of love.

Love in all its many and great manifestations. The love of the mother and the child; of the woman and the man; of man and the universe; of the painter and his canvas; of the composer and his music. The energy of love!

For myself, I can only say that I come to the centre more for spiritual renewal than for my physical health. Is it really possible to come just for the sake of one's health?

It strikes me that we come to the centre in order to gain a greater understanding, an explanation of things, and in order to find the answers to questions – to discover them for ourselves and not simply have them handed to us.

For can someone really recover their health if they don't work on their spiritual being as well, if they don't try to understand why they fell sick in the first place? Indeed, sickness of the body is the consequence; it is sickness of the soul that is the cause. And it is very important to understand this.

We can't, of course, see the correlation between things that happened ten or twenty years ago and our present illness. It was, after all, so long ago. For all we have now is sickness, which gives us no respite, day or night. It hurts and torments us. Isn't this all that matters? No, it isn't! If we once had a reason for getting ill then that means we also have the power and the incentive to overcome it. All we need is to be aware that we did something wrong in our lives, that we hurt someone, wished someone harm, let someone down, or didn't share something with someone. We must go back and beg forgiveness. But even this is not enough.

We must first be renewed spiritually, and only then is physical recovery possible. And to do this we must have faith. We must have faith and not just trust to luck. But what is the difference between these two ideas? As far as I'm concerned, a great deal. To trust to luck is for now, for the moment, it is transient. It is merely to be on the safe side; but having real faith is a state of being, forever. With faith you cannot have doubts. Doubt is a poison which destroys faith.

We need to believe in God, in ourselves, in the energy of creation [a term coined by Dr Konovalov which will be explained in this book; ed.]. Only such an unshakeable belief can help those people suffering from diseases deemed by conventional medicine to be the most serious and incurable – the people you invite up onto the stage. If they give in to doubt they will not be cured. For this journey through pain, horror and suffering towards spiritual and, after that, physical recovery is all about faith in God and in ourselves. No matter how frightening and difficult and protracted this journey may be, it will end with your victory over illness, but only if you have faith.

Search for that saving grace, that island of hope within yourself and work on it, develop it until it has turned into solid ground, on which you can stand upright and say to yourself: "I am well again." It is you, dear Sergey Sergeevich, who, for the last ten years, have been teaching us how to take up this difficult task, to learn how to believe in God, in ourselves and in the universe.

I would like to say this to those who are in doubt: where else on earth will you find a place, or a person, who will teach you these things? What doctor is going to listen to the whole of your story, tell you what to do and inspire you with confidence in your own innate strength, and help you to become one with the energy of creation? Who else is there who will share in all the trials and tribulations of our illnesses, other than you, dear Sergey Sergeevich?

Forgive me if what I've written sounds over-emotional. I was overcome by my feelings and the desire to share with you and your patients what I have learnt as a result of coming into contact with you at the healing sessions. I am not a beginner; I've been attending our centre since 1991. You have to know how much we love you and value you.

My thanks for the long-suffering and courageous way in which you help us get better. With love and respect ...'

*14 July 1999, St Petersburg*
*(In October 2001 all was well)*

**From case history 1002226 (born 1945)**
'I am, as it happens, in constant contact with you, but from a distance. I get

answers to many of my questions at the healing sessions, and I thank you for this. It's impossible to overestimate the things that you now inspire in us. My God, there are times when we can't even explain to ourselves what is going on in our lives, why we behave as we do. Sometimes it seems to me that I'm of no use to anyone, and that maybe that's how things are. And then I suddenly hear your words: "Learn to love yourself". ...

And really, to love oneself and not pass through life unnoticed, to find the time to associate with people dear to your heart .... I have no doubt that you yourself Sergey Sergeevich are one of these people, and you're there not just for me. God gave you the good fortune to be able to recognize not only human suffering, but also the joy of communicating with people's souls. Maybe I'm wrong, but it seems to me that, as a rule, a person's soul is pure, trusting and easily wounded, which is why it is often closed off to others in order to avoid being hurt. What a joy it would be, if it were possible for a person to go through all the stages of growth and development on earth and remain the true person they are, without playing a role, or several roles.

You know, somehow or other, I seem to have spent my whole life looking out for other people. This can happen in entirely unexpected situations – on public transport, for example – or in regular contact with relatives, friends and acquaintances. There are so many dramas and crises going on all around, in which we, in one way or another, find ourselves taking part. Today, at our treatment centre you addressed us with the words: "Begin with yourself!" And you are absolutely right. How simple it is, if you love yourself, respect yourself, and don't get into quarrels (for whatever reason); if you look upon the people around you as fellow human beings, make people happy, and perhaps make a small gift to someone who isn't, and do it with a smile. Such things give me a kind of joy, a happiness at the thought that this child (woman, man, or elderly person), whom I've met by chance as I make my way along, will in turn have the desire to give some small happiness to somebody else ...

You know, the last time I came, it struck me that things must be very hard for you right now. Forgive me if it seems a little tactless to write like this. But the thought keeps coming back to me ... You are so attentive and caring towards each and every one of us. Yes. These are very difficult times we live in, when, every now and then, you find yourself thinking that you are living out of your time. So many lies, such bad behaviour, I don't even want to talk about it … And it's so difficult to hold on to our human sympathy.

The purer a person is, the more they have to go through. That's the way things are; it's outside our control and was so before. And coming into this life, to a greater or lesser degree, we have broken down under the pressure of reality. I wrote to you previously about how I've spent my whole life looking out for people and that I'd long since come to the conclusion that Leo Tolstoy so succinctly expressed: "The eyes are the windows of the soul." Sergey Sergeevich, your eyes are the eyes of someone with a capacity for unlimited, unconditional love towards people. It is no accident that God gave you the good fortune to lead us sinners towards regeneration.

You draw to you the pure light of love for everyone of us. So long as others do not hurt me, then I, in turn, have no need to hurt them; and I can in all truth say that love such as this is a reciprocal thing. The more you come to understand it then the happier you are. It's true, Sergey Sergeevich. How well I understand the woman who declared her love for you. I've met such people in our treatment centre.

Having gone through a lot of things in my life and still not knowing what it finally has in store, I bow my head before your great achievements. You keep telling us that our coming to the healing sessions is a duty. This is true; the truth being that many people have to struggle just for the chance to get here. But all this pales before your work, which in truth is superhuman. Thank you for your persistence, your intense effort, the sleepless nights, and the love you give for the preservation of humanity on this earth.

Your light attracts not just people who are suffering. It's a shame that there are people among us who have attended dozens of treatment programmes yet, as you so rightly observe, still understand nothing. There is so much darkness in our everyday lives and it does not want to make its peace with the light … Who knows, perhaps years will pass and we, your patients, will, together with you, generate a mighty power that will conquer the darkness.'

*December 1999 St Petersburg*
*(In October 2001 condition stable)*

PART I

# THE LIFE OF DR SERGEY SERGEEVICH KONOVALOV

# CHAPTER 4

# THE DREAM OF FLIGHT

*'Progress in science can only be achieved when the practitioner, of whatever level or capability, is prepared for the most improbable and at times contradictory turnarounds in his own fixed way of thinking. It is only in this way that the most important discoveries providing man with the opportunity to move ahead will be accomplished and will continue to be accomplished.'*

Sergey Sergeevich Konovalov

## Those Who Lived on Earth, but Whose Work was in the Sky

It is said that dreaming is a state of flight – a soaring up into the clouds. The adult starts out in life a small child, with its own view of this vast world, and a way of thinking upon which his family leaves its own indelible imprint as he develops and grows.

Sergey Sergeevich Konovalov was born in the Chernigov province of Ukraine, in the small military town of Priluki. Many of the people who lived here, on the land, worked in the sky. 'If you want to know where your father is, then throw back your head and look up at the sky. Can you see, up there, that little white dot in the blueness? That's your father.' The sky becomes a natural extension of the earth when you are always gazing up at it, searching for the person dearest to you. And you want so badly to grow up as quickly as possible, so that you too can go up there and be with him. It was at this time that the small boy for whom a special path had been mapped out dreamed of flight, a boy who was destined to set his sights higher than even his father had done – a father who was an elite sportsman and world record-breaker in parachute jumping, and a commander in the paratrooper section of a strategic bomber division.

Dr Konovalov's father was a strong and courageous man. He tested the special parachutes used by the Soviet cosmonaut, Yuri Gagarin, when he landed back on earth at the end of his historic space mission in 1961. The son was keen on parachute jumping and discovered for himself that the most important thing on any jump was the landing back on earth. Because that was where his home was – as well as the parents who loved him and who devoted all their tenderness to their children. They didn't spoil them, no, they didn't indulge them. They brought them up with respect and love for each other and the people around them.

Their grandmother lived in the same town. She was a woman of devout faith and took an active part in the life of the local church. She was often asked to preach in the language of the church – Old Church Slavonic – to the families of parishioners and in the church itself as well. She took her grandson with her. And this for him was also a kind of flight – an extraordinary sense of ecstasy at the greatness of God's works, at the harmoniousness of the ritual chants and melodic beauties of Old Church Slavonic. 'Remembering my school days between 1961 and 1971', Dr Konovalov says, 'I cannot recall spending a single day in indolence and idleness. I attended both state school and music school, and in the ninth grade I took up parachute jumping. I conducted an orchestra that played popular music, played in a brass band, sometimes played in a symphony orchestra too. In the tenth grade, in addition to all this, I took extra lessons in physics and chemistry in preparation for medical school. I had no free time. Much later on my father told me, when recalling my adolescence, "I was so sorry for you, son! I never ceased to be amazed and in admiration of you, of how you could take all this on. It was beyond me."'

## The Dream of Helping a Loved One

When, not long after finishing at both state and music schools, the question arose as to where Sergey Konovalov should continue his further education, a new dream was born – to heal people, and to help his grandmother get well. She had been very ill and walked with a stick, her back bent over. In medical terms this was defined as 'a metabolic disorder with affection of the joints of the arms, legs and spinal column'. This second dream now took hold in him – the dream of helping someone he loved: to learn the language of medicine and make his grandmother well, take away her pain and straighten her spine.

And so, in 1971 Sergey Konovalov gave up his dream of parachuting, to which he would in any event return later, and took up medicine. To be precise, he became a student at the Pirogov Medical Institute at Vinnitsa. It was no easy thing for him to tear himself away from home and distance himself from his warm family environment, and so, at every opportunity, he went back to visit his family, to draw upon their support and love. Even a distance of 375 miles (600 kilometres) would not prevent him from going home, if only for one night, to soak up the family atmosphere and recharge his energies.

## A Marriage Made in Heaven

Years passed, and Sergey became more and more caught up in student life and his studies. And then at the age of twenty he found love – a pure, deep, sweet love which consumed him entirely. First love, first girl. That love continues to this day, because it was God-given, because it is one of those rare marriages made in heaven. A year later Dr Konovalov's son Yaroslav was born and, with him, the hope that when he grew up his parents would be proud of him. In 2000, after six years of intensive medical studies, Yaroslav graduated from the Pavlov First State Medical University as a Practitioner of General Medicine (GP). He later read for an MBA in the UK, and is now overseeing the translation of his father's books for the English-speaking world.

## The Path to Traditional Medicine

In 1977 Dr Konovalov graduated from medical school. He was young, happy, and full of strength and a desire to extend and enrich his knowledge, to take up medical practice and become a true master of his profession. The joy of being young, the enthusiasm of a young specialist, widened his physical horizons: the state of flight continued. Dr Konovalov had a devout belief in medicine, in science, and the miracles that it could work.

Medical practice inevitably began bringing him into contact with cases that medicine terms as 'hopeless', the kind of cases where he had neither the specific qualifications of the specialist nor the specialized equipment required. But he knew that somewhere in major cities there were first-class professionals and clinics, equipped with the latest technology. In such places even the dead, it seemed, could be brought back to life and they were certainly able to do there what he himself could not. And he still wasn't put off when he began coming across one and the same phrase, regurgitated in article after article in medical journals and manuals, that the causes and mechanisms that trigger this or that particular disease are 'unknown' and still being studied.

Dr Konovalov was extremely anxious to get to the best clinics in the world, in the hope that he could there add to his knowledge and gain some real practical experience. During 1981–2 he undertook a specialist course in therapy at the Soloviev District Military Hospital in Leningrad (present-day St Petersburg) and in 1982 a three-month supplementary course at one of the faculties of the Kirov Army Medical Academy. After that, in 1986, he was sent on a two-year supplementary course to the Molchanov Clinic of the Army Medical Academy.

## A Sign from Fate, or Unconventional Logic

After Dr Konovalov entered the Army Medical Academy something happened, the true significance of which can only be understood today. It often happens in life that fate gives us signs, to which we pay no attention or which we look upon, at the time, as unexpected obstacles or misfortunes. It is only many years later that we understand that what happened then was meant to be.

The officers who had been sent on this advanced course had to take part in a psychological test, involving a hundred or so questions touching on practically every aspect of life. Such tests were usually very routine and nobody, including Dr Konovalov, worried about their results. However, on this occasion, the outcome was quite different. On reporting the results of the tests to General Evgeny Salamatov, the group of psychologists who had conducted them remarked that Major Konovalov's answers 'did not fit the standard responses of an officer'.

General Salamatov was extremely puzzled and alarmed. For such 'unconventional logic' on the part of an officer would close the doors of the elite Army Medical establishment to him. The general summoned Dr Konovalov for a talk, as a result of which he was, nevertheless, admitted to the course. To this day, Dr Konovalov remembers the general with deep gratitude for the things he taught him and all that he did to support him.

Of course, looking back now, one might confidently assert that the psychologists were right. Dr Konovalov's way of thinking was indeed unconventional. For otherwise, his method of energy healing would never have been adopted. Thousands of examples of miraculous recovery by 'unconventional' methods would never have taken place, and there would never have been one last source of hope.

# CHAPTER 5

# DOUBTS ENCOUNTERED ALONG THE WAY

## When Medicine is Powerless: The Thousands of Questions to Which There is No Answer

It was in the Army Medical Academy that Dr Konovalov first experienced a sense of anxiety and unease. Despite their access to a whole arsenal of remedies and techniques as well as an excellent range of diagnostic equipment, people with chronic illnesses did not always get well. Sometimes they died suddenly, without the doctors being able to help them or being able to detect what exactly had caused their deaths. Dr Konovalov's first patient had been suffering from myocardiopathy. He has remembered him all his life: the lacklustre, listless look in his swollen, yellowish eyes. The patient didn't recover, despite the best efforts of the doctors and everything that medical science had to offer. There's another patient he remembers too: a young woman with Takayasu's Disease (systemic vasculitis), who suddenly lost consciousness and a few hours later passed away, despite all the efforts of a whole brigade of highly qualified doctors.

Incidents such as this wore away at and undermined Dr Konovalov's faith in conventional medicine; they prompted thousands of questions to which none of the leading specialists could give him an answer. For all the time, the same question kept coming up: is the template for good health, as followed by modern medicine, the correct one? Is it possible that those physiological processes going on at cellular level and on the surface of the body's system are actually the key factors in health? And does it follow that the treatment of pathological processes going on in the organism is also not being correctly applied, because it is not directed at the real source of the illness and thus does not eliminate the primary symptoms?

## Gaining Acceptance among Patients

'But surely the resources medicine has to offer are defined by the development of science as a whole?', Dr Konovalov argued. 'On the one hand scientific progress provides medicine with new possibilities all the time; yet on the other hand, medicine increasingly looks upon the human organism as a mechanical object.' It was only then that he sensed, without daring to admit it even to himself, that his faith in medicine had been shaken, and that his doubts were not the passive reaction of a sceptic, but signified the as yet unacknowledged search for a different path – his own unique path in medicine. It was these very same doubts that prevented him from completing his dissertation. 'For many of my colleagues,' says Dr Konovalov, 'the dissertation was a way of gaining acceptance in one's chosen field. Defending a dissertation is a means to an end: securing a job, establishing oneself, getting promoted over other doctors. But the doctor needs to gain acceptance among his patients too – that is his true objective. To become a doctor is not to enter a profession, it is a way of life in which one dedicates oneself to the service of sick people. Degrees, honours, official posts – all these are unimportant to the real doctor.'

And it was his adoption of this different path which made Sergey Konovalov into an exceptional doctor, with his own theories, his own particular methods, and a unique lifestyle. As a professional medical practitioner and a highly educated person, he understands that it will be a long time before his methods are recognized. Indeed, as personal fame is not something he seeks, he avoids interviews, TV broadcasts and advertisements. He does not allow sensation-seekers – of whom there are a growing number with every year – any access to himself or his work, because the results of his treatment are in themselves genuinely sensational. He devotes himself entirely to his work and to the patient; for in truth, it is for them that he lives.

## Personal Experience Brings with it Acceptance of Dr Konovalov's Methods

A well-known journalist once approached Dr Konovalov wanting to write an article, and maybe then a book about him and his healing methods. The journalist's wife happened to be seriously ill and he asked the doctor to examine her. Dr Konovalov met both of them. The woman had terminal cancer and the doctor strongly urged her to start coming to him for treatment. The couple didn't live far away, but they did not come to the healing sessions: neither he, nor her.

Some time later the journalist telephoned to arrange another meeting, but Dr Konovalov turned him down, telling him it was impossible for someone to write about something in which they didn't believe. For the journalist clearly didn't believe – either in the doctor's abilities, or in the possibility of his wife's recovery. So what, in that case, could any book he wrote have to offer? This was the crucial thing: how could the journalist persuade people that the hope of recovery does exist, that there is another way in life? Before writing about all this, one has to experience it. It's possible that some journalists can get by without doing so, but for Dr Konovalov there is no room for such hypocrisy.

At the present time, the acknowledged luminaries of orthodox medicine are undoubtedly still in no position to explain Dr Konovalov's methods, and thus not prepared to accept them either. This is of no importance to him, even though, as an experienced doctor and researcher, he is constantly drawing new conclusions from his work, studying the results and laboriously extracting statistics based on medical assessments of patients taken before and after his healing sessions. And he doesn't do this work on his own any more. He now has his own staff, consisting only of those doctors who are able, as selflessly as he, to devote all their efforts to the sick patient.

The other doctors at the centre are also extraordinary. Once they themselves were the doctor's patients and now, having recovered, that is, having experienced for themselves the healing powers of energy, they are able, without the shadow of a doubt, to help the doctor restore patients to health. They don't have days off; there's no such thing as 'free time'. They often have to go to patients in the middle of the night, at the other end of St Petersburg. And this is after the evening healing session, during which they also have a considerable amount of work to do. Today there is no disputing the facts: swellings which have not responded to conventional treatment shrink and disappear; sight is restored; the composition of blood changes; chronic illnesses, considered to be incurable, go into remission.

### From case history 1017956 (born 1951)

'I'm reviewing my treatment over the last year. My major problem – a gynaecological one – is a major victory – there is no myoma (after about 15 years). I had an examination and the results were good. My menstrual cycle has started again. The herpes, which had tormented me since childhood, has gone. My gums are better and don't bleed. I have become a lot calmer. My bowels are working like a child's. The skin of my heels doesn't get cracked, and it used to be very bad and painful before. I'm not anxious any more, and my hair has gone dark in places. I've begun doing the exercises at home with enthusiasm. So that's it for now. Thank you very much for the healing sessions and for the books.'

*18 June 2001 St Petersburg*

### From case history 1013490 (born 1970)

'This is the fourth year of our acquaintance and of my spiritual and physical recovery. I want to share my successes with you. They did an ultrasound of the organs of my small pelvis and of my kidneys. When the doctor was checking me, I asked him to examine me with particular care. He couldn't understand what I wanted him to find. For I had not told him that, since childhood, I have had prolapsed kidneys, glomoerulonephritis and pyelonephritis.

And this was what he concluded: there were no clinical signs! I had written to tell you that I had chronic left-sided adnexitis, and that my uterus was displaced to the right. There were no signs on the ultrasound. During the treatment programme my menstrual cycle started again, without interruption, and whereas before I had to take painkillers then everything is fine now. Thank you, doctor. It is a joint victory!'

*28 May 2001, St Petersburg*

*From case history 1009041 (born 1957)*

'I'm attending my 20th treatment programme. My primary diagnosis is disseminated encephalitis, of fifteen years' duration, plus a whole range of other clinical diagnoses.

Dear Sergey Sergeevich, my 20th treatment programme is coming to an end. I first came to the centre three years ago, in January 1995. Time passes so quickly. How much has changed in my life during those years! I thank fate that I had the good fortune to get to know you and many more wonderful people. I'm not aware of anything happening to me during the healing sessions. Yet some kind of change takes place. Three years ago I never imagined that I would be able to work again, but I've been working for three years now, after so many years of illness as an invalid. Three years ago I could not have imagined that I would one day be able to get to the healing sessions without help. The metro, and especially the escalator, were a real trial for me. But, for this treatment programme, I've been coming on my own and practically never experience any discomfort in the metro ...

I've become fitter, stronger. I'm happy that I'm able to wear high heels again. For me it was a tragedy to have to go around with my footwear tied to my feet. I walked unsteadily, was afraid to go out of the apartment block, to come downstairs from the second floor ... This summer I swam for the first time in the Gulf of Finland and sunbathed, lying on the sand. Thank you for helping me get back to my old life, to the things which I had been deprived of for so many years. I work and 'support' my family (a sick father and a twelve-year-old daughter). Thank you very much for everything that you have done in my life.'

CHAPTER 6

# THE VICIOUS CIRCLE

## The Beginning of the Doctor's New Work – Helping Others

In 1988 Dr Konovalov was assigned to work at the Soloviev District Clinical Hospital. A year working in the intensive care and resuscitation unit meant that for a short while he had to abandon his search for a different path. Working in a place like this left no room for reflection or doubt. His work demanded knowledge, practical experience, and rapid decision-making. For people were being brought in hovering between life and death; everything possible had to be done to save them and bring their life-threatening condition under control. This invested the doctor's work with a higher sense of purpose and compelled him to devote his entire strength and knowledge to saving human life. Indeed, it's impossible to describe the sense of triumph and joy which both he and the nurses – themselves only young women – experienced when, thanks to their efforts, a heart that had arrested for 30, 40 or even 50 minutes, started beating again. It was as though the yearning inside him, for one thing and one thing only – to help people – had finally been satisfied. But it would not be for long.

## The Signs Given by Destiny Along the Path

The path which fate had chosen for Dr Konovalov, continued, even here, to yield up its secrets to him in the most unexpected of ways, compelling him to ponder everything and carry on searching. It goes without saying that every doctor working in a resuscitation unit repeatedly has to confront death. There's no getting used to it. It's there in the pain and grief of the relatives, their tears and suffering. All of this weighs very heavily on the emotions of the doctor, especially when a patient dies in his arms. Once, after a patient had died, a heavy-hearted Dr Konovalov went into the house-surgeon's room. Barely a couple of minutes later a distraught nurse, quietly, almost surreptitiously, came in after him, 'Forgive me but I have to say it!', she burst out, 'I'm scared'. The doctor looked at her in surprise: sad though it was that the resuscitation team couldn't always beat death, the nursing staff had never before demonstrated any kind of superstitious fear of the dying. 'There's something strange in there…'. Sergey Sergeevich hurried back to the resuscitation room. There, up high in a dark corner, both he and the nurse, by now frozen to the spot, distinctly observed a shapeless patch of light.

This happened only once. Or at least it was only once that the doctors noticed it. But to dismiss something like this was not that easy. What exactly is death? When the heart stops beating? When the vital processes cease to function? Is that it? But why, when the doctor saw this strange patch of light, did thoughts of the human soul leaving the body come into his head? Is such a thing possible?

He couldn't stop to think about it; his work didn't allow him the time. Yet, now and then, inexplicable things would happen – inexplicable, that is, from a scientific point of view.

For example, a patient in a coma suddenly regained consciousness and sat up in bed. The nurse went over to him in astonishment, for it's very rare to come out of a coma. The man began gathering his things together. The nurse, not understanding what was going on, asked him: 'What are you doing? Lie down.' 'Would you give these to my wife', the sick man asked, handing her his things, 'I don't need them any more.' 'Why are you saying that? Get back into bed, calm down, I'll get the doctor…' 'I don't need the doctor; I'm no longer here, I've already gone, give them to her …' And with these words the sick man lay back down in his bed and died.

All of this not only caused considerable consternation, it stimulated both the imagination and the intellect. Could it be that death is not the end, but only a crossing point, beyond which there is another entirely different life? Is the religious concept of the immortal soul really such a naïve one? Is it really so far from the truth? And if it isn't, then where does the truth lie?

## When the Patient is Not Just a Patient but Someone Who Matters

After a while, Dr Konovalov realized that he would never experience total satisfaction in his current work. He was, after all, only in contact with patients for a short time: he would save them, bring them back from the brink, beyond which lay death and oblivion. After that the patients would be transferred to an ordinary hospital ward and Dr Konovalov would know nothing of their ultimate fate. Maybe this all seems perfectly normal.

If a doctor were to take an active interest in what happens to every single one of his patients, if he followed up on every detail, then what would be the result? He'd have no time left for his own life. And the doctor is, after all, an ordinary person; he has his own worries, his own family commitments. And is it possible anyway to burden oneself with such an endless stream of human pain and suffering, of the kind which a doctor encounters daily, simply because that is his job? He wouldn't be able to handle it emotionally. Because of this, some doctors have learnt to bottle up their feelings, performing their duties with great skill, yet in no circumstances allowing someone else's life, with all its sufferings, to get to them. Others, at some time or another, simply grow so accustomed to the suffering of others that they become immune and develop an indifferent attitude to their work. They tell the patient: 'You're not the only one', 'You're not as badly off as some people', 'Your problems are nothing new'. Sounds familiar? I should say! We all know it. The reality is, that the more the doctor gives of himself or herself to every patient, the more such patients – dozens of them – come to them every day.

And if the doctor in question isn't a Konovalov, he or she won't be able to cope. They will lack the strength, day in day out, to put themselves through the mill of the pain and suffering of thousands of patients. For Dr Konovalov doesn't look upon a person as 'the patient', but rather as 'someone dear to me'. This attitude has become the hallmark of the unique way in which he works. His patients repeat it in their letters, like a prayer or a mantra. Sitting at home in your armchair, you may doubt this, but there, in the centre, at the doctor's healing sessions, nobody doubts it in the least.

### From case history 10021162 (born 1927)

'You have given my life back to me. Given me back myself; saved me from not wanting to go on living. ... From you, and through you, I have found my connection with the universe, and it has made me stronger and even a little bit wiser. I now know that I will never be left in need of support in time of difficulty, because you are with me.'

*(In October 2001 condition stable)*

### From case history 1007366 (born 1941)

'I can't help but add my own most sincere gratitude to the hundreds of expressions of thanks – which are impossible to put into words – for your ethical, spiritual, professional, physical and humanitarian achievements. For healing our "broken" spirits, for giving us back the chance of living. I've heard of many who've been "singled out by God" in the world of art, but your exploits, or rather – your mission – leave no room for doubt as to which is the more important ...'

*(In October 2001 condition stable. Continues treatment)*

### From case history 1007728

'Thank you for treating every one of us. Nobody who comes to you at the healing sessions feels they are ignored. They find themselves in an atmosphere of goodness, understanding and love. When you address the auditorium, it seems to me as though you are addressing me personally, that you sense that I am in pain and want to help me. You are there calming, supporting and comforting me. And all my friends who come to you experience exactly the same feelings.'

# The Vicious Circle – When the Doctor is Powerless

After that, Dr Konovalov worked for three years in the cardiology unit. It was here that he realized the full extent of his powerlessness as a doctor, a fact signified by his lack of a long-term perspective on the patient.

A patient would be sent to a ward. They'd treat him – and how! Using a whole arsenal of modern medical means, nothing slipped their attention. Here the best of care as well as every aid in assisting recovery – all in all the most modern types of treatment – were at the patient's disposal. The patient was discharged in a satisfactory condition, but sooner or later, would be back on the ward again. It was a vicious circle.

On this ward people were treated primarily for heart conditions. Modern medicine has, as a general rule, divided the human body into its various components and trained up a whole generation of doctors dedicated to treating each one separately: the heart or the intestines, the kidneys or the liver, but only one thing at a time. 'But doctor, I've also got ....' 'That's not my field. I only specialize in kidney complaints.'

What happens is that people who've suffered heart attacks or who have other heart problems and come in for treatment, are often also suffering from other chronic diseases, ranging from everyday things such as osteochondrosis, to serious problems affecting the organs and tissues, where major, systemic diseases occur. Many accompanying illnesses are exacerbated by heart attacks, when, as usually happens, the patient is confined to bed for two weeks or more.

Dr Konovalov's patients would thank him for making their heart problems better but he continued to be concerned about the fact that a patient's other, accompanying physical complaints persisted. And not just these, for, having had a heart attack, the patient would be discharged, still suffering from coronary heart disease. The heart had been weakened, which meant that its poor blood circulation would worsen. Sooner or later the patient would be back in the ward again.

With resuscitation it's simpler. Here, the doctor can feel he has won through. He's saving life, fulfilling his sacred duty. And the surgeon too has reason to feel proud and can gain a sense of satisfaction: he can cut things out, sew someone up, transplant organs, save and extend a person's life. But what kind of life will this be? Well, that's not his problem. The important thing is that he's made it possible for that person to remain on this earth for a little while longer, and even to think that they are in some way better. But the treatment of chronic diseases is not, unfortunately, always like this. A moment comes when the doctor begins to avoid the patient and avert his gaze. How often, in out-patients' departments, does a 'struggle' arise between the patient and the doctor when the patient is about to be discharged? 'But doctor I'm still sick. Nothing has got better. Why are you discharging me?' The patient can't understand. And he goes away dissatisfied, disillusioned even, both with his doctor and with medicine as a whole. It's because he doesn't understand that in medicine the bottom line is the regulated turnover of hospital beds and not the patient. The main thing is that the patient doesn't die on the ward, doesn't damage the department's good record, or that of the hospital as a whole. And that's how they see it. As one doctor has observed:

*'In essence, doctors today are all becoming hostages to an inflexible doctrine: chronic disease cannot be cured. Every doctor knows this, especially in the major specialist clinics, not just in Russia but all over the world. Why the major ones? Because the doctors in clinics and small hospitals send their patients to these specialist clinics in hopes that they will be able to help them. And there's no doubt that they will, that is, that they will ease their suffering and extend their lives, which is also very important.'*

## The Doctor Rejects His Own Helplessness in the Face of Disease

Dr Konovalov could not accept any of this. It just didn't fit into his way of thinking. His feeling of helplessness when confronted with chronic disease gave him no peace. He couldn't and didn't want to become one of the millions of doctors who, when coming up against serious symptoms, find they are at a loss. It is clear that Dr Konovalov's mission as a doctor and healer had long been preordained. The path which he follows today was even then pulling him inexorably in its direction, leaving him no choice, heightening his sensitivity and receptiveness to things for which others had only a cold sense of detachment. Having the deepest feelings of gratitude towards his teachers, of whom he remains proud to this day, and confident that they had given him a great deal, Dr Konovalov set off in search of his own path.

*'The medical way of looking at things is a very conservative one. Anything, no matter how obvious, that did not fit into the standard form of treatment for this or that particular symptom, was met with objection or was categorically dismissed. Things became difficult for me when (in 1989) I tried to introduce the anti-oxidants now commonly used today into the treatment of coronary heart disease. These preparations, partly composed of vitamin E, were being manufactured by national pharmaceutical factories, and had been producing good clinical results in cardiology. But because at that time not a single cardiology clinic had officially adopted them, I was told: 'It's not necessary. You don't need anything more. And anyway, what if ...'*

'What if?' ... Doctors carry not only ethical but also legal responsibilities. For this reason, they won't be drawn by even the slightest divergence from the 'norm' in the accepted treatment of a given disease. The doctor is held to account for so many things, so why add another burden? And in any case, the patients being given this medication as part of the complex treatment of their arteriosclerosis had already noted a significant improvement in their condition after the third or fourth injection.

But the most surprising thing was that other doctors, including cardiologists, who were directly observing the results of the course of treatment devised by Dr Konovalov did not attempt to adopt this preparation in their own practice.

## Confronting the Major Enemy – Chronic Disease

In the end Dr Konovalov finally came to grips with his implacable enemy. And that enemy was *chronic disease*, which modern medicine hasn't the powers to defeat. His enemy had devoured the lives of hundreds of thousands of people, turning millions more into slaves, dependent on pills, injections, inhalers, constantly reminding them of its presence with attacks of pain and endless discomfort. This enemy had deprived old people and children, men and women of all ages, of happiness, turning their lives into nothing but an intolerable existence, of living from one period of suffering to the next.

Dr Konovalov realized that if he were to stick to the accepted medical way of thinking in his search, then he would achieve very little. A new medical preparation might be devised, or one of the links in a particular pathological process might be detected, but chronic disease would not be vanquished. The more he made a concerted search for the answers to the questions with which he was confronted in his clinical practice, the more clearly defined became the goal towards which he was striving: to seek out the real causes of chronic disease, and find them, so that the diseases themselves could be totally eradicated from the human organism. But at that time he still did not know which path fate had in store for him. It was 1990, and he still had not reached an understanding of the path he should choose in resolving the most complex of the challenges which he had set himself.

# CHAPTER 7

# THE MERCILESSNESS OF DISEASE:

## GOD WORKS IN MYSTERIOUS WAYS

Dr Konovalov had no idea of the ordeal that awaited him in the near future; nor did he imagine the effect that it would have on his quest. For something terrible happened: his mother phoned to tell him that his father was in hospital, under observation for pneumonia, and that they had detected growths in his spinal column, pelvis and clavicle. He immediately knew what this meant, got in touch with the doctors at the hospital where his father was being treated, and they confirmed his suspicions: it was cancer of uncertain location, with metastases of the skeletal structure. There was no hope.

He gathered together all his father's case notes and transferred him to the district hospital where he was working at that time. His father's illness had come like a bolt from the blue for the members of the family, as well as for all those who knew him, because he had been fit and healthy all his life, and had never complained of anything, even though he was seventy-five by that time. Yet all that the full range of modern medicine could do was to confirm this terrible diagnosis.

Dr Konovalov simply could not accept it, although the reasons for the illness were utterly mundane: a year before, his father had been on holiday at a spa hotel in a resort not far from Kiev and had swum in the Pripyat River, the waters of which had until recently run from Chernobyl, the site of the catastrophic nuclear explosion in 1986, which had polluted the countryside for many miles around. His father wasted away in front of him. In the space of a few months, the strong, fit, healthy man was reduced to a helpless cripple. And, as a medical man, his son was only too well aware of what lay ahead for his father. He knew that, with a strong heart such as his,

his father would have to endure terrible suffering. As they were progressively eaten up by this terrible disease, his bones, his vertebral column, his ribs, would begin to break, but his heart would keep on beating to the end, until his entire organism had finally been destroyed.

It was only then, when he sensed his utter helplessness that the son, having no other way of helping the person he loved most, began to call on God's help and to pray desperately and fervently that he would soon take his father to him and not make him drink the cup of unendurable suffering to the dregs.

As he lay dying, the doctor's father suddenly became like a small child. He called for his mother, and wept, and then quite suddenly 'burned bright' before crossing into the next world. He had gone, and so too had his son the doctor's belief in the traditional methods of medical science. Dr Konovalov was at least grateful to God for hearing his prayers, but he was now even more acutely aware that there must be another way of treating the sick, that it already existed and would reveal itself to him, and that indeed it was already calling him.

This tragic episode, which is all too common in the life of many families, was, for Dr Konovalov, a turning point. Today he is full of joy that sick people with exactly the same diagnoses as his father are cured during his healing sessions, although it torments him, of course, to think that, at that time, there was nothing he was able to do to help his father. But God works in mysterious ways. Who knows, if this tragedy had not occurred, whether the secrets of the 'living universe' (a term coined by Dr Konovalov) would have been opened up to him, or whether his search would have been in vain. His father is still very much with him, even now – in his thoughts and in everything he does. And the results the doctor achieves today through his treatment methods speak for themselves.

*From case history 1001204 (born 1937; primary diagnosis – prolymphocytic lymphoma)*
'Before the healing sessions literally everything was troubling me. For two years solid I had been confined to the oncology ward of the hospital at Pesochnaya. During that time I had undergone chemotherapy twelve times without the desired results, so that after each chemotherapy session the process had been repeated at double the intensity. It's rare for someone to

endure so much chemotherapy; they die simply because their other organs can't take it. All of this is very hard to describe, but to go through it is absolutely unbearable. It's terrible thinking about it, even now.

I was discharged with the diagnosis "prolymphocytic lymphoma, with lesions of the retroperitoneal peripheral lympho-collectors, the spleen, the tonsils and the skin". There's only one person still alive out of all those in that same ward at Pesochnaya, and that is the person who now sits in the auditorium of your treatment centre. I so regret that we didn't know about you before, Sergey Sergeevich. How many lives might have been saved! It's clear that God saw fit to leave me among the living, so that I might encourage people who are incurably sick to your wonderful healing sessions, to these wonderful celebrations. Many people come here from the suburbs and get home after midnight. But none of them get tired; they are all so happy, uplifted and full of energy. I've now attended nine treatment programmes. The other day I had a blood sample taken and couldn't believe my eyes: everything was normal. I even went to work. There aren't the words to express my gratitude to you for my life, my children. I now live, work and help them.'

*(Case history recorded in 1993. According to active clinical observations taken in October 2001 the patient's condition was good)*

### From case history 1007776 *(born 1955)*

'Here's my anniversary questionnaire – after ten of your treatment programmes. How quickly time has flown. Is it really that long ago that I first "crawled" into this centre, not knowing where to go or who to turn to? My life was losing its meaning; for "cancer in remission" had been written in blue on my diagnostic chart. Since then, a great deal has changed in my life and in the lives of those near to me. I've told you about this in every one of my nine questionnaires.

So what has stopped bothering me? My knees don't ache (arthritis for twenty years). Autumn and winter, and then even in spring too they were nothing but torture. I don't have any pain in my liver, kidneys or pancreas and my osteochondrosis doesn't trouble me any more. The veins in my legs have stopped aching. But the main thing is that I no longer have to have chemotherapy, and there are only one or two tablets left! I've had my hair done nicely, yet before I had hardly any hair. In the winter they discovered a cyst in my thyroid gland. After a month it had shrunk by a third; and during the treatment programme was reduced by half. This Wednesday the ultrasound check confirmed that I could forget about it: it had gone!

This summer, before the latest programme, I wrote in about a gynaecological complication – an enlarged endometrium. But now the ultrasound shows that it's normal. ... And there's more. I got very worked up when, after each treatment programme my weight went down by a kilo. All in all, I've lost nine kilos in the nine treatment programmes. I was worried that my weight loss was due to the cancer. But now, after my holiday, it's gone back up by two kilos. And I'm so bothered by these extra kilos that I would much rather lose them again at the treatment sessions. I'm terrified even to talk about the cancer. In August, my doctor said that I needn't come in again for controlled observation for another three months.'

*(Case history recorded in 1994. According to active clinical observations on 10 October 2001, the patient's condition was stable)*

**From case history 1010312 (born 11 March 1951)**
'In the previous questionnaire I wrote that hopefully I had got rid of my allergy. July had not yet come, when it most commonly flares up in me. Now it's already the end of July and I can tell you with all confidence that it hasn't reappeared at all. This is quite a milestone for me: a whole phase of my life which I hope has gone forever. At any rate, I'm no longer scared of the fluff from poplar trees or the pollen from too many flowers.

On Sunday we had a day off. I sat in the park and walked around. There were so many flowers, such an abundance of smells, everything in full blossom and I didn't have the least mucous reaction to it. ... Sergey Sergeevich, you take from our lives such a huge, enormous burden of suffering. Whenever I walk past the Hermitage Museum [in St Petersburg] and look at the statues of Atlantis "holding up the sky in his hands of stone", I am reminded of you. Because you hold all of us in your hands in exactly the same way; there's no changing that, nobody can make you stop and rest. And all that those of us who are recovering can do is to try to help support you from below. You have already done the most important thing – you've made us change mentally and spiritually. It's hard, but that's the way things are: it's always hard at the beginning. But whatever happens, we are already changed people. I say this because the people around me at the centre have changed and you can see it too among the new arrivals. I am going to try to change myself.

At last, I can now turn my head without any pain, and my right clavicle no longer aches.

Dear Sergey Sergeevich. I never cease to thank God that we are always here with you. Thank you for what you teach us and your love.'

*August 1999, St Petersburg*
*(In October 2001 condition stable)*

# CHAPTER 8

# SUMMONED BY A NEW PATH TOWARDS MEDICINE AND HEALING

## The Mysterious Power that Revealed itself to Dr Konovalov

After his father's death Dr Konovalov began to stop off almost every day at the 'Greek Hall' at the cardiology centre. (It had previously served as the hospital chapel and had been where the Russian composer Mussorgsky's funeral service had been conducted in 1881.) He thanked God for hearing his prayers, and prayed he might be shown the path towards knowledge, so that he might, if only by a fraction, pull back the curtain on that secret, that panacea, that might give help to the sick and the suffering. Having lost his own father, Dr Konovalov was now praying for others, for those who might still be helped, for those who might still be saved. He was now more open than he had ever been to receiving help from a higher power. As a seeker after knowledge, he hungrily strived to break through into the unknown and was prepared to make any sacrifices to achieve this.

And God heard his prayers. Perhaps this all sounds rather far-fetched, especially to scientists and atheists. But that's how it was. No, there was no angel with a sword of fire. It was all quite different. Maybe one day Dr Konovalov will tell us all about it – some day, when we are ready to listen and understand. But will we? It is not for nothing that those who have been initiated hold on to their secrets for so many centuries.

Since that time Dr Konovalov has felt the presence of a power within him. It's something that cannot be expressed in words and cannot be described. Understanding came gradually and with it knowledge too. He gained experience, and his practical work gradually eliminated all doubts, confirming that this was not a fantasy, not some trick of the imagination. To convince another person of something extraordinary is difficult enough; but it is even more important to convince oneself. As a man of science Dr Konovalov was not inclined to believe in things that couldn't be backed up by scientific analysis, or in any kind of power or force that could not be quantified using the most sophisticated instruments. Only practical experience could convince him; only the recovery of sick people, whom nobody apart from he had been able to help.

It would be good to have been there and to have been able to follow Dr Konovalov along the path, every step of the way, because every step has its own profound logic. Sergey Sergeevich did not simply wake up one morning as a great healer, no. He moved towards his goal by degrees, drawn by the mysterious powers directing him on the path towards his destiny.

## The First Manifestations of the Doctor's Extraordinary Gift

After the death of his father, Dr Konovalov continued to work in the cardiology unit. About a month later, he began to be aware during his rounds that a kind of intense pressure was bearing down on him and that his hands felt unusually flexible, as they do today. These were the first strange sensations, the very first manifestations of an extraordinary gift. But as he was still a long way from even the most basic understanding of bioenergetics, he didn't pay any attention to it at first. He simply registered it as a fact and that was all. He didn't read literature about the occult or extra-sensory powers; he had no interest in it, and anyway there was no time. What would he, a serious-minded person, want with such rubbish? What kind of interest could such theories offer him if they had no practical use? Every day he would read clinical articles of all kinds in attempting to keep up with the latest medical developments, in the hope of coming across something that might help in the treatment of his patients and their attendant chronic illnesses.

One day, a nurse called him to a patient who had had a heart attack, brought on by diabetes and complicated by endarteritis of the lower extremities. The man was suffering terrible pains in his legs. Dr Konovalov ordered that drugs and analgesic preparations be brought for him. The sick man lay there in agony as the nurse was preparing them. Three or four minutes after his injection, he was still groaning with pain. And then, suddenly, something happened which would prove to be the first step on Dr Konovalov's path towards the uncovering of his unique abilities, the development of his treatment method and the establishment of his own centre.

It's difficult to describe exactly what he felt at that moment. The patient's suffering was, for him, unbearable; but even more unbearable was the realization that he could do nothing to help him – even with drugs. 'Dear Lord,' he thought to himself, 'please help this person.' And at that very moment, as he tried to soothe the patient, he ran his hand down the leg that was causing the pain. Who knows why he did this. He was standing about three metres [approx. two feet] away from the patient, and he went on passing his hand over what seemed the painful part of the man's leg. And as soon as he had done it, the pain stopped.

As Dr Konovalov did not believe in miracles of any kind, he paid no particular attention to this first occurrence. And anyway, only three minutes previously, the patient had been given pain-relieving medication, and the doctor was convinced that this was what had stopped the pain.

The same thing happened the next day. Indeed, in order to make the pain go away sooner he did exactly the same as he had the day before. On the third day, during his rounds, he suddenly found himself going up to the patient and running his hand over his leg. He still doesn't know what made him do it: a superior power? – a doctor's gesture of despair? – a need to find any means possible of relieving the patient's pain? For him it didn't matter. What did matter was that the pain went, there and then. And a few minutes later, an incredulous patient informed him, even on this, the third day, that he thought his leg felt considerably warmer that it had done before.

The doctor was himself no less astonished than the patient. 'For me this was a real shock – in the full sense of the word – because I didn't understand, I didn't know, couldn't even stop to think about what exactly had happened.'

*From case history 1013960 (born 1956)*
'I am one of those women whose large, cyst-like formation went away during the course of October's treatment programme. I told you about this in a note. I was so delighted and overjoyed; you and the creation energy have really worked a miracle. It's hard for my mind to accept this, but it is so.

There's something in one of your books about how patients get used to miracles and even take them for granted. But it's not like that with me. This miracle aroused the strongest feelings in me: indescribable joy and gratitude, as well as an element of fear at losing all the things I had gained with your help. I don't think one can ever get used to the miracle of healing; it will always seem somehow supernatural, magical and will stay in a person's mind for the rest of their life.

My life was turned into no life at all – simply an existence – as a result of my previous trouble: a huge cyst, 17 centimetres by 8 [approx. $6\frac{1}{2}" \times 3\frac{1}{4}"$] and the need for an urgent operation at the Pesochnaya Hospital recommended by my doctor. And then, dear doctor, I experienced for myself the full force of your priceless gift. You cured me in a matter of days and hours.

I was so acutely sensitive to the personal effect you were having on me, like never before, that it felt as though it wasn't me at all. I rang the patients' information line and asked what was happening to me. Why was I so calm and composed when I was faced with such a thing? And they told me that Dr Konovalov does this to us in order that the creation energy should have a better effect on us.

My disbacteriosis went in the middle of October, and on the 1st November the test results showed that there was not the slightest sign left of that enormous cyst.

Since October you have been with me every day, not just on healing-session days. Right up until the New Year, I did my energizing exercises for an hour every day, morning and evening, after healing sessions. Now I do them once a day. I read your books and then read them all over again.

My enormous gratitude and respect to you my dear, beloved doctor.'

*26 January 2001 St Petersburg*

*From case history 1014386 (born 1969)*
'I've been coming to healing sessions at our centre since December 1997,

but it's only now that I am happy to tell you that my main problem – genital herpes – doesn't bother me any more. The problem has not recurred for four months now. But how long my road to recovery was, how many treatment programmes! And sometimes it seemed as though I wasn't getting anywhere. But now all my doubts are behind me. How wonderful it is to know now that your blessed gift, my own body and God, together have restored my health. I am trying not to remember how it was when I was going to the Influenza Institute, how they prescribed me very strong and expensive drugs – all to no avail. And now the disease has gone and doesn't bother me. It's still like a miracle to me, even though I understand what goes on at healing sessions, both at the centre itself and beyond its walls. I cannot help but be amazed at the great power!

And that's not all. A few days ago I had a colposcopy and the erosion of the cervix is healing naturally.'

*28 May 2001 St Petersburg*

**From case history 1017961 (born 1945)**
'I've been coming to you with my daughter for five treatment programmes now. I never thought about myself – only about her. Not long ago I became ill – with high blood pressure. The doctor said I needed an ultrasound to check my kidneys. I already knew that I had chronic pyelonephritis and that both kidneys were located on the left (they'd done an X-ray four years ago). But now, this time, the ultrasound showed that I'm like other normal people – with one kidney on the left and the other on the right. I just couldn't believe it. Could a kidney really move itself over to the right?

I still have chondrosis of the neck and chest. I couldn't raise my left arm. But now I can raise it normally. I'm also going through the menopause and was having terribly heavy periods. But they're lighter now.'

*18 June 2001 St Petersburg*

# CHAPTER 9

# TAKING THE FIRST STEPS

## Stereotypes Cannot Be Broken in a Day

Dr Konovalov was unconsciously aware that something inexplicable was happening to him, something that did not fit either into conventional medical knowledge or into our general perception of the human being, of nature and the surrounding world. But at that time he was still trying to determine some logical explanation for what was going on. In part, he put the anaesthetizing effect he produced on patients who were in pain down to his own soothing personality, for that had always come easily to him. He thought perhaps this might have a psycho-therapeutic effect. Vaguely thinking that there was no other possible explanation, he nevertheless held to his orthodox medical position, not yet daring to believe that other ways existed, not yet daring to take them up.

Stereotypes cannot be broken in a day. In the days that followed he would have to become a different person in the full sense of the word: he would have to accept another world, another path, and faith in a different kind of reality. He would have to achieve a turnaround, not just in medicine but, first and foremost, in his own ideas and his own way of life. And it wasn't rational thought that was propelling him in this direction, it was practical work. More and more facts, testifying to his 'miraculous' and inexplicable effect on sick people, were accumulating. And they were leading Dr Konovalov towards a new way that nobody had ever tried before.

## Formulating a New Way of Thinking

Extraordinary things began happening to him at this time. A whole world, not normally seen by the human eye, was gradually revealing itself to him: he was gaining spiritual insights. These new revelations did not fit into conventional logic, but slowly and inexorably they began, nevertheless, to change his preconceived view of things. As Dr Konovalov relates:

*'And so, I set out on the path towards a completely new and untried knowledge ... And, as with any path which one has never travelled before and along which there is no one to show you the way, I knew full well that that it was a path that did not promise to be easy. But I set out on this path without hesitation and with a deep faith, sensing the power that was, little by little, investing me with the mysterious knowledge which (and I now understand it only too clearly) was enabling me to work to the maximum of my capabilities. Even at the very outset of my journey, of my getting established, these small amounts of energy helped me become more self-assertive, helped me gain self-belief, and allowed me not even the slightest reason to doubt its reality. And, more importantly, this gradual, drip-drip of knowledge was happening (and continues to do so today) in such a fashion that it did not provoke a crisis of conscience in me or in my way of thinking; in other words, it didn't take away my ability to think rationally. (For this is perfectly possible. We know from a multitude of examples in history that people have lost their reason after making contact with the information-fields system of the sensitive world. Or the reverse has happened: it is only after extreme traumas, catastrophic events or illness affecting the brain that some people suddenly find themselves able to see the sensitive world.)*

*And although I was insistent on an explanation of some kind for the things which had happened, for the causes of this or that disease to be made known to me as soon as possible, although I prayed to be given the ability to save this or that seriously ill patient from suffering, the rate at which knowledge was imparted to me (as I now understand it) remained strictly regulated by the level of consciousness I had by then attained. Many different things, affecting both me and my family, happened during this time. I can talk about some of them now, but as for the rest, the time has not yet come to do so.'*

## The Surgeons Get a Shock

Around this time a patient was admitted to the clinic with a very serious diagnosis: gangrene of the toes due to diabetes. When the woman was

74

brought in, the doctors could all see that amputation was unavoidable. The pain was so agonizing that it wasn't giving her a moment's peace. And drugs only killed the pain for a short while. On top of that, the patient also had heart problems: she wasn't young and it was likely her heart wouldn't be able to take the strain of the terrible pain that was wracking her body for much longer. And now gangrene was developing in her legs. Dr Konovalov first saw her on one of his rounds: she was emaciated, worn out with the pain; there was a look both of supplication and of hopelessness in her eyes. By that time Dr Konovalov no longer doubted that the power of healing was being transmitted to him. 'But you need to understand my state of mind at that time, when I first started on the path', he explains. 'I felt, with my whole heart and soul, that I could help and I was seeing the results of this. But there was still a battle going on inside me between the traditional logic of the doctor and the logic of a doctor-healer that was now developing inside me.' He passed his hands over the patient's legs. Nothing! He did it a second time, and again – nothing. And then, suddenly, it came to him: he had the knowledge. He instinctively realized that he had to act on the spinal cord in order to take away this pain, that is, he had to work on the seat of the pain, having blocked off the peripheral nerves from it.

He therefore, as it were, 'drew out' the woman's spinal cord towards the body's outer, sensitive layer, where he blocked the pain, with the help of the special energy, by channelling a type of anaesthesia into it via his own hands. At that time, of course, he didn't call this power 'the energy', but simply knew that he could take the pain away.

To all outward appearances, nothing seemed to have happened. The sick woman just lay there with the doctor standing silently beside her. After three minutes the pain went, the woman's face got pinker and went smooth. Dr Konovalov carried on channelling the energy, now directing it towards hopefully improving the microcirculation to the blocked blood vessels in the woman's feet. When he finished the 'procedure' the woman said to him: 'Doctor, I can feel warmth in my legs. Something is throbbing in them. Doctor, I feel all right.'

For about ten or twelve hours the woman didn't feel any pain. The surgeons who had been preparing her for amputation were extremely taken aback. They all knew about their colleague's capabilities, but as Dr Konovalov himself had only just begun demonstrating them, they thought that his power to anaesthetize pain was the result of a gift for psychotherapy or, at least, hypnosis. They understood no better than Dr Konovalov did that there is no psychotherapy or hypnosis that can take away pain of the intensity that is resistant even to drugs. This incident finally convinced Sergey Sergeevich that the power which he had tapped into had nothing to do with either psychotherapy or hypnosis. And, what is more, he had never ever dabbled in either of them.

## A Medical Orderly Gets a Shock

Dr Konovalov could now feel this power growing in him with every day, and how, under its influence, his outlook on life was changing too. If he held his breath, he could stop and watch his own rebirth taking place. A little while later, when he was on duty one day, a patient who had been admitted to the ward after a heart attack, had a stroke. A blood clot in his artery left him paralysed in the left arm and leg. The nurse rushed to get Dr Konovalov, who immediately lowered his hands over the patient's body, not knowing at that time that there was no need for him to do this. But for the time being he continued to make the hand movements that had once helped him. He 'drew out' the diseased part of the blocked arterial system towards the sensitive layer and treated it. Five minutes later the circulation of the blood to the brain was restored and the patient did not even know what had happened to him. Everyone in the ward was rooted to the spot. The short silence that followed was interrupted by a young man – himself a medical orderly – who had been doing things for other patients on the ward. He had a broken arm and had been in terrible pain for several days. 'My arm doesn't hurt!' he said in amazement and moved his fingers, unable to believe it.

And so it was that practical experience such as this gradually helped Dr Konovalov formulate a whole new outlook on the world and equipped him with a new way of thinking. He slowly moved away from the old stereotypes. It is impossible, of course, suddenly to start believing one day in the existence of some kind of supernatural power if you have taken a pragmatic view of things for 35 years, especially if you are a doctor. For being a doctor makes you a pragmatist twice over.

# CHAPTER 10

# THE POWER THAT POINTED THE WAY FORWARD

Despite knowing that he possessed a special kind of power, Dr Konovalov did not stray from the well-trodden path of modern medicine. He continued to see sick patients suffering from this or that disease of an organ or with problems with their physiological system as a whole. He would examine the patient, arrange for the conventional tests, make a clinical diagnosis and prescribe medication. In other words, he remained the same doctor; it was just that he enlisted an additional and very real power in his treatment of the sick body – a power as yet uncharted. He carried on his former way of life, considering himself in all honesty to be just an ordinary person in whom extraordinary abilities had been revealed. That these were not just abilities but an indicator of his future path he could only guess at then. But he didn't yet dare cross the line and break away completely from the way of life he was used to.

## An Ordinary Person with Extraordinary Abilities

Dr Konovalov's personal life had always been subordinate to his work, right from his very first days in practice, when he had been sent to work in Murmansk. His daytime duties had been followed by emergency calls at night, and then he would be back on duty the next morning. He had to save people suffering from frostbite; soldiers injured on duty; deliver babies in cars when he couldn't get the mother to the maternity hospital in time. When he did have an occasional evening off, he would invite friends over. And wherever fate took him and his wife, Antonina Konstantinovna [this is Mrs Konovalov's given name and patronymic; ed.], they always turned out to be the best of company. The lovely, charming woman and the young doctor, who played the piano so beautifully, were a very striking couple and nobody was ever bored in their company.

And what about Dr Konovalov's music? It would need another book to tell you all about it. Dr Konovalov was born with many gifts – and he could have made use of all of them. So making a career choice was difficult: more than one path beckoned. He could continue in practice as an army doctor; as it was, he had enough material at that time for more than one dissertation. Doesn't everyone dream of honours or scientific awards? He could also have taken up music professionally – by that time had had already become well known for his compositions, his songs and other musical pieces. The Leningrad figure-skaters, Oleg Makarov and Larisa Selezneva, had become national champions to his composition, 'The Stream', and went on to win the European Championships. And then Dr Konovalov's music was heard in 1988 at the Winter Olympics in Calgary and the World Ice Dance Championships. In the space of two years Dr Konovalov wrote more than eighty musical compositions; his songs and musical improvisations were played on Russian radio stations and used on television in arts and popular science programmes. But, meanwhile, the mysterious power which gave him the ability to heal people was all the time gaining a stronger and stronger hold over him. His views were changing, and so was he.

This process continued over several years, during which he continued to open up a whole, mysterious world for himself and for his patients, drawing them not only out of their sickness but also away from the narrow horizons to which their lifestyles had confined them till then. He was opening the door for them to a wonderful future; not to go through that door is to remain a hostage to disease, the prisoner of a life that has done nothing but cause anguish.

## Learning to Accept the Doctor's Methods

Dr Konovalov is a panacea; he is not a medicine. You can't simply 'take' his healing sessions instead of pills and then go back into that same suffocating little world that gave rise to your pain and suffering. Otherwise the pain will start again, and your disease will come back. Only those who grasp the fact that they need to set out on a new path and who accept that they must change many things in their lives can recover completely and retain that precious state of health afterwards. Sooner or later almost all of the doctor's patients realize this.

*From case history 1011222 (born 1964)*

'I'm currently on my 14th treatment programme since 1996, although with some interruptions. I came to the sessions with deep erosion of the cervix of the womb (they suspected cancer), inflammation of the adnexa, fibroadenomatosis of both mammary glands, autoimmune thryroiditis, osteochondrosis and radiculitis, chronic bronchitis and tonsillitis, varicose veins in both legs and severe myopia in both eyes. On top of all this, I was plagued by insomnia. There wasn't a medicine I hadn't tried – the strongest kinds of sleeping pills. I was treated at places – you know the kind I mean – where they claim to treat you spiritually, but instead … instead, you are left still feeling wounded, battered, sick in spirit and in pain. And a divide opens up: between the world of "Before" and that of "After". I thought I would never be able to endure the pain, the humiliation and the shame that I had to go through. As a result of coming to you and to your wonderful healing sessions (for me they aren't just healing sessions, but more a process of revelation and the constant possibility of gaining knowledge, of moving ahead, from out of the shadows and into the light), I have now not only got rid of the insomnia but also of the terrible anguish that welled up in me whenever I thought about that time in my life. I can tell you all this calmly now, but I don't see how I could have won this victory over my own recollection of the past without the extraordinary part you have played.

You tell us our about body's potential. Today, 28th April 1998, as I write these lines, I want to tell you, dear doctor, that at today's session your words flowed into my soul like a powerful beam of light. … They brought with them a unique knowledge, not merely the wisdom of a man who has come to know the laws of the universe's development, but also the astonishing divine revelation about the good and omnipotent power. … "Start with yourself", you told us. How difficult that path is, doctor. How difficult and complicated it is to start with myself, feeling so helpless in comparison to you … I came to you at a most difficult time … A brutal diagnosis, a husband who told me that it was my problem … and I was so … You remember … endless tears, no work, I already felt as though there was nothing I could do, that nobody wanted me. How I sobbed when I heard you say: "Look at your hands..." My palms looked back at me so reproachfully: "What have you done for us? You're always plunging us in bleach and detergent. But we once played the piano ... And we are so defenceless, especially when you get worked up and bite your nails." Yes, Sergey Sergeevich, I'm so ashamed, but in all my 33 years I've not been able to stop this dreadful habit. And then I burst into floods of tears ... After that an agonizing series of complaints followed: first my legs ached, then I had problems with the blood vessels in my head. For a while I just wanted to give up and run away. Run away! But where? And from what? From myself! Yet again – from myself. But inside, in my heart of hearts, I already had hope and faith that the doctor with the miracle-working (yes – miracle-working) eyes would help me.

I groped my way through life as though through a boggy marsh at night. Feeling my way forward, I bumped into things and stumbled. Sometimes I was frozen to the spot, worn out with the struggle for life. How could I even stop to ask myself: "Life ... what is it to me?" How could I be so blind, so deaf, so insensitive to all the complexities of this many-sided life, with its flashes of light and thunder, which sometimes tormented and wounded me but which nevertheless called me to it ...

A ray of light appeared in the darkness, and when you came into my life new hope dawned in me. My friends say to me: 'You've changed so much, we can hardly recognize you. You've got slimmer, prettier ... If only they knew how difficult this path has been for me, and if it hadn't been for you and your astonishing wisdom and your great patience, I don't know what I would have done. I'm beginning, only just beginning, to realize what it really means "to start with oneself". It's not enough to see what it is in yourself that prevents your recovery. That's only the beginning of the journey. Trying to become a better person, day by day, hour by hour, is much harder. You see, I get home feeling calm and then not long after, I begin to get worked up: the floor needs washing, the ironing hasn't been done. It's up to me to do these things. And I want to take out my frustrations on somebody else, and unburden myself. But is that the right way to go about it? Is it really that necessary to get rid of the burden of sorrow and worry by offloading it on to somebody else? I left my old self behind, doctor, and returned to it a new person, who had just started changing and was becoming more patient. But I was still touchy and hypersensitive, was hurtful and sometimes dreadfully spiteful to those nearest to me. Now I always think about what I do. I've started trying not to upset people with an unkind word. For I suddenly realized: my God, how wonderful life is! Every minute of it! Every second.

I've just got back from the Mariinsky Theatre with the wonderful music of Sergey Prokofiev still ringing in my ears, yet there's a blizzard outside and the street is covered in wet snow – in April. Somebody said to me – "What terrible weather." And suddenly, in the midst of the blizzard I saw the Nikolsky Cathedral in front of me, so beautiful in all its majesty. ... And then as I watched my native city float past me through the glistening window of the tram, I began to think that these moments, these god-given flashes of light, are also moments of real happiness. For me happiness is harmony, a striving towards spiritual peace. And it was then that I realized that everything lay ahead of me: personal happiness, and love. Five years ago I had written myself off. But today, a day on which spring has finally set in, and it's warm on the street, like June, I walked along the embankment of the Neva on my way to one of your healing sessions. Thank you Lord for that moment, I am grateful that I am here and not there. There were two occasions – during my two operations – when I could have been there already. I didn't know about you then, dear Sergey Sergeevich. But I didn't know about myself either, absolutely nothing about my body, about my soul, which was being torn apart. I was just like a ship without sails, adrift in the open sea. Where was the captain? Where was the crew? They were all sleeping a deep sleep and the deck was deserted. And the wind was whistling. At the healing sessions I not only lost excess weight but I also began to sleep well and peacefully. To describe all this and then just close my notebook might suggest that I've understood nothing about your healing method. But, of course, I'm only just beginning to understand and it's hard for me at present. But I can feel your help and support.

We are always in such a rush, hurrying for tomorrow. "But what about today?" you ask us. "But what is there for me today?" "Why am I living?" I think I'm beginning to understand: it's for love and for joy; to bring joy to myself and to others and to give love. But how very difficult it is to understand this and accept this simple truth.

People often write to you asking, "get my husband back for me", "get my wife back" … But I'm not asking you for this, or for any other quick fix for family happiness. There's no such thing in my opinion. We all have to discover it for ourselves, find our own path. And so I ask just one thing of you: to support me along this path, and I will try and discover it for myself, because nobody else can do it for me.'

This letter has not been edited down, as some of the others have been. Everyone who has passed through Dr Konovalov's 'school' writes their own deeply felt and honest testimony. The candour and genuine feeling that goes into these testimonies shows how much they are written from the heart, in one sitting, without pause for breath or reflection. They show the extent to which so many people coming to Dr Konovalov's healing sessions are inspired by their experiences there to set out on the search for a new path in life, and with it a re-evaluation of what matters most to them. For Dr Konovalov offers them a new beginning – both mental and spiritual. He believes that it is the essential basis of a full and lasting recovery from ill health.

# Chapter 11

# CONNECTING WITH THE ENERGY

## Knowledge of the Energy brings with it Self-Knowledge

When he first started on his new path, all Dr Konovalov did was take away pain, restore the workings of the gastro-intestinal tract, and normalize blood pressure. At first he worked with individual patients, then with a whole ward, and finally, in a small hall, with the entire hospital unit. When it reached a point where there were more patients wanting to join in than the hall could hold he began working in larger auditoriums and much larger halls. But that didn't stop the people coming.

At first he thought that the power, the energy that was helping him to help his patients, was being channelled through his hands. There was no doubt about this because he could feel it physically, could sense the power and energy flowing into his hands. They would burn and even ache after long therapeutic procedures in the hall when he had been conducting a healing session for an hour or so. And it was then that the doctor came to the conclusion that this energy which he called upon was activated mentally, that it was subject to his control and he could direct it.

A week after first encountering the energy of creation, as he later came to call it (and about which you will find out more in his other books), Dr Konovalov sensed that a mysterious power was drawing him to the hospital's Greek Hall:

'*I understood this call, this summons. Something very forceful had brought all its weight to bear on me, but my heart was trembling with joy at this. And this force, under the influence of which I had first sensed the mental power entering my consciousness, drew me to the hall. I collapsed into my chair. The weight kept*

*increasing and soon became so intense that it was literally pinning me to the chair.
My eyes closed and I let go. What was it I then experienced? A dream? A reverie?
A state of meditation? It was, rather, a state of indescribable bliss, of union with the
vastness of infinity. And it was a feeling that seemed so familiar, so natural and
comforting. I wanted it to go on forever. It was an indescribable sense of spiritual joy,
of tears, love and gratitude to the almighty.'*

Dr Konovalov felt as though his mind was being charged with a huge
bank of information. This first contact or 'charge of energy' lasted only for
about 25 minutes, but it transformed him into a completely different person.

After returning to the house-surgeon's room he now had a sense of the
direction in which he had to go and that he possessed the ability to
recognize and open up for himself a vast and wonderful world. And, most
important of all, he suddenly realized that he knew precisely what it was he
now had to do, that very moment, with the sick patient, with all
sick people. The next day he went to the ward where the most
seriously ill patients were to be found. And there he held his first
healing session of a kind he'd not come across before, but which
he now knew he had to conduct, right down to the smallest detail. And
it wasn't just the doctor, but every single patient who could now feel
the power, or the energy, as the doctor would later call it, feel its
warmth, its gentle touch. It was something that shook the imagination,
stunned the senses.

*'It inspired and encouraged me. I understood that all my appeals, my daily
prayers for help with my patients were not empty words but a reality that was
drawing near.'*

## The Period of Discovery that Laid the Foundation of the Doctor's Present Healing Method

It wasn't long before the hospital staff began noticing with amazement the
effect the doctor's daily rounds had on the patients. For Dr Konovalov's
ward round was slightly different from others. He made it at precisely the
same time every day; the patients had to be in their beds, nobody was
allowed to wander about in the corridor, and there was to be no casual
conversation. His superiors often reproached him for never answering his
phone if it rang when he was doing his rounds. But that time was 'sacred'

to him. The effect his visits had on patients became clear when the majority of them showed the same, practically normal, pulse rates, and a blood pressure that was also almost identical too. He now went on his rounds with a real sense of joy.

Spurred on by this new – albeit relatively small – amount of knowledge, as well as by his practical experience, Dr Konovalov began conducting daily healing sessions in one of the wards. Soon the ward began to outdo the other wards in the unit in the rate of recovery of its patients. But that's not all. Other unexpected and pleasant surprises and developments started happening. 'Look, Sergey Sergeevich! There's nothing on my arm,' said one patient in amazement, who had suffered from eczema for years. 'Last night when I went to bed it was covered in sores, as always. But today I got up and there's nothing.' And so, gradually, the path the doctor had chosen was reflected in his practice, as he carved out new experiences. On one occasion, a patient told him how after a healing session he had accidentally splashed some water from a jug on his bedside table onto his arm. And straight away the itching on his skin had stopped. This provided the impetus for the later use of energized water in treatments (see Chapter 19).

The doctor became so caught up in this first phase of discovery that he hardly slept. It was like being in love – the greatest love of his life. He had neither the desire nor the willpower to resist it, for it was a voice which since then has resounded around the world. For it is also the voice of the human heart.

## Practice Opens Up New Horizons

Practice now opened up new horizons in the doctor's work, highlighting new possibilities and perspectives. Soon, his healing sessions were relocated to a small hall at the hospital in order to fit in the twenty patients who were coming for regular treatment. Dr Konovalov no longer had a sense of inadequacy and helplessness when confronted with incurable disease of the kind that previously would have made him unable to look patients in the eye. He now knew how to help them and what he had to do. Any heart specialist can tell you how hard it is to manage the care of a cardiac patient. Confinement to bed unavoidably leads to intestinal problems, to various types of radiculalgia and disturbed sleep patterns. But these were no longer a problem for Dr Konovalov's patients. And soon they began asking him to treat their relatives, their wives, children and friends as well. After only two or three months 75–80 people would be gathering in the hospital hall.

Dr Konovalov would feel completely drained after holding his healing sessions. These 'charges' or link-ups with the energy would last for about ten minutes to an hour, and he got a great deal out of them. But the most important thing for him was improving the patient's state of health and getting rid of their accompanying ailments.

*'And so, these three months of work and of contact {with the energy} became my whole life, my whole existence. It was all that interested me; nothing else. I thanked God for the strength he had given me, for, at that time, I felt that I could do anything. And why not? Here's an example – that of a handsome nineteen-year-old athlete. He was suffering terribly with intense bouts of pain that came on 3–4 minutes after he tried to eat anything. His mother brought him to see the surgeons at our hospital. They did an ultrasound of his abdominal cavity and found that his internal organs had prolapsed. What could they do? The surgeons threw up their hands in despair. His mother brought him to me and I took him with me to a healing session. While it in progress, I heard someone cry out. It was the young man and he was in terrible pain. "Don't give up, I told him." As a result, all his organs are now back in the right place. And that was after literally one session.*

*By then, thanks to the fact that eight out of ten of my patients had recovered from all sorts of illnesses, I'd been given reason to have faith in the power of the energy. I thought that now, at the hospital, we'd be able to work miracles, making use of traditional methods of treatment in conjunction with the new medium now being revealed to me. But I was fooling myself. My colleagues, especially those whom I respected and who'd had many years' practical experience, not only responded coldly to the practical results produced by this inspired new method, they made no attempt to conceal their hostility to it either. I was naïve, despite the fact that on previous occasions I'd been more than prepared to take a genuine interest in the work of my senior colleagues in their attempts to introduce innovative methods of treatment. It wasn't just a matter of their attitude to me; it was rather a general symptom of how things had been in the past and of the way we live now.'*

# The Knowledge That Constantly Backs Up Practical Work

By now, it wasn't simply that Dr Konovalov had learnt something new, he'd also had specific, practical experience of working with the energy which had helped him reach his own conclusions about sickness and health. He'd already come to his own understanding of the living human organism and, in the process, had formulated what he terms his 'information-energy theory'. What is more, he continued to refrain from reading any books that might influence his new way of thinking, determined, for the sake of the 'integrity of the experiment', to make use only of the information he received during his 'contact' with the universe. Of course, today, under the influence of the never-ending flow of information emanating from it, he knows, understands and can do so much more. Dr Konovalov looks upon his theories then as being only in an embryonic stage. They've developed over the years; he's added new knowledge to them and made adjustments based on his practical work. But I can assure you that the knowledge which he possesses today has no boundaries, nor has he yet arrived, even now, at the definitive truth. In days to come he will glean new knowledge from the depths of the universe, find new possibilities and ways forward and reveal them to us. He is moving ahead of his time, leaving far behind him the most up-to-date medical theories.

# The Attitude of Medical Colleagues to Dr Konovalov's Work

The reaction of colleagues to Dr Konovalov's extraordinary abilities was extremely varied. On the one hand, they saw with their own eyes the patients who had recovered thanks to his inexplicable gifts; on the other, they kept their eyes, and minds, firmly closed to what was really happening, ascribing these successes to Dr Konovalov's charisma. But they too were ordinary people, just like their own patients, and even doctors can fall sick. When this happened, Dr Konovalov's colleagues would come to him privately, ask him take their pain away and heal them. Sergey Sergeevich would do all of this and yet, instead of being thanked for it, he'd hear the same words over and over again: 'Don't go telling anyone I came to see you ...' And what is more, those who came to him weren't just ordinary doctors, but professors too – his former teachers. And they'd all leave saying the same thing: 'You know, all this is ...'. For none of them had studied 'all this' in medical school, no-one had told them about 'all this' in their medical faculties, and they concealed 'all this' even from each other. Yet if you'd gathered them all together, then half of the clinic's medical staff had, at some time or other, been to see Dr Konovalov. The doctor's colleagues had come to him to be treated, yet were not prepared to admit to 'all this'. And these were doctors of the highest qualifications, who'd been treated by the very methods which they refused to acknowledge.

Dr Konovalov has always hated hypocrisy, especially of the professional kind. It was one of the reasons why he left the hospital, and with it, conventional medicine. And then he came up against an even greater lack of understanding – or rather, an unwillingness to understand – among his colleagues. After an international conference on cardiology was announced, to which the only Russian medical men invited had been Dr Konovalov, Professor Almazov and one of their assistants, the hospital issued a paper and submitted it to the conference. Dr Konovalov had done the primary work on the paper, having informed his colleagues about the results of his treatment method and some of his basic theories. The paper was heard with interest, after which one of the leading therapists at the clinic announced that 'all this' was nevertheless nothing but psychotherapy, despite the fact that only a week earlier Sergey Sergeevich, with the help of 'all this', had relieved that very same therapist of his back pain. Yet the man made out that this was something any therapist could do.

*'It's difficult, if not impossible, to turn one's back on the whole vast core of knowledge and experience one acquires in the course of one's life. But when a new concept is rejected simply because it contradicts the accepted canon, our preconceived notions and experience, without any attempt at getting at its essence, then that, in my view, is conservatism in the narrowest sense of the word. But it doesn't just apply to my colleagues; it's relevant also to the patients who are absolutely convinced that a sick person can only be treated in a bed in a hospital ward, with tablets, or by surgical intervention or other "traditional" methods.'*

### From case history 101473 (born 11 July 1967)

'This is my sixth treatment programme with you. I believe in you; you support me in many ways. At the healing sessions I experience feelings of bliss and joy. After the latest session, I woke up with the feeling that our life-giving energy, the energy of creation, was bringing me to life, and that, with its imperceptible touch was working miracles on me. It is healing me. It is teaching me. It is protecting me. It is mine – this tiny particle of the universe – and mine alone! It's as though you cast a spell over me; I can even see the waves of energy emanating from you. It's as though they're trying to strengthen my faith in myself. Good lord, how wonderful all this is. And now, when you say my face will be massaged, straight away my cheeks are massaged with the energy's gentle, tender touch.

It knows me better than I know myself. It looks after me. What happiness! It will help me. I now feel instinctively that when I leave the hall, having left the energy behind, I need only summon it up again and it will come, will support and help me. And when I stop to think for a moment that it is not just mine, but belongs to everybody there, I feel almost jealous. And then three women come in who have now almost recovered, and I once more have a feeling of incredible joy that this energy of ours has saved them, that it helps all of us. May everyone get well. Thank you, thank you, thank you.

I now know that this energy of ours is making me – my body – fight, and go on fighting against my disease. It has been sent by God. I'm being touched by God, and he is looking after me. He knows each of us better than we do ourselves. He is helping us. How dear and tender the energy is, how dear.

Thank you very much indeed for what you give and open up to us. I've always believed in God, and now I know that he is really with me. And it's you who have given me this feeling and revealed it to me. Thank you and may God protect you.'

*24 July 1999*

*From case history 1009502 (born 1939)*
'I've come to your healing sessions for the first time, but the road getting here lasted a year. I came already believing in you, thanks to my wife, who is also a doctor. She had been a patient of yours for a year and had had considerable successes ...

The first healing session: it's 11 a.m. While the patients acclimatize themselves to the hall and relax listening to the gentle words of Antonina Konstantinovna my worries and anxieties disappear. Then your music begins. I have an idea of what psychotherapy and music therapy is – I've tried them more than once. But this is something incredible, unfamiliar, and much harder to fathom....

The second treatment programme: ... forgive me if there is less and less to say about my case history. I'm not being lazy, it isn't my fault. It's just that there's no trace of my former problems ... So I'll just recap on those that have gone or stabilized by now:

1. No signs of osteochondrosis or the pains in the joints and in the spine; no giddiness.
2. No chest pains or shortness of breath. The attacks of pain I used to have in my head every week have stopped. I don't take the medicine any more.
3. The gastritis and agonizing spasms in my oesophagus haven't got worse and there's no sign of the cholecystitis. I'm sticking to the diet less and less and there's no pain, no heartburn, no feeling of heaviness after eating. My bowel movements are regular.
4. No pain in my kidneys. No difficulty passing water. All the problems with my prostate have gone and my sex life is normal.
5. Hearing couldn't be better. Sight is getting better all the time. I no longer take my glasses to work with me.
6. I've forgotten all about acute respiratory diseases, flu and colds.
7. Now for what's left: blood pressure. Here's the pattern: when I came to you it was 180 over 110. Now it's stabilized at 150 over 100. What is more, immediately after the first session it was 160 over 100 and the following day was 145 over 95. After the eighth session it was 140 over 90.'

*(In October 2001 blood pressure was normal, condition stable)*

### From case history 1007107 (born 1949)

'Two years ago I was rushed to hospital by ambulance. When they opened me up they discovered that my right ovary was infected and on the point of bursting. And there was a massive cyst with a huge number of commissures on the left one; at the time, the doctors said they'd never seen so many. The operation lasted for four hours. The cyst turned out to be none other than a metastasis of a malignant tumour. On top of that, three days later my body rejected the stitches, and on the fifth day they had to open the suture and drain it. And then the final blow– it was CANCER.

At the Oncology Centre on Berezovaya Avenue I asked the doctors what my chances were. Nil they said. Just imagine being given a death sentence at the age of only 43.

I then went through four courses of chemotherapy. I felt worse and worse. Many of those who were being treated alongside me have since died, and I was getting ready to die too.

I came to see you on the off chance, without faith. I thought things couldn't get any worse if I did so. My blood count was a nightmare: leucocytes 2/haemoglobin 69. I was in agony in my spine and lumbar region. The fits of dizziness were so bad I couldn't go outside on my own. My face was waxen. There was a hard swelling in my left breast of about eight centimetres. They were going to operate in the autumn, but I was convinced I wouldn't last that long. ...

After the very first healing session I was still in terrible pain and desperately wanted to sleep (prior to this I'd only been able to sleep for about two hours in every twenty-four). That same day I slept the sleep of the dead – for twelve hours. And when I woke up I couldn't believe how I felt: nothing was hurting. In the middle of the second treatment programme I had a blood test. The oncologists couldn't believe it and asked for the test to be done again. But the result was no different the second time – my blood count was excellent. They asked me what on earth I had done. I told them I was coming to you for treatment. "Ah well", they said, "that explains it."

Gradually all the pain in my spine went away. During the summer I worked in my kitchen garden and didn't feel at all tired. I'm dark-skinned by complexion, but for the last five years I haven't been able to get a suntan, although I didn't know about my illness then. But this summer, although I didn't sunbathe once, I went as brown as a berry. I went for my operation in the autumn, but the doctors couldn't find the tumour. They sent me for an ultrasound which showed there was nothing wrong. And that's because the most terrifying thing, my tumour, had gone. My blood count hasn't got worse since then. When I'm at the healing sessions my mind and my body are at rest. I come out spiritually uplifted and ready to climb mountains! Thank you very much indeed, my dear doctor.'

*(According to the results of practical observations in October 20001, condition was stable).*

Many of those who attend the hall in St Petersburg for healing sessions have already been under treatment for three or four years, or even longer. People such as these sit in the exact, same places because they know that it's easier for the doctor to work that way. He knows the feel of the hall and tunes in to every sick patient there and recommends that they don't change their places during the treatment process.

Whenever I go to observe a healing session, I feel terribly self-conscious because I'm not suffering from any kind of chronic disease. One or two minor things, but that's all. I'm preoccupied by a sense of guilt that I'm taking someone else's place, that somebody else needs these sessions a hundred times more than I do. The only justification I can raise in my own defence is my sincere desire to write this book with Dr Konovalov about his work, so that as many sick people as possible, who have nothing else left to hope for, might know that the chance of a miraculous recovery does exist.

Since then, I've noticed how often people complain about their health. Too often! Before, I used to listen sympathetically to such complaints. Not any more. Now I immediately say, 'What? You mean you don't know ...? Don't you know there's this amazing doctor and that getting better can be an enormous pleasure rather than just a matter of standing in a long line at a clinic waiting to be seen by an indifferent doctor. You say that nobody can help you? – But you don't know how lucky you are! How lucky we all are!'

There's a man sitting not far away from me breathing heavily. 'It's probably his first time here', I remark to my neighbour, who has been coming to healing sessions for four years now. 'What do you mean! He's been coming for three years!' she says. 'So?' I ask in amazement. 'It's not helping him is it?' 'What are you talking about? They carried him in the first year. The second year some woman brought him.' I look at the man again and it's only then I understand how much he's been through, what a hard time he's had and how much these sessions, which have given him his life back, mean to him.

*From case history 1009678 (born 1943)*
'My illnesses first began after I'd turned 40; by 49 I was classified as disabled (category 2) with a whole catalogue of complaints: gall-stones, a stone in my left kidney, chronic pyelonephritis and left-sided nephroptosis.

On 6 March 1995 I had an attack of colic in the left kidney; on 15 March an X-ray revealed a stone of 0.5 centimetres in the upper third of the bladder, 2nd–3rd degree hydronephrosis, a stone of 0.5 centimetres in the upper calyx of the left kidney. Within a month the kidney had stopped working. ...

When I first came to your healing sessions they were still being held at the hospital. My attitude was the same as that of many others – I had no faith in them, didn't take them seriously. Now, every healing session is a painful reminder of what I've lost. If only I'd known about you sooner, then I might have been able to save two people dear to me. I came to you in hope, trusting that I could and would be well again, and this belief gets stronger with every healing session. I still tire easily but the left kidney hardly bothers me at all. ...

Today I had an ultrasound: the kidney is working, there's no hydronephrosis and the second stone has also disappeared. Thank you for being here among us.'

*(In October 2001 there were no symptoms of disease)*

How many more doctors will there be in the future, who will be utterly dumbfounded when searching on an X-ray for the tumour that had been there yesterday, or for the skin lesions which the patient had not been able to get rid of for the last thirty years, or the signs of arthrosis, of ulcers, or gall-stones? You don't know? But I do: as many as there are patients coming today to be treated by this extraordinary doctor.

*From case history 1011583 (born 1931, a gynaecologist)*
'At first, I didn't believe what people coming to you for treatment told me about you. I even laughed at them. How on earth could I believe? You go to the hall, sit down and all your illnesses just go away? But chronic diseases never go just like that. You take your pills when things get bad, you don't eat or drink anything you shouldn't. And if something more serious

develops – then there's nothing for it but an operation, and sooner rather than later. That's how I used to think. But people kept saying to me: go there. Watch and listen, and then you can draw your own conclusions. So I went. ...

And now I'm a different person. I trust in every word you say. Medicine really is far from being perfect. Poor doctors – every day faced with the same thing – the chronically sick. And there's only one answer they can give them: "You'll have to get used to it."'

*(In October 2001 feels well)*

CHAPTER 12

# TRUSTING IN THE UNIVERSE, TRUSTING IN PEOPLE

## The Demands Destiny Makes on us as We Set out on the Path

The universe has now opened up to Dr Konovalov and to this day continues, by degrees, to reveal to him the true path to knowledge. He has dedicated his whole life to following this path; to do otherwise is impossible. He is no ordinary person, who yields to human weaknesses, for if he were he wouldn't be able to work miracles two or three hours every day during healing sessions. The path to knowledge demands that you give your all: all your thoughts, desires and feelings. There is no room for the slightest lack of commitment, or for any straying from the path, for there is no road back. Dr Konovalov has been chosen and must complete his task. That doesn't mean he hasn't stumbled or fallen as he's made his way; it's because, still lacking sufficient knowledge, his steps have been hesitant.

To choose such a path is, however, to condemn oneself to a solitary life.

'During this time', Dr Konovalov tells us, 'we gradually lost all of our friends and close acquaintances. They couldn't understand why we couldn't meet up with them, why we didn't visit, why we didn't phone. And I couldn't explain things to them, knowing full well that my whole life, and that of my wife, my closest friend and confidante, had now been dedicated to other people.'

The extent to which the doctor would gain trust in the higher powers communicating this knowledge to him, and with it further initiation by them, now depended on his every action, as well as the innermost workings of his mind.

# The Path to Eternity

Dr Konovalov has now been pursuing this difficult path since 1990, never ceasing to bring his patients back to good health, but in addition offering them spiritual warmth and measureless kindness. Every time he goes out onto the stage at the treatment centre, Dr Konovalov experiences an extraordinary, boundless joy at knowing that just before he begins this healing session he will come into contact once more with the energy of creation. By channelling it through him he can direct it towards helping the thousands of patients sitting in the hall. Many look at Dr Konovalov, up there on the stage, as their last hope. And the doctor is only too aware of this. For he is the embodiment of a hope; and that hope will, with time, be transformed into an implicit faith in the doctor's powers. For through the doctor the sick person discovers the limitless possibilities of their own organism's ability to recover.

It's still hard to believe that fourteen years have already passed. Dr Konovalov and his patients can hardly believe it. For the path they have set out on is the path to eternity and one lifetime isn't long enough in which to attain it. There are many people who now come to the centre, not to be cured of their diseases – they have already recovered – but because they are drawn by the new path that the doctor has revealed to them. What then is he to them: spiritual healer or mentor?

*From case history 10013189 (born 1966)*
'When I try to explain in the questionnaires how I feel about you and your healing sessions, I always feel frustrated because I can't find the right words to tell you. Words aren't the right medium; they aren't the right 'code'. If only I could put it into music, but I can't. But if I really had to say it in a single sentence then, until recently, it would have been a very long one, containing words about sanctification, about the universe, God, the divine energy, the information fields. Now, having been in contact with you for three years, all I need to say is that you represent for me the road to myself. This takes in everything: physical and spiritual health, man's destiny, as well as the divine universe that is in all of us. I come to the centre to listen to you and conduct a dialogue with myself – to be cleansed, for an escape from everyday worries, to enter a state of grace – all of them things which can't

be described in words. Although the road to self-discovery is difficult, it's a very interesting one. And it's a process of discovery that lasts an entire lifetime.'

### From a case history (born 1939)

'If I were to be asked what kind of person Dr Konovalov is then here's what I'd say: First and foremost, Sergey Sergeevich Konovalov is a doctor, endowed by God with unique skills and capabilities. He is a doctor ahead of his time, who treats people using new methods and means known only to him. Peace, faith, hope and love prevail during his healing sessions. People believe in his healing powers and can feel them at work. They become stronger in body and spirit from one session to the next – it takes them over. Their faith in the healing process becomes absolute, and slowly but surely the network of disease is destroyed, Gradually, almost imperceptibly, people begin to get better and, as practice has shown, it's forever, because the cause of their disease has been destroyed. And here lie his unique gifts in healing chronic diseases that are labelled incurable. All in all, I'd say this is the doctor who can help you too.'

### From case history 1007714 (born 17 July 1924, a doctor)

'My dear doctor and wise mentor. I am already 75 and for me to address you in such a fashion might seem odd. But I genuinely look upon you as my teacher. I've studied many things in my life, I've never scorned the advice of good and intelligent people and I've never had occasion to regret it.

Like many of your patients, I came to you by accident, on the advice of an acquaintance, as a person who was superficial and shallow in their judgments. Not having been told anything specific by my friend, I was surprised to find I suddenly understood, or rather sensed instinctively, that fate had smiled on me and had brought me to a place where I could improve my health and prolong my active life. Despite my advanced years, I still didn't want to give in to old age, there were too many interesting, challenging and joyful things going on in my life. And besides, conventional medicine had led me into a dead end, with medicines that offered no hope of improvement.

During the first healing session I developed an unconditional, instinctive sense of trust in you and my hopes were raised. I was in such a joyful, uplifted state. It was a moment of spiritual regeneration, as though my soul had been washed with fresh morning dew. My husband, who came to meet me, immediately noticed my change of mood and soon became a loyal and regular patient of yours. Much time has passed since then and I'm now attending my 27th treatment programme (since mid-1995) ... Regular contact with you has, for me, become one of life's necessities.

I was brought up an atheist (although one of my uncles was a very devout priest and my grandmother a true believer), so perhaps I am taking the first, timid steps towards some kind of acceptance of faith. I come to you as though I'm attending a sacred temple. Every visit gives me real joy. I soak up the atmosphere of goodness and kindness. I see faces lit up, I hear the extraordinary timbre of your voice, and a feeling of spiritual peace comes over me. The things you talk about are always interesting and of importance to me because they bring us centuries of accumulated wisdom and knowledge. Whether we always take up your advice is, of course, another matter.

But there's one thing that still bothers me – and that's the lack of peace and quiet at home, with my son's family. This means that the wonderful injection of energy I get at the centre is soon dissipated. But at least there's a marked improvement in my general state. The chest pains don't trouble me as much and are less intense than before. I suffered from insomnia for many years, and often had to resort to sleeping pills. Now I get to sleep without them ... and I've learned to cope better with the attacks of arrhythmia, thanks to the healing leaflets. I do my energizing 'heart' exercises, as well as taking the usual medicine, which together give results that I didn't get before. My vasomotor rhino-sinusitis has completely gone. I don't go down with colds the way I always used to. I haven't had flu for three years now. ... With respect and love ...'

*28 July 1999, St Petersburg*
*(In October 2001 condition stable)*

## The Insignificance of Awards and Accolades

Looking back over the path he had travelled, Dr Konovalov never once regretted the things he left behind: his long unfinished dissertation (he

98

finally received his PhD in August 2003), prestigious appointments, professional honours.

*'When I came to realize that the entire medical establishment, with the best professionals and the very best medicines at its disposal, was still not in a position to save the actual sick person from chronic disease, I decided to leave. It wasn't the sick I was leaving, but the attitudes and way of thinking that had been instilled in me over a period of twenty years in medicine.*

*I didn't seek out alternative sources of knowledge in other branches of medicine – such as folk cures, or cult medicine, etc. Already having under my belt a considerable and solid foundation of knowledge gleaned at the Institute, the Army Medical Academy and on supplementary courses, and having also had direct collaboration, in the course of my work, with wonderful, knowledgeable and experienced colleagues, I decided that I should now rely on my own intuition. The time had come to give myself up to the inner self and to try and draw out from the depths of my memory the inherent knowledge which protects our organism but which is buried deep in our consciousness. I shan't expand on this theme here because it deals with what I call the path of initiation.'*

## Dialogue with the Energy of Creation

The doctor therefore decided instead to take stock of those signs passed on to him by destiny as it nudged him along this new path. It was as though the energy was trying things out on him as it attempted to find a common language between them. In Murmansk, much to his own surprise, the doctor started writing poetry; one day, when he was about to note something down, he picked up a pen and there and then wrote a poem. It was a wonderful feeling and, from then on, he wrote a poem every day, unaware of where this was coming from and why it was happening. Then, a few years later, just as unexpectedly, he found himself beginning to compose music. That is, he didn't think about it or sit down at the piano, working out a melody note by note. The music took shape, of its own accord, inside him. He sat down at the piano and it responded to the touch of his fingers with the most magical sounds. Sergey Sergeevich never set out to be a poet or a composer. Even when his music was popular he never once thought of giving up medicine. Maybe this is why the real, full force of the energy was directed towards opening up to him the path towards healing people. It was as though it was putting him to the test.

When evaluating the path he had taken many years later, Dr Konovalov observed:

*'The gaps in my knowledge and their lack of application in the way I was working were compensated for by an enormous faith in what I was doing. My knowledge and experience as a doctor made up for these shortcomings, as of course did the recovery of my patients. But the most important thing at that time was that I didn't feel as though I was lacking in knowledge. Although I still didn't understand all that was happening to me then, I never ceased to feel its presence – within me, alongside me – in whatever environment I found myself.'*

The feeling was strong; it was real, and palpable. Every day, as evening drifted into night, Sergey Sergeevich would go into the kitchen at the other end of the apartment, so as not to disturb his sleeping wife and son, and always at precisely the same time. He would sit on a chair, always looking in one and the same direction, and would enter into the dialogue. Only it wasn't even a dialogue at first: as yet, he still wasn't asking questions, wasn't challenging anything. All he could feel was that something real, something tangible was there, standing behind him. It was as though some kind of power was holding him by the shoulders, stroking his head, and filling him with knowledge. He was afraid to move, or turn around and take a look. He was afraid that it was all an illusion, and that if he turned round he would see nothing; he was afraid he was deluding himself. And there is nothing worse than self-deception. He began gathering up his courage in order to look round, but wasn't yet ready for what he might see.

## The Reality: Sick People Do Recover

Sick people did recover and that was the reality. Dozens of sick people already felt so much better, thanks to the power he had learned to channel through himself. It wasn't a fantasy or mere invention. As a result of the healing influence he had over patients, those with problems such as poor circulation in their extremities began to feel warmth in their legs again. Sick people walked again and, not only that, they were able to walk further than they had ever dreamed of being able to. Then they'd excitedly tell the doctor and the patients in their ward all about their successes with such a sense of joy. There are so many victories over disease achieved by patients thanks to the doctor's help that can be listed since then.

Dr Konovalov himself could feel the power as nobody else could, he could see the results, and yet

*'There was still that logic, the doctor's way of thinking – it didn't give me any peace. It was like a millstone round my neck, weighing me down and it wouldn't let go.'*

But he couldn't turn back now. He was afraid to – for then he would not see, and not to see would be to abandon his faith in the energy. In other words, he did not want to destroy that new, as yet tentative, way of thinking that was only just taking root in him and which in the future would bring him to an understanding of the causes of disease and his theories about the healthy human organism.

## One Last Important Test

He had faith, he understood, he was sensitive to things and he didn't turn back. And then the power revealed itself to his wife, Antonina Konstantinovna, who hadn't had the least idea what was happening to her husband. Or rather, she had of course heard about her husband's new treatment methods, but Sergey Sergeevich hadn't told her everything, as he was afraid of alarming her. Antonina Konstantinovna had always been a serious-minded person, totally detached from other-worldly things, and interested only in the real world. Nevertheless, the universe also revealed a tiny living part of itself to her. For, after the doctor had already been in contact with the energy for many months, Antonina Konstantinovna also had material contact with it. Dr Konovalov now knows why this had happened, but at the time it became a test, and not just for him. It's hard to imagine what the doctor's future path might have been if Antonina Konstantinovna had not been able to cope with it.

The woman with whom a man chooses to share his life is his destiny. Every man of genius, every true innovator who has come down through history, has often had an extraordinary woman who has worked alongside him. The union of man and woman is indissoluble and the 'weaker' half should always be given credit alongside the 'stronger'. Could the doctor have filled his patients with his soul's pure light if his wife hadn't also taken the path chosen by him? And would this light have been so bright? Would the doctor's eyes have revealed a hidden sorrow? One can only guess at this now. The fact that Antonina Konstantinovna was able to understand and support her husband was of course a great joy not just for the doctor but also for his patients.

I cannot help but cite the words of Antonina Konstantinovna herself at one of the healing sessions held during the November 1998 series. She practically never talks about herself and for this reason not all patients can say that they know her as well as they do the doctor. So such a rare statement by her is worth citing here. The utter sincerity of this testimony, made by the person closest to Dr Konovalov, reminds us also of what is important: of just how difficult the path to knowledge and to inner growth and development is. And so, when you read this book, don't try to measure it against your own standards or compare it with what you know already.

*'Good morning, dear patients.*

*I first came on to the stage here, at the treatment centre, more than six years ago to set the scene for the doctor's entrance. At that time I wanted to devote my whole life to one person only – the doctor – and to help no one but him. At that time, everything else seemed only to exist in relation to this – it all took second place. There was much that I didn't understand and for which I was ill-prepared when I set out on the path. And now, six years later, at the beginning of every new treatment programme I still worry. I'm anxious and have doubts. I lose my spiritual equilibrium and sense of peace, because I now know what a heavy burden we have taken upon ourselves and what a huge responsibility we now have – both to you and to God. Our mission has turned out to be, in essence, a rejection of the self; it has become our life's goal, our religion, our world, our path in life.*

*After you've completed the treatment programme that follows, you will go your separate ways, to your own homes and back to your everyday business, but you will still be with us, and in us, for we never take a moment's break, even between programmes. A good deal of strength is needed sometimes to be able to come up with anything new. Right now I'm talking about the direction medicine is taking as a whole, about the future of our methods of treatment and educating people about them. It's said that the doctor should not get emotionally involved with his patients, but Dr Konovalov, as well as those of us who help him, come under such intense mental and emotional pressure on a daily basis that we completely forget what Aristotle warned us about the root of real tragedy, about pity, and about fear. But how, today, can we not feel for and sympathize with those unfortunate sick people, especially the elderly and children, who are so defenceless and who do no harm?'*

It is for this reason that Antonina Konstantinovna is there beside her husband today, supporting him and giving inspiration to his patients. Because she, and those assisting her at the treatment centre, stand in the wings during the healing sessions, they do not feel the beneficial effects of the energy. Or at least, they don't sense it in the same way that the patients, comfortably settled in their seats, do. But they are, nevertheless, still tuned in to what is going in the hall – to its pain, suffering and misfortunes. And Antonina Konstantinovna in particular finds it hard to stick to the advice the doctor often gives to his patients: don't allow pain to enter your heart, for she constantly allows this pain to pass through her.

But this is now. Twenty-seven years ago when she and Sergey (as he then was to her) first met in the pop group in which he played the piano and she sang, if someone had told them of the life that lay in store for them, neither would have believed a word. On the outside, they were no different from the other cheerful young people around them. Which is why Antonina Konstantinovna simply smiled when one of her older friends, having met her husband for the first time, said with a thoughtful look: 'He's going to be a great man one day'.

## The Family That Knows Real Peace

Family life for the Konovalovs was always chaotic, especially during the first years when Sergey was posted to the north-western seaport of Murmansk. There were the night calls, as well as other emergency situations and unfortunate incidents that occurred outside working hours, all of which required the doctor's urgent assistance. Antonina Konstantinovna got used to sleeping with one ear open, so that if, in the middle of the night, someone was sent to fetch the doctor, they didn't wake her young son by knocking loudly at the door. In her sleep she'd hear the downstairs door bang and manage to get to her apartment door before they knocked. Why Sergey Sergeevich was specifically sent for, and not some other doctor, was no surprise to her. There were three doctors covering their area, but she knew that her husband was a doctor sent by God. It was not he who had chosen his profession, but destiny.

Despite all the external things that disrupted their life, the family did have peace – real peace of the kind that only real love and mutual respect can bring. But then, one day, Antonina Konstantinovna fell ill. Having by then learned how to use the energy in healing patients, her husband sat her down in a chair, told her to relax and then transmitted its energizing power to her. His wife looked at him in amazement, suddenly realizing that this power of her husband's was something she had been subconsciously aware of for a long time. She'd had a sense of a heavy weight bearing down on her on and off for years. She'd gradually got used to it and had put it down to tiredness, or atmospheric pressure, or weakness. But that, of course, was not how it was.

## Fulfilling the Mission Becomes a Way of Life

Even though it was not difficult for Antonina Konstantinovna to believe in her husband's extraordinary abilities, it was nevertheless an entirely different matter to embrace the new way of life that they dictated. For Dr Konovalov's life was now synonymous with one thing: work, work and yet more work. He would get up at seven in the morning and set off for the hospital; in the evening he would then go and conduct healing sessions in a small hall somewhere in the suburbs. He'd return at midnight, but often it was 2 or 3 a.m. In the morning it was back to the hospital again, and in the evening – another healing session. What ordinary human being could endure such a punishing schedule? And what kind of woman would be happy that she only saw her husband for half an hour every day? Naturally enough, it provoked misunderstandings and even hostility towards her husband's work. Small disagreements would blow up into rows. They were always short-lived because there simply wasn't time for them, but nevertheless they were unusual in a family where peace and harmony had prevailed till then. Once, in the heat of the moment, after Antonina Konstantinovna had furiously demanded that her husband give up his healing sessions, she was overcome by an intense and heavy wave of energy which prevented her from finishing what she was saying. It was so unexpected it choked her and she fell into a stunned silence. It was as though the energy was saying to her: 'Don't touch him, don't interfere!' Antonina Konstantinovna sensed a real threat in this. But it didn't frighten her, just helped bring her to an understanding of the fact that her husband was not merely excessively devoted to his work but was carrying out a preordained mission. But from whom? Was it possible that the power which had invested him with this extraordinary gift was now demanding total submission and was removing from his path anything that might get in its way?

Antonina Konstantinovna began to take a closer look at the work her husband was engaged in and the level of results it was bringing. The results of his treatment were, even then, exceeding all expectations – both those of the patients as well as the doctor himself. That surely meant that the energy was good? Yet Antonina Konstantinovna could still feel its 'mortal grip' on her and she was still rather frightened. A short while later she became unwell. She stayed at home, intending to have a lie down, but once again, became aware of the energy. Only it wasn't the kind which threatened a person's strength and sapped it – the kind she had experienced previously. Now the energy was surrounding her on all sides and after a few minutes she felt better. This time, the energy had been more tender than a mother fussing over a child, more gentle than a kitten, more caring than the most attentive of sick-nurses. It was no longer a rival, but was now a friend and ally.

After that, everything changed. Tired of trying to catch her husband on his way from the hospital to the healing sessions in order to give him his sandwiches (for he never usually managed to have time to eat, or simply forgot), Antonina Konstantinovna decided to give up her job and devote herself entirely to him. And to him alone – or so she thought at first. But it didn't turn out that way. She couldn't avoid the one thing that gave meaning to his life – his work. She too was soon drawn into it, unable to close her heart to the suffering and pain so intensely felt by so many of the patients who came to every session. Within a few months, overcoming her terrible nervousness, she began going out on to the stage in order to create a calming atmosphere in preparation for the healing session to follow. This is how she described it:

*'It isn't just healing that takes place in our hall, it's the creation of a well person, of a healthy individual. We don't just ease the patient's condition, taking away their pain, we don't just remove scars and deformities. Here, the real causes of disease that are hidden deep in the human psyche, in the soul – the mistakes a person has made in their often harsh attitude to themselves and to those around them – are uncovered and removed ...*

*Our organism is such a complicated machine that it could only have been created by a genius. And only God can know how difficult it is for both the patient and the doctor to get to the root of disease. At our healing sessions, the patients find their way back to health in ways that are natural, for we are learning the laws of nature gradually, by degrees. Nature is the greatest doctor, it has all the secrets of healing at its disposal and, if we have a teacher who enlightens us as well, then half of our problems will have already been solved. The rest is up to each one of us.'*

## 'We've Never Seen So Many Cars in Our Neighbourhood Before'

Antonina Konstantinovna was born in a rural district where there were no school, clinic or doctors. Until now, people living there had to go into the nearest town to attend school or see the doctor. So, of course, whenever she goes back with her husband to visit her family the whole place starts buzzing. News quickly circulates that a doctor from the city has come on a visit to his aunt; the visit to relatives inevitably turns into a series of healing sessions.

'On one occasion, Sergey was healing an old man who was paralysed', Antonina Konstantinovna tells us …

'I didn't heal him' Sergey Sergeevich says, being a stickler for accuracy. 'I couldn't, I didn't have enough time. His wife asked me to go and see her husband, who'd been confined to a wheelchair since an accident ten years before. He couldn't move his legs at all. I took my son with me and we set off for the patient's home. During the healing session the patient's toes began to move and then his legs literally started twitching. He was stunned by this, and so was Yaroslav. Of course there wasn't enough time to treat such a serious problem properly. I think he would have needed at least six months.'

However, news of what had happened went round the neighbourhood like wildfire and crowds began to gather. No one had ever seen so many cars, parked bumper to bumper along the road for hundreds of yards. And whenever the Konovalovs visited there'd be as many people crowded into the house as it could take. People brought water with them for it to be energized and they hung on the doctor's every word. These were the most receptive patients he had ever had in his life and his work with them went easily and without a hitch. The neighbourhood was small but God had not abandoned it, for its people had retained a pureness of heart and mind. They opened up their souls to greet the doctor and followed him wholeheartedly, with a faith both in him and in themselves.

'The people here are closer to the earth, to nature and have not yet forgotten its laws', remarks Antonina Konstantinovna. 'I clearly remember how my grandmother looked after herself. She lived alone, and no matter how many times my mother asked her to come and live with us she refused. Grandmother carried on looking after her own home even when she was seventy. But as she got older her legs began to ache a little. Every evening she'd boil up different kinds of grasses and soak her feet in them in a bowl, reciting something along these lines: "My poor old legs, you've worked so hard today, take a rest.".... And that's how she managed to stay on her feet until the end. Then, suddenly one day, in the middle of summer, when she'd just turned eighty, she turned up at her daughter's. She came into the yard, sat down on a bench under a mulberry tree and said: "I've come to die, my dear." Her daughter was shocked to hear this but, composing herself, said: "You're not dying yet, Mum. After all, you've managed to get here on your own two feet." She sat down on the bench next to her mother and tenderly put her arms round her. They talked for a while, and then the mother laid her head on her daughter's shoulder and quietly and peacefully – with the utmost ease – passed into that other world.'

It wasn't at all like death in the terrifying sense of the word, the inevitability of which we are all marked with from childhood, but rather a painless transition from one human energy field into another, different one, the one the doctor talks about in his healing sessions.

## Unexpected Things Happen When the Doctor Makes a Visit

Sometimes the effects of Dr Konovalov's powers can bring a smile to the face. For example, on one particular visit to Antonina Konstantinovna's parents' home, even the drinking water from the well was affected by his presence. It too became charged with the energy, because even here, in the countryside and 'off duty', the doctor still held healing sessions. Antonina Konstantinovna's father enjoyed taking part in them, but had his suspicions now and then about some of the 'side-effects' of the doctor's presence. For example, he liked to have a drink from a special, small cup before dinner. It was a habit, a tradition that he'd stuck to all his life and which irritated his wife. Why this special little cup? One day, he had sat down at the table after his daughter and son-in-law had come on one of their visits, picked up the cup, raised it to his lips ... and suddenly froze. Antonina Konstantinovna and her mother noticed this, looked at each other, and exchanged a covert smile. Her father turned the cup this way and that in his hands, put it on the table, tried taking it in the other hand, again raised it to his lips and once more put it back on the table.

'Why do you keep on swapping it around?' his wife teased. 'Drink it!'

'There's something wrong with it,' he said in disbelief. And then, with a wry look at his daughter, he said, 'It's that wretched energized water of yours.' And after that he would run over to the nearest well where the water was unaffected, in order to fill his cup.

(By the way, the energized water's powers can be utilised in the treatment of alcoholism. In their questionnaires, many patients tell how a husband, son or daughter has, much to their own surprise, been able to give up alcohol after drinking only the water brought home from healing sessions.)

## News Spreads that the Doctor is in the Neighbourhood Again

So, in this way, even a holiday back home turned into yet more work. For many years on end the doctor and Antonina Konstantinovna never had much of a holiday or an extended break from work. It wasn't until the summer of 2003 that the Konovalovs were finally able to take a proper holiday abroad for the first time. On an earlier, brief holiday many years earlier, there was a woman on the beach who had an asthma attack. Naturally enough, Sergey Sergeevich immediately went to help. He'd brought the attack under control before the ambulance arrived. Other holiday-makers who'd witnessed this soon themselves became patients and Dr Konovalov had to take up work yet again. On another occasion, a young girl – the granddaughter of a woman who was waiting her turn to be seen – was running around and skipping and Sergey Sergeevich stopped to take a look at the sore patches disfiguring her hands. 'Let's make you better,' he said. And, once again, word about the doctor spread like wildfire and an endless stream of people came wanting to be treated.

Does Antonina Konstantinovna have any regrets about her former, uneventful and ordinary life? She does. She bitterly regrets spending so very little time, or that's how it seems to her now, with her grandmother. Grandmother would come out with such wise words and meaningful observations about all kinds of things. Yet Antonina Konstantinovna feels she didn't place enough value in all her wisdom at the time. She regrets, too, that work took her away from her child and that she had precious little time to spend with him. She regrets not knowing and understanding then what she does now. If she had, she feels she would have been able to offer more spiritual warmth, and give much more attention and love to people.

Returning from holidays like those described above, Sergey Sergeevich and Antonina Konstantinovna would once again resume their on-stage healing sessions in St Petersburg. But they are not actors; nor are those gathered in the auditorium their fans attending some kind of performance. As for the hall itself – it is a place where much sadness dwells. It is filled to the brim with suffering, a place where, instead of being inundated with ovations, the stage is inundated with pain. Those who get better bring flowers – there are always bunches of them lying on the stage at every healing session – and then they leave. Others, who are yet to embark on the difficult, long and protracted path towards recovery, come and take the places of those who have moved on. There are also those who come here because there is nowhere else left for them to go. They look at the stage with mistrust, constantly expecting to discover that it's all a sham – for they've been deceived many times in their lives. They are ready at any moment to get up and leave. And then the doctor, with his extraordinary gifts, comes out on stage to them, accepting their disbelief, as well as their ingratitude – which are characteristic of many sick people – and sensitive to their sense of confusion. He comes out so that he can teach them to believe, to love and to learn to have hope.

*From case history 1005787 (born in 1936)*
'I want you to know that I'm on my 16th treatment programme, straight on from the 15th one. Things are going really well for me. Having experienced the usual emotional and spiritual uplift by the end of the last programme, none of us was able to 'come back down to earth', to cool off from the heightened state that has accompanied all the healing sessions in this programme.

... A few words about the special water*. The energized water has been very good at helping my gastro-intestinal tract get back to normal. I drink a cupful in the morning, and sometimes I can't even manage to get out of bed before it starts working. It's very good. When I used to drink 'dead' water, my stomach wouldn't work for up to five days.

Sergey Sergeevich, a small 'miracle' has unexpectedly happened for me, thanks to the healing sessions and the energy. I wasn't expecting it and didn't tell you because I needed time to be sure that it was really true. But now I know for certain.

The thing is, I've always liked having a couple of glasses of vodka before dinner. Seeing that we aren't in any financial difficulty, there's always something to drink – and then some. I've been doing this practically every day, except when there's a healing session. But suddenly, after the 14th treatment programme, an amazing kind of 'paralysis' took hold of me: I forgot to put the bottle on the table at dinner time; I did it several times, all week. As a result, I very rarely have a drink: I don't drink and have no desire to. This has in no way told on my general well-being; it hasn't affected my moods or my personality. It's wonderful that it happened so easily, almost without me noticing. In fact I didn't notice it myself until three or so days later, during dinner. It suddenly occurred to me that it would be nice to have a drink with the meal, but for some reason I couldn't be bothered to go and get the bottle from the fridge and, what's more, I had absolutely no desire to do so. And when I really don't want to do it then there's no reason to drink. So this is how my life is now and I'm not at all upset about it.

This unexpected bonus from the healing sessions and from the energy has filled me with joy and the conviction that I am on the road to recovery. Goodbye Sergey Sergeevich. What a joy it is that you are here with us.'

*20 July 1999 St Petersburg*
*(The patient stopped coming to healing sessions. In October 2001 condition unstable. Problems with his legs)*

(* The use of the special, energized water will be explained in Chapter 19.)

# PART II
# PRACTICE

# CHAPTER 13

# THE HUMANITARIAN REHABILITATION CENTRE IN ST PETERSBURG

## The Clinic Where, Every Year, Thousands of 'Incurables' Recover

The Humanitarian Rehabilitation Centre, Dr Konovalov's energy clinic in St Petersburg, has now been in existence for fourteen years. Its fame has long since spread beyond St Petersburg and across the whole of Russia; word of the doctor's work is now bringing many patients from Europe, America and even Israel to the centre, to add to the thousands of Russian patients who are already cured here every year. Each healing session brings together up to 1,500–2,000 patients, depending on the size of the hall. Even though the number of people wishing to attend is constantly growing, Dr Konovalov never conducts a session before more than 2,500 patients at a time. In this way, the centre at St Petersburg now addresses the needs of between 6,000 and 8,000 patients a week.

More often than not the people who come to the centre for treatment are those who have nothing left to hope for – people who have been suffering for many years from long-standing, chronic illnesses, many of them cancer patients, whom the doctors have told are hopeless cases; people who are exhausted by the frequent calls for an ambulance, by endless hospital visits, and who are worn down by pain – in short, the kind of people who cannot be cured by conventional medicine.

Here, little by little, day by day, month by month, they recover their lost health. The doctor heals them. But he heals them not with tablets and not through surgical intervention. There are no medical drips at the centre, no syringes, and no arsenal of proprietary medicines, although the centre does, of course, have its own team of fully trained doctors and nurses who are always on duty to deal with emergencies and who carry with them all the equipment needed to assist those very sick or disabled patients who need their help. But as for the healing sessions themselves and his overall treatment method, the doctor heals through the transmission of the energy that was revealed to him. And before you raise your eyebrows in disbelief, just take a look at the testimonies of the patients themselves and read the many case histories that are to be found throughout this book. It is doubtful whether anyone could describe better than they what happens in this extraordinary centre, or could tell you about the miracles that take place there every day, about the illnesses which retreat when confronted with Dr Konovalov's healing gifts.

*From case history 1015743 (born 1938), a professor and doctor of technical science*

'This is my second questionnaire, before I begin my 14th treatment programme. I have not the slightest doubt that the diagnosis "prostate cancer with metastases of the bone" does not accurately correspond with the facts. I am grateful to God that he brought me to you. I have to say that after my course of radical radiotherapy in March–April of this year I felt no better, for I knew that they were still giving me the worst possible prognosis. But I didn't for one moment think that I would give in to it.

And here I am, at your temple of health*. I quite appreciate that I will be a regular patient of yours, not just for a few treatment programmes but for many, many years to come. But it has its values and its advantages. My dear wife and I have come to look upon everything connected with you as an alternative, happy life. At long last, twice a week, we can leave behind our ordinary and mundane daily routine and can appreciate that, besides work and nothing but work and worry, there is a place where we can see just how far removed we are from the ordinary way of living and how much there is to do and learn in order to rid ourselves of those unpleasant qualities of which we are well aware and from which we need to free ourselves. It is precisely their presence, their reappearance in the previous few years, that has been the cause of all my own "ills".

The most important thing is my belief in success, my belief in you and in God. Everything will be all right.

During the 6th treatment programme you singled me out for attention. After the session I had a strong sensation of heaviness in the lower part of my body. My legs ached. During this session and those that followed, I could feel the circular movements you perform with your hands on other patients whom you single out. When I experience these movements I am lifted by a wave of energy, which rotates in the opposite direction and bears down on me from above. My general condition is normal, blood pressure 115/80.

By the 8th treatment programme, my haemorrhoid ganglions had disappeared. I noticed that my rapidly thinning hair had darkened and that new growth had appeared on my bald patch. When, during the first ten treatment programmes, I managed with difficulty to get to the centre, after a few minutes I had mentally left it. In the time that followed, I became more and more acutely sensitive to the heightened atmosphere in the centre, whenever I was there, and it turned out to be the energy of creation that was engulfing me. It was a very powerful feeling, not just of warmth, but rather a bright, irradiating heat which penetrates the region of the pelvis, and clenches itself into a fist, placed between the legs.

Dear Sergey Sergeevich, your work with children has had a very great effect on me. Your beautiful music, to the sound of the chirping of birds, always brings tears to my eyes. Perhaps I am sentimental, but this is how it is with me at every healing session.

Thank you very much, doctor, for urging me to think about my sins and try to come to terms with them and the bad things I have done, the ways in which I have behaved, and the unkind words I have said.

I consider myself to be a truly happy person; I believe in you and in God; I believe in the fullness of my recovery; I believe in the wider sense of love towards all people and, of course, my love for the person most precious to me – my wife.'

*13 July 1999 St Petersburg.*
*(According to clinical observations made on 3 October 2001, the metastases had gone. The patient feels well and is continuing with the treatment)*

[* NOTE: The centre is not a religious institution in which people gather to pray and address God, although many Russian patients, who gain a deep sense of spiritual peace and faith during their treatment there, often refer to it as though it were a church or, more specifically, a 'temple'. What they are in fact describing is the state of being that individual patients achieve during the healing sessions – a sense of harmony with the whole body and with the worlds that go to make up the individual's organism. Some of this will be explained later in this book and can also be found in the doctor's many other publications.]

### From case history 1011767 (born 1939)

'I am now attending my 15th treatment programme. I came to you with tachycardia – an irregularity of the cardiovascular system – as well as osteochondrosis, fibroadenoma of the mammary glands, and lymphadenitis of the subclavian nodes on both sides of the mediastinum. There's no treatment; you live life as it comes and go and see the oncologist every six months. I felt I was being kicked when I was already down, but destiny is now revealing things to me and sending me the light at the end of the tunnel. So here I am now, with you. What can I say about my life now? The nodes have disappeared, the osteochondrosis has cleared up, my spine is perfectly alright, my heart beats calmly, and I sleep a deep, healthy, almost dreamless sleep. I wake up full of strength and energy, eager to do things.'

*(In October 2001 nodes in the lymph glands and the fibroadenoma had gone. Treatment continues)*

### From case history 1010907 (born 1933)

'I am attending my 14th treatment programme. I cannot continue without remarking on the miracle that has happened to me. If you take into account that I was born in 1933 and that my rheumatism first started in 1944, then it is a miracle among miracles. On 16th June 1997, at Diagnostic Centre No. 1, I had a heart examination which included a cardiac ultrasound. I had last had a physical examination in 1993. The results were as follows: the openings of the cusp of the aortic valve had enlarged from 1.6 to 1.8*; no calcinosis was detected; no deficiencies; the area of aperture of the mitral valve had reduced from 2.2. to 2 square centimetres; the marginal deformation of the cusp, the cupola-shaped opening, and pronounced calcinosis were no longer in evidence; mitral insufficiency had reduced from stage 3 to stage 1. There was no fluid in the pericardium. The doctor herself told me that my valves are in good condition. Three doctors examined my results. For several years now my consultant has been I. A. Gorbacheva, a candidate of medical sciences from the First Medical Institute. She is very attentive, very knowledgeable and doesn't miss a thing. She told me that she had never come across a case where calcinosis has disappeared. Thank you very much.

Dear Sergey Sergeevich, looking back, I now understand that my recovery began at the very first healing sessions. I had so many problems then, and all of them at such a critical stage, that I was incapable of noticing it physically. I made it to the healing sessions, dragged myself there, with the greatest of difficulty. After the first four treatment programmes most of the varicose veins in my legs had disappeared, the remainder became less pronounced. My gout began to clear up. My stomach started working properly. The size of my liver went back to normal. During the 7th treatment programme I felt as though my whole body had begun to get better, especially my respiratory tract. By the 8th of April I knew that I had recovered. I felt incredibly relieved. The 13th treatment programme was a real holiday for me: I felt a significant improvement in my right sub-costal. The skin on my legs became much brighter. I could breathe better through my nose. I came back to life, literally from the brink. This all took a year and a half, at a time when life had been very hard for me. Now I want to live again. My gratitude to you is limitless, dear Sergey Sergeevich.'

[* Note: smaller, fractional measurements in metric have not been converted, because to do so would create inaccuracies]

## Inexplicable Things that are Sometimes Obvious

This is what the same patient wrote a year later, after having continued her treatment with the doctor:

'Now, three years of treatment are behind me .... In fact, for a long time now I've not been filling out questionnaires but writing what I'd call testimonies ... When I came to you the first time I could barely stand, I was on my last legs. That's no exaggeration.

The calcinosis of the mitral, aortic and tricuspid valves of my heart has gone. What a miracle that was! In only a year and a half! The proof came in the cardiac ultrasound. And the electrocardiogram shows that there is no deterioration. The arrhythmia is now in a normal systolic form. And yet in the early 1980s they suggested a heart operation. In fact, at the Academy of Medical Sciences they insisted on it and painted a terrible picture of my future. I wept but nevertheless refused – and then the miracle happened. My liver now feels a lot better. Before, I hardly ate a thing, only cereals, boiled potatoes and watery soup. I couldn't even eat black bread and cabbage. Now I eat everything that I can afford to buy. When I'm visiting people, I eat everything I'm given. My varicose veins began to go down from the very first healing sessions. My oedemas went down and my kidneys began to function better. They had had serious lesions since 1944. I had to take so many antibiotics – and still I couldn't get rid of my rheumatism. I took bicillin, penicillin and all sorts of anti-rheumatic medication, year in year out. My poor kidneys! What they went through! The gout began to disappear from the very first treatment sessions. My fingers are now much less swollen, the wrinkles have reappeared on my skin, whereas before it had been taut with smooth lumps. My thyroid gland has shrunk. My breathing has got easier. The spasms have practically stopped. My backbone has straightened and my spine hardly aches at all. The stomach is working a whole lot better, my haemorrhoids have shrunk considerably and don't bother me. Something that came up in my right breast has got smaller and doesn't trouble me and the nipple has got noticeably better. I'm no longer flat-footed. The long, calcified ridges in my fingernails are disappearing, and they are smoother and brighter. The skin is beginning to regrow over places where I received burns in the autumn of 1941.'

*December 1999*

**From case history 1014789 (born 1938)**
'This is my 5th treatment programme. I first came for treatment in April 1997, although I had been to several of your diagnostic evenings. I began to make progress from the very first treatment programme. First of all, the stone in my left kidney shrank to 0.2 centimetres (it had been 1 centimetre). The right kidney raised itself by 2 cm (having dropped by 6 cm). Secondly, my nodular goitre has reduced in size, and I get by without medication. After four treatment programmes the stone in my kidney had completely dissolved, the right kidney was back in its proper position and became smooth. I hardly ever get headaches. My joints ache a lot less.'

*(In October 2001 condition stable. Treatment continues)*

*From case history 1012459 (born 1936)*

'I am attending my 7th treatment programme in two years. During this time we have achieved a major victory – my bronchial asthma, which had tormented me for about seven or eight years, has completely gone. In all this time my osteochondrosis hasn't got any worse. The hip joint which I injured in 1996 is working normally, even though I haven't cut down on my workload. In the last year I haven't once complained about my health, and consider my fitness level to be that of a 45-year-old. And it is your extraordinary gift for channelling energy that has made this miracle possible. Thank you so much for this.'

*January 1997*

*From case history 1012617 (born 1944)*

My 11th treatment programme … At the present time I have been getting very good treatment results: at my regular check-up the doctor couldn't find any signs of disease – in other words, the fibromyoma had gone. They have withdrawn the diagnosis of "anaemia"; my haemoglobin level has risen from 80 to 141 units. I don't keep coming out in patches of flaky shingles, yet before it broke out all over my skin every spring and autumn. I am amazed and very happy about this, because it has been bothering me for more than thirty years. I sleep well. My paradontosis has gone. My sight has improved. My joints hardly bother me at all. The diagnosis of "coronary heart disease" has been withdrawn.'

*(In October 2002 condition stable. Treatment continues)*

*From case history 1009188 (born 1936)*

'The 18th January 1998 was three years to the day since I first dragged myself to your centre. I now want to summarize it all and try not to forget anything. So: my insomnia has gone, the acute and painful spread of extensive osteochondrosis has stopped, as has high blood pressure. I'm hardly bothered at all by the chronic gastritis, cholecystitis and enterocolitis, and practically all my allergies have disappeared. I'm not troubled by the acidic fibroadenoma of both my breasts (in December I went to see the oncologist, who said that everything had settled down). My chronic bronchitis hardly ever flares up, and I now only have a mild form of vasomotor rhinitis. The veins in my legs do not throb; my leg and elbow joints don't ache. The corns on my heels and soles have practically gone, and the calluses on my fingers have disappeared; my bent fingers have straightened themselves out. The twitching in my legs has practically stopped and my arms don't go numb. My thyroid gland is going down little by little (it protruded quite a lot before). During the 10th treatment programme my right kidney raised itself, during the 12th and 13th programme my uterus rose significantly on two occasions. My short-sightedness has not yet gone, but the glasses are already annoying me. My memory and hearing have improved. My physical capabilities were nil before, but now I feel normal; I've become much calmer, more patient. In general, right now, my spirit is being reborn, although there's still some way to go before I reach complete harmony. Many dark hairs have appeared in the midst of all my grey, my gums and teeth do not ache. I walk as I did when I was young – with a light step, and my neck-line and breasts are now more attractive than I dreamed they'd be when I was young. I feel young at heart and look younger too. They've started asking to see my pass on public transport, and don't believe I'm a pensioner. Someone even once referred to me as a woman in the prime of life. ... I got married, had a family, and many other good things have happened in my life. I thank you from the bottom of my heart for everything and shall go on praying to God that he sends you and your family health and happiness.'

*(In January 2002 condition stable)*

**From case history 1011695 (born 1927)**
'I am on my 16th treatment programme ... When I was in hospital, I asked the doctor if the extrasystoles would ever go away. I was getting them very frequently, every third or fourth day. He replied that, taking into account my age and the fact that I had already had a myocardial infarction, this was impossible. But I haven't had a single one in the last year, which has greatly surprised the doctor, who had been in charge of my case for six years. And now a real miracle has happened: my aneurysm has disappeared, and this was shown when they did an 'echo' on me on 5th January this year. All these years they've been telling me: no sudden movements, no sharp turns – in

short, watch what you do. At first I didn't believe it and then, on my way home from the clinic, the tears began pouring from my eyes – tears of immense gratitude to you. You often tell us: "Say thank you to your body." But what was my body without you? The only way in which I was able to help myself was by having faith in you from the very first healing session. And so here I am writing to you. My words seem so feeble; I just can't find the right ones with which to say thank you, dear Sergey Sergeevich.

*(In October 2002 condition stable)*

## A Phenomenon Imperceptible in its Vastness

'I cannot express myself in words', 'I cannot find the words', 'I don't know how to thank you': these are the kinds of expressions that can be found in almost every questionnaire. Which is why it is one thing to hear about someone else's miraculous recovery and quite another to experience such a recovery for oneself. Besides, people mainly come to the centre to be cured of a single, major illness – the one which causes them the most distress. It is precisely then, during the healing process, that they realize that there were other things wrong with them – that they couldn't breathe properly through their nose before and now they can, that they had stomachache every week and now it doesn't hurt, that they had a wart on their finger and now it's gone. Thousands of questionnaires contain one and the same expression: 'I've only just noticed' – for example, 'before, I couldn't bend my head without feeling giddy, but now, look, I can sit down, fill in this questionnaire.' Or: 'I came across my drops in the drawer of the table and I've only just realized that I couldn't get by without them before.'

And yet, how is it that many people know so little about Dr Konovalov's work? First of all, it is because the doctor has no need and no desire to advertise. He categorically rejects all forms of publicity. In fact, he often says to his patients: 'I've made you better, but don't go telling anyone about it.' There is a great and profound reason for this: the healing process requires peace and quiet, and certainly not fuss and public fanfares. The three treatment halls in St Petersburg are full of patients; Dr Konovalov simultaneously conducts sessions in all of them, working alongside his assistants almost round the clock. In addition, he has absolutely no time to give interviews or be filmed, although he has now begun putting his many ideas about health and healing into the series of 'Books That Heal' as well as giving lectures and writing medical and academic papers. But work – and that means the patient – always comes first. To tell the truth, work also takes third, fourth and even hundredth place. He needs no acknowledgement for this – he gets acknowledgement enough from the thousands of his patients who have recovered and from the doctors who themselves have been to the centre for treatment. There are many of them, and they subsequently send their own patients whom conventional medicine has failed to help.'

*From case history 10103315 (born 1964)*
'I am attending my 6th treatment programme. My dear Dr Sergey Sergeevich, I am very grateful to you and to God for the disappearance of my illnesses and the improvement in my general state of mind. My fundamental problem has gone: throbbing, pounding headaches which have tormented me for years on end, since I was at school. My headaches were particularly bad from the morning until 4 or 5 p.m. As the years went by, the pain would ease off for a while and then get worse, to the point where I could barely manage to think straight and talk coherently. I first began noticing it in the 9th to 10th grades. Somehow or other I managed to get into the technical institute, but had to abandon my studies within the year: the pain had got much worse and prevented me from continuing my studies.

I twice went to hospital for treatment and was examined, but the doctors simply couldn't pin down what was triggering the pain. They suggested various diagnoses: vascular dystonia and high blood pressure. And then, on top of this, I was called up for military service. There the pain got worse again and I ended up in the military hospital in Tbilisi. Here, after examining me, they formally concluded that I had inflammation of the membranes of the frontal cortex of the brain, together with other dysfunctions. But they couldn't explain what was causing my headaches. And though they exempted me from active military service, they still transferred me to the reserve.

Six months after leaving the army and back home again, I felt more like myself and went back to work. It was physically taxing, and after working for the next six years my spine began to hurt; I had pains in my heart and my blood pressure went up. The doctor said: "If you carry on working like this you'll end up an invalid." I had to give up my job. In 1995 all these became simultaneously much worse, and once again it became difficult for me to talk and move about. It thought I was going to die. But it was then that God showed me the way, and brought me to you, as my last hope. After the very first healing session, I began to revive. Afterwards, they told me that I was as white as a corpse when I came to my first session but that I left it with a rosy complexion. Gradually, I got better and better. Everything became coherent again: my speech, thoughts, wishes, dreams, love and compassion. It was as though I had been born again. My energy came back. I couldn't sit in the same place for a single moment, slept only four hours a night, managed to think up an interesting business enterprise. I began attracting people's attention and they began taking an interest in me.

The frequently relapsing tracheitis from which I had suffered since I was thirteen disappeared. Before, when I had even a simple cold or rhinitis, it had always turned into a hacking cough with green sputum. They had told me at the Pulmonology Institute that I'd never be free of this problem. But the chronic rhinitis which had also plagued me for years also disappeared. After the latest treatment programme I managed to lose 6 kilos [14 lbs] of excess weight. I am enormously grateful to you, dear doctor, and wish you happiness and a long life. God protect you.'

*(In October 2001 condition stable. Feels very well)*

### From case history 1007680 (born 1928)

'There are a lot of good things I want to tell you about. I first came to you, or, I should say, I was dragged here under protest, when you first started treatment programmes in the Vyborg district. My whole body had seized up and I was almost paralysed: severe osteochondrosis of my arms, intercostal neuralgia, terrible headaches. I couldn't hold a spoon let alone cut a slice of bread. It was a nightmare.... By the 7th treatment programme I suddenly found I could lift up my arms and that I could get myself into a wheelchair more easily. When everybody around me had gone off to sleep, I would sit there weeping, hearing you say: "Don't cry my dear, everything will be fine." Nevertheless, for the whole seven treatment programmes I was angry: why was my husband bringing me and making me sit here? Later on I wept with joy that someone had made me do it. My heart slowed down and got calmer; when I got home I didn't want to take my nitro-glycerine. I suddenly noticed that my terrible operation scar had somehow disappeared, and my distended stomach had gone back into place. My husband bathed me and kept remarking on what had happened to me. During the fifth healing session of the 2nd treatment programme, I was suddenly able to raise myself, holding on to the wheelchair, and join in the exercises with the others. I didn't wait for my husband to come back with the wheelchair as I usually did. Some kind people helped me drag myself to the cloakroom, put my coat on and led me out to the car. Meanwhile, my husband was dashing around looking for me, wondering where his wife had got to. Now I can walk and can dance thanks to you. On the 23rd July I will go for my official disability assessment. I'm sure they won't register me this time. In fact, all my assessments are excellent. And although I'm thinking what a wonderful thing it is to be well, I will no longer receive the additional disability allowance in my pension. Everything is fine now. Thank you for everything.'

*July 1998*
*(In October 2001 condition stable. Does not attend treatment sessions)*

*From case history 1009851 (born 1936)*
'It is four years this May since I began coming to you for treatment. I've not missed a single session. When I filled in the first questionnaire I had been diagnosed with more than 30 medical complaints. I'm happy that I am now free of a significant number of them. Today, I want to tell you about the worst one – the cancer. I came to you with fibromyoma and a tumour of the breast. But what a victory! The fibromyoma has gone! And my breast has also got better. The flare-up in the condition, which happened in January, was all my own fault. I'd gone around boasting to all and sundry about how happy I was. I was telling everyone. On top of that I had been really squashed up against people in a crowded bus; so all your work came to nothing. My God! How distraught I was when the oncologist told me that only an operation would save me. Do you remember the panic-stricken

questionnaire I filled in at that time? My friends rang the treatment centre and asked for their support. And you, my dear doctor, started all over again and corrected my mistakes. At that time I was preparing for the operation and having tests. When I went to the doctor for my regular check, she noticed an improvement. They postponed the operation. And then my condition got even better and they stopped talking about an operation. I told the doctor about you. You know, I go everywhere with your leaflets taped to my body.* At the consultation, when I was getting undressed, the tapes got all tangled up and the doctor was intrigued, having helped me undo them. And so I told her. She asked me to thank you for the help you had given. And really, I can't tell you just how grateful I am, my dear doctor.'

*(In October 2001 condition stable. Treatment continues)*

\* The use of the healing leaflets is explained in Chapters 19 and 21.

### From case history 1004723 (born 1938)
'I am attending my 26th treatment programme, 24 of them at the Lensoviet Palace of Culture ... My sleep has improved, my head doesn't ache as much ... the myositis in my left shoulder blade, which I've had for 25 years' has gone, the fibromyoma I've had in my left breast for 35 years has dissolved, and the knobbly growth on my right metatarsus has disappeared. ... After my 17th treatment programme the fibromyoma in my uterus disappeared (an ultrasound on 21st October 1997 proved it), the nephroptosis has gone (no symptoms were found during ultrasound on 21 October 1997). Hooray! We have won the battle against some of my problems and I am convinced that we will continue along the difficult path to the pinnacle of good health.'

*(In October 2001, condition improved. Continues treatment)*

### From case history 1013990 (born 1993, letter from mother)
'We are attending our third treatment programme. In the interval between sessions my son has not been ill. We've been to the circus, to the theatre. Before, we were frightened of large gatherings of people, but now my child

is able to enjoy life. There's no more flu, not even a cold, which means his immune system is recovering. We've been to the Oncology Institute for checks. The tests showed that everything was normal and only his haemoglobin levels were slightly down (111 units). The professor joked and couldn't believe how, in such a short time, we had managed to get a child with fourth-stage cancer back on his feet again. He said he'd take my son to a conference in Canada as a unique case.'

*(The child was supervised under treatment at the centre for a further two years. In February 1999, condition stable. In October 2001 he was well and attending treatment sessions.)*

We hope that, having read these wonderful uplifting testimonies, the reader can now begin to understand why Dr Konovalov's work is such a unique phenomenon. All of us, at some time in our lives, have come upon wise and wonderful words that have moved us deeply and that get to the heart of things – words that tell us how we should live and what really matters in life. Sometimes, reading about isolated, individual success stories, about the chance chain of events that have helped people overcome all kinds of disease, set us wondering about how such stories could be relevant to us, in our own lives. It is hoped that these accounts by patients of the effectiveness of Dr Konovalov's treatment programmes will convince the reader of the endless possibilities for recovery, not just from adversity in our personal lives but also from crippling and even terminal disease.

A miracle is often described as a phenomenon which cannot be contrived, controlled or repeated any more than it can be categorized or described on paper, or its results explained away. But the miracle of the work of Dr Sergey Konovalov is a living miracle that is repeated regularly, at every single healing session. And its witnesses are many.

# CHAPTER 14

# 'I CAN TAKE YOUR PAIN AWAY'

## A Man Who Is Unusual in Every Respect

Even the most sceptical of people who come to the centre for the first time, perhaps by chance, not believing in any of what they perceive to be nothing more than 'clever tricks', or having been talked into it by close friends, will be taken aback by what by what they see, hear and experience when they get there.

On stage stands a man whom nobody could possibly think of as ordinary. Even if he wanted to, Dr Konovalov would not be able to lose himself in a crowd. Everything about him is extraordinary: his face, eyes, movements and his low, soothing voice which penetrates to the depths of one's soul. One has the impression that this man is the embodiment of goodness and purity and is utterly untainted. The energy generated by his goodness can be felt with exactly the same intensity by those sitting up in the balcony at the very back of the hall as those in the front row.

## The Structure of the Healing Sessions at the Centre

The healing session begins. Antonina Konstantinovna comes onto the stage. She uses her voice as a kind of a tuning fork, setting the atmosphere for the session. Her soft voice, her intonation and the words she uses all have a calming effect. They inspire hope and are reassuring. The healing process has already begun and patients eagerly latch on to her every word: for indeed, she speaks for and on behalf of the doctor. Her explanations are fundamental to what each patient is about to experience, despite the fact that, on the surface, they seem to have no specific relevance to any particular person's state of health. She talks about human qualities, about the difficulties encountered in life, about spiritual renewal. When she has finished, the auditorium is completely silent. Then the doctor appears.

## The Doctor Comes Out to Meet his Patients

A certain ritual accompanies Dr Konovalov's appearance. On each occasion, the form it takes depends on the atmosphere among the audience, which the doctor senses differently every time he appears. For people, of course, arrive in different states of mind, with different preoccupations and worries.

The lights are dimmed and enchanting music begins to play. However, even though the doctor improvises on the piano, he is not giving a performance. He is a healer who has already set the difficult task of healing in motion. And so there is no applause. In this respect, one might ask why the doctor needs a stage at all. And indeed his answer is that he doesn't need one. The stage is there for the benefit of the patients:

*'It is there for you, all of you, so that you can more easily see and hear me. I never distance myself from you; I am not your superior, and do not place myself above you. I am among you, in the auditorium. I am beside you my dear patients, and with you in your pain and in your suffering.'*

During the healing session all that can be sensed is the flow of pain being drawn from people in the auditorium towards the stage, a pain which Dr Konovalov channels through himself, soothes, and takes away. During any one session, there may be as many as 2,000 pairs of eyes straining towards him with hope and faith, and these people must not be deceived. They come here to regain their health and nobody leaves without having experienced the alleviation of their physical as well as their spiritual pain.

## Words That Will be Remembered for a Lifetime

The doctor takes away the acute and chronic pain which has brought more than 90 per cent of all patients to the centre. Sooner or later, he is sure to say: 'I can take your pain away; the pain is now leaving you. It's no longer there.' In patients' case histories one frequently encounters one and the same thought, best expressed by one elderly woman in her questionnaire: 'I listen to you and I weep. I cannot believe that there is someone capable of taking my pain away. For do tell me please, who, in the times we live in, would entertain the idea of taking upon themselves the pain of someone else?!'

And then Dr Konovalov begins to talk and his words constitute a message that is passionate, comforting and uncompromising. His voice reverberates around the auditorium and the pain recedes, sickness goes away, and spiritual wounds disappear, leaving no scars.

Many patients sink into a deep sleep at this time. The energy which the doctor has summoned up and channelled through his body penetrates into every cell of the human organism, engendering the warmest of feelings, the most common of which is identified by his patients as a feeling of tranquillity.

## The Knowledge Which Many are Seeking

Some wonderful, energizing exercises now follow. The patients do them sitting in their seats. In this way the body's sensitive layer (a term devised by Dr Konovalov in 1992) is regenerated. If this is your first visit, then many things will seem a puzzle to start off with or will seem to be an eccentricity of the doctor's. But this is by no means the case. Those who have been travelling the long road to recovery with Dr Konovalov can confirm this. At every healing session these people have, by degrees, acquired an extraordinary knowledge which the doctor has shared with them. This knowledge has slowly built up to form a well-balanced system of healing not just for the body but also for the mind.

Many people down through history have set out in search of knowledge such as this. For some, even a few odd fragments have seemed to be sufficient in order to set themselves up as some kind of healer or psychic. First here, now there, new quack healers are constantly emerging out of nowhere, armed with various scraps of knowledge. They are too busy to listen any further; they think they've understood it all, have got everything they need and can now set to work. Their kind of 'healing' is like a well-rehearsed platform performance – and it's always exactly the same. Why does Dr Konovalov say nothing? 'Why do you write so little?' 'When is your next book coming out?' asked patients in their letters when Dr Konovalov first began his healing sessions. This situation has of course changed and he has now written 16 books. But back then, when he first started, there simply weren't enough hours in the day to sit down, think back on things and write it all down, because the doctor felt that he had to keep on moving forward.

His incredible journey is still not complete, and the amount of knowledge he gains is greater with every year, so where to begin? And where indeed is the beginning? It is there, where he finds himself at any given point in time, and can still barely be distinguished. ... But what if others make use of this knowledge? It doesn't matter, because Dr Konovalov is continually moving forward. Practical experience brings its own adjustments – to the healing method, the patients' own testimony and their own knowledge of the universe. The main thing is that these people have a right to receive what they came here for – and that is their health: health in body and in spirit. This is the real triumph, and Dr Konovalov shares it with his patients.

## The Triumph of Overcoming Illness

*From case history 1004326 (born 1940)*
'Apart from praising you and your noble achievements, I am hugely grateful for the tremendous work you do in the name of people's well-being. I am indebted to you for everything from the bottom of my heart.

I am 53 years old. I was a Soviet boxing champion by the age of 18. Then I finished my studies and took a job. In 1981 I went to Afghanistan as a senior army economist. Out of our group of reserves living in the civilian compound, only three survived. One night, the Mujaheddin opened fire on the people in the hostel, and I received two bullets in the chest. One tore through my oesophagus, the other destroyed part of my right lung. In Leningrad I underwent an eight-hour operation (they lifted my stomach, because my oesophagus had been shortened, and part of my lung was removed). And of course, I felt terrible after this; I weighed only 40 kilos [88 lbs], and I'm 180 centimetres [5' 9"] tall. But I hadn't lost my will power; I had my ten-year-old son on my hands, as my wife had perished during the attack that night. My fitness level as a sportsman helped me, as well as regular training. On the surface I made an almost complete recovery, and my son helped me keep up my resolve. Years passed, but I still continued to feel unwell. My son has been studying in Germany for the last few years and had brought me all sorts of expensive medication for my heart, pancreas, liver and kidneys, but none of it had any effect.

And then fate brought me to you. If only God would bring such good fortune to everyone. At my third healing session I felt feverish and very unwell, but you had been warning us that this was all part of the diagnostic period. At my fourth session I sensed a significant improvement in my condition: the heartburn went away, my pancreas and liver stopped aching. With every session I felt a dynamic intake of energy and my health improved. My mistrust completely vanished. After my eighth session I picked up my skipping-rope and worked with it for a whole minute, like I used to during my sporting career. After the ninth session, I did a minute's shadow-boxing for the first time in the twelve years since my operation. I began to discover joy in my life, and in having control over my own body. Thank you so much.'

*(Left the country)*

*From case history 1001622 (born 1941)*
' I now want to share my happiness with you. For the last fifteen years I have been registered with a surgeon for my mastopathy. He examined me regularly and each time would shake his head: the disease was progressive. ... It spread to my other breast ... At the Army Medical Academy, they decided to operate. ... After your healing sessions, at the end of 1992, my surgeon spent a long time examining me, and was somewhat disconcerted. At the end of the examination he admitted that the indurations had become smaller and softer. In March 1993 he warmly congratulated me: the mastopathy had gone, and he took me off his list. ... Encouraged by the results I went to the gynaecologist's consulting room. ... The previous year, when filling out the details in the chart for my sanatorium treatment, the gynaecologist had forbidden me to take narsan mineral baths. And here I was in the most nerve-wracking room for women. A doctor who had been keeping a close watch on my condition for ten years knew me very well and after examining me could not disguise her astonishment: there was no fibromyoma ...'

*(In October 2001 condition stable)*

## Medicine and the Wounds to the Human Spirit

There was a time when Dr Konovalov totally and utterly trusted in medicine. If it had not been so, he would never have finished medical school or become a doctor. He is not the kind of person to take something up without having absolute faith in and dedication to it. But one thing kept him forever on his guard: a surgeon removes a cyst, but it reappears again in exactly the same place. A person is cured of one particular disease, only to succumb to two new and far more serious ones. So can it really be said that a person is fully recovered when you can still see that lingering look of fear in their eyes, the same sense of doom? It's clear that they will soon be back in the clinic, if not in a month, then in a year. What is it we are missing? Could it be that the wounds in the human spirit are no less important? Could it be that these wounds give rise to cancers, to osteochondrosis, to pains in the joints? Could it be that we need to treat these things in a different way?

*From case history 1006417 (born 1950)*
'You have opened up for me a whole new physical and spiritual world, a greater sensitivity to life's experiences ... day by day, week by week, layer by layer, I am changing.'

*From case history 1013316 (born 1962)*
'But the greatest victory of all is the slow but sure way in which, almost without noticing it, I am changing in my attitude to myself and to the world around me ... I have gained confidence in myself, a sense of peace and equilibrium, a sense of my own worth. I have learned to enjoy life. I've discovered aspects of my personality of which I was never aware before...'

*(In October 2001 condition stable. Continues treatment)*

*From case history 1013309 (born 1974)*
'My major ambition is to recover not just physically but also spiritually, so that I can be confident in what I do and the things I wish for – that they are for the right reasons. ...What was the attitude with which I came to the first sessions? It was one of unshakeable self-confidence, with hang-ups,

with a distorted, even unhealthy impression of life. ... Now I have begun to take stock, to examine my attitudes.'

*From case history 1009990 (born 1951)*
'I am taking part in my 30th treatment programme, during which I have been experiencing a gradual improvement. I'm getting better and my sores are clearing up. Before, I was very nervy, and nearly always worked up about something. I regularly blew my top at the first person who happened to be there. But this doesn't happen now, thank God. I feel ashamed to think about it. And the constant, throbbing pains in my head have also lessened without me noticing.

In the mornings, when I opened my eyes, I could hear the throbbing in my head; now I get up with a clear head, and so long as I don't put on weight and I do my energizing exercises then I get a burst of energy and am cheerful all day. I used to write to you saying that I got tired very quickly. For instance, on my days off I had to do the housework that had accumulated during the week, but that I'd do a little, a bit more and then soon feel tired. Now, whatever job it is, I want to do it better – properly, because now I have almost enough strength to last all day. I'm very happy about this.

My major problem – a duodenal ulcer – has completely gone. I eat everything: salty and sour things, as much as I like. It is now two years since I followed any diet strictly. My alimentary canal has recovered.

I must tell you that the longer I go on attending the healing sessions the more I sense the power of the energy of creation. Every healing session has a powerful impact on me, but the feelings vary: I'm being stretched, my head and shoulders are being twisted and rolled around; sometimes it seems as though I have grown taller by a whole head. My back often arches at the waist, my stomach swells out like a ball, and then my waist contracts back in, my fingers begin to stretch and bend. And it's the same with my feet. They are profound sensations, and all without sharp pain of any kind. Often, when I've left the centre, I have a feeling of energy, as though I've been massaged somewhere around the hips.

When I came to you for my first healing session, I didn't have a good figure. I couldn't wear trousers although I'd always liked them. But this summer I put some on and everyone told me they looked good on me, and in general my whole figure has changed since then: it's got better, firmer, and I've lost weight. People tell me I look much better, the skin on my face is smoother, I've got some colour in it. Morning and evening, I wash my face with the energized water. I've given up using face creams.

And there have been other changes, in my relationship with my husband. There had been a long period of dissatisfaction in our close personal relations, an air of misunderstanding. It was upsetting. We'd even thought of separating. And now everything has changed. Naturally, it didn't happen at once, but gradually. First of all, I changed inside, and then you helped to change my husband, through me. Little by little I changed as a woman: I stopped being shy and embarrassed with him and now have a better idea of who he is. I began at last to know what makes him tick, to gauge his mood, whereas before I was absolutely oblivious to it. And of course, he too behaves differently – has become more considerate, and sometimes I don't even have to ask him to do something, to help me, because he's already done it. The days of our youth have returned to us. How can you put a value on that? You can't as far as I'm concerned. It's priceless. The improvements began at the start of the first healing sessions, when you instructed us to direct our energy towards our own homes, our bedrooms. I've sensed changes in my relations with my husband since then, and with every day they have become warmer and we have begun to smile at each other. So, bit by bit, during the last year and a half to two years, our relationship has finally sorted itself out.'

*July 1999 St Petersburg*

## When Age Retreats: The Tale of Valentina Travinka

Despite an almost total absence of advertising, Dr Konovalov's centre, as has already been mentioned, is known to many people. All kinds of people come here to be healed: from leading academics to ordinary engineers, famous actors to housewives, doctors, pensioners, writers and journalists. During 1992–3 one of the seats at the healing sessions at Dr Konovalov's Humanitarian Rehabilitation Centre was occupied by an, as then, unknown journalist. During the course of many years she had been dogged by a serious illness, which she had been fighting as hard as she could, studying and trying out all kinds of natural remedies. The doctors had long since given up on her, but she had gone on fighting, and had turned to many healers, in the end coming to Dr Konovalov.

A year later this courageous woman wrote her first book, for which Dr Konovalov wrote the preface. Then there was a second book, then a third … Six months later her books had become bestsellers. The name of the journalist we are talking about, and who without doubt is now known to millions of Russian readers, is Valentina Travinka. Unfortunately, she did not manage to complete her treatment, her urge to help others proving greater than her own desire to get well. The need to write about it was too strong. Her books and the meetings she had with readers left practically no time for her to look after her own well-being. She passed away, but her books, to this day, rank among the leading works on health matters in Russia.

What compelled her to begin writing books at the age of 60, when others are by then coming to the end of their own work, finishing things off, having decided that it is now too late? It was undoubtedly her meeting with Dr Konovalov that made her take up the cause of helping people who suffer. It was his example of self-sacrificing love for others that inspired her to play her own part in the service of goodness and love.

'And now let us turn to your wish', says the doctor, 'the most cherished wish you have in life. And remember, it must not be to do with your health. You will all be well, there's no doubt about that. But for now … What is it you wish for? What is the greatest wish you have in life? Stretch out your hands towards me' …

The whole audience silently stretches out its hands …

'I give protection to your wish. At the count of three clench your hands into a fist. Now press them against your heart.'

Who knows, maybe it was at this precise moment during a healing session that Valentina Travinka vowed to write books that would help people. Indeed, she began doing so that same year. The fact that these books were hugely successful and had massive print runs leaves no doubt that this could not have happened without some kind of miracle. … This is how Valentina Travinka described her own experiences during healing sessions, in a letter to Dr Konovalov:

'You ask us to describe those changes which we have noted after your healing sessions.

The most significant outcome (in my opinion) is the tears. Yes, those bright, joyful tears of a kind that have never before been shed. They came with the intense release of feeling that I experienced during the sixth healing session. And now, every time you come on stage, I am seized by an overwhelming desire to weep. Your low, muted voice sends shivers down my spine and long before the music starts I fall into an energizing state of sleep (or rather I fall into a state of complete immobility in which I immediately lose all sense of my body).

Your voice, accompanied now by the music, makes my right arm lift up (it started happening at that 6th healing session) and place itself on my chest, although it feels to me as though it lies right over my heart. My left hand bends at the elbow, my palm opens and stretches out in the direction where you are standing. It is as though I am begging for salvation.

And throughout the whole session, salt tears run down my face. Might it be that long-suppressed sorrows, which during the course of my life have burrowed deeper and deeper inside and have gnawed away at me in there, have begun to work their way out again through these tears? Whatever it is, it makes me feel brighter, easier in myself.

... I was never one to complain, even though I had a whole host of troubles. The time has obviously come for me to have a good cry about them. ... They say that illnesses are most commonly provoked by grief.

I weep at home too, every time I think of you in the auditorium (as you tell us to do), up there on the stage. I wake up during the night and again in the morning, in tears. It's as though the floodgates have been opened!

Thank you for my tears. Thank you, dear doctor, for being here among us.

*Weeping Blade of Grass\*, 26 January 1993*
P.S. In my diary, I'm writing down all the beneficial physical changes.'
(\* the Russian word *travinka* means 'blade of grass')

The key to the success of Valentina Travinka's books in Russia is undoubtedly due to the fact that they contain within them that spark which Dr Konovalov daily ignites in the hearts of all kinds of people. There are many such examples that I know of. His patients become poets, painters, composers; they successfully defend their doctoral dissertations. Valentina Travinka discovered her own talents when she was over sixty. Many people rediscover themselves when at the centre. Age has no meaning. A true and fulfilling life opens up for people, one for which they have been searching, without knowing, for many long years.

## The Miracle in Which We Can All Share

Those who have never examined different, esoteric ways of thinking perceive everything that Dr Konovalov does at his health-giving sessions as a miracle. But people experienced in this field, who are familiar with the work of Elena Blavatskaya, Gurdjieff, Shri Aurobindo and Plato will undoubtedly take note of Dr Konovalov's gifts as both practitioner and doctor. A teacher? – Yes. A theoretician? – Yes. But it is always his practice and always the patient, that come first.

Many people coming into contact with the doctor's knowledge have in turn become teachers and advocates of his methods. Yet in the annals of history there are few documented cases of people who have given themselves up entirely to healing others. How many obvious candidates are there? In ancient times, the legendary Greek father figure of medicine, Hippocrates (c.460–c.377 BC), for instance, or the Persian physician Avicenna (980–1037); in the modern era one might cite the German physician Paracelsus (1493–1541). But there have also been many other unsung and unacknowledged people down through history who have devoted their lives to helping and healing others in all sort of ways. Dr Konovalov is part of that long-standing tradition; he ranks among those special people who have been chosen to put the sufferings of others first. In so doing, he has accepted the pain of others as his own pain. For true empathy for others is the foundation upon which the gift of healing has always and will continue to be given. Perhaps this is why so few have been willing to take up the burden – because it's easier simply to carry the torch of knowledge than take upon oneself all the many different forms of human suffering, both physical and spiritual. This is a difficult path even for those who have been initiated and few have the courage to travel along it.

This is the path that Dr Konovalov is following. Today, right now, people can join in this miracle, because it is near at hand. For even though

Dr Konovalov is based in the centre of St Petersburg, you, the reader, can follow his treatment methods wherever you live in the world. For they are your last hope if traditional, conventional medicine has been unable to get to the root of your problem, if everybody gives up on you as a hopeless case, if even those closest to you are incapable of understanding what you are going through.

Even if you live outside Russia and have no chance of visiting Dr Konovalov's Humanitarian Rehabilitation Centre in St Petersburg, this book can still give you strength and hope, because, above all, it talks about love. About the love and selfless devotion of the doctor in relation to his patients, whomsoever they might be – be they unfortunate, lost, or rejected.

# CHAPTER 15

# THERE'S MEDICINE AND THEN THERE'S MEDICINE

## Present-Day Medical 'Philosophy'

Today, we are all of us accustomed to seeing doctors at our bedside, in the hospital ward, in the surgery or clinic. But all these familiar settings seem to us bogged down by medical convention and stereotypes. In Russia in particular old people attending out-patients departments are frequently told: 'What do you expect? It's your age.' Yet, these are people who today are in their prime – our mothers and fathers, our beloved grandmothers and grandfathers – who might yet look forward to many more years of active life. Sadly, all too often they believe what they are told and accept what the medical men tell them. A woman looks at herself in the mirror, sees the wrinkles on her face and thinks: 'There's nothing I can do about it – it's age!' A sprightly grandfather who is younger at heart than his own grandchildren, reads in the paper every day that the average life-expectancy for a man, in Russia, is ten years less than he himself has already lived and he sadly concludes: 'I should be dead by now too.'

Just try calling an ambulance for a sick person who is over ninety in Russia. 'How old did you say?' they ask you. 'Save his life? What for? It's time he was in his grave, so why use force to drag him back?' Such ruthless attitudes don't embarrass anyone. In Russia we understand this cynical way of thinking and we accept it. So much so that what Dr Konovalov says at his healing sessions may appear crazy to many.

But if you stop and ponder things for a minute, then it's hard to think of anything more unsatisfactory than the medical thinking we currently live by. Where Dr Konovalov's method differs so dramatically from others, is that he takes time to look at the whole person, going beyond their mere physical symptoms. He also goes beyond their medical treatment by conventional methods such as drugs, X-rays, surgery, and so on. His diagnosis is based on getting to the very heart of a patient's problem and to do so he takes into account not just their physical state but their mental and spiritual outlook as well. For Dr Konovalov believes that all three aspects have to be treated in conjunction with each other in order to bring about the essential healing process. Once this diagnosis has been achieved and the healing process initiated, the patient is thus empowered to continue with their own self-help and healing.

## The Basic Philosophy of Dr Konovalov's Centre

*'The fact that people today enjoy so little of life that they die afflicted by illness, with backs bent, toothless, and withered, is not normal. Primordially, the human organism was programmed for a long life, measured out in hundreds of years; programmed to flourish and then to quietly pass out of this world. There was a time when people, leaving this existence, looked and felt almost the same as a healthy, forty-year-old person looks and feels today. And this is precisely how nature has constructed our organism.'*

Who knows, perhaps if this attitude, described by Dr Konovalov above, had not been instilled in us since childhood, if it had not lain at the root of our philosophy and in particular the way we look upon medicine, then maybe women would not become prematurely aged and men would not die before their time from heart attacks and strokes. How you think Dr Konovalov advises middle-aged women visiting his centre when they recover from illness? He advises them to protect themselves. From what? From unwanted pregnancies! Because questionnaires from patients testify to the fact that after treatment the body is revived and rejuvenated; that the menopause retreats, that the menstrual cycle can reappear at any age, and that the workings of the body that fade away with age can all be restored – including the ability to conceive.

What do you imagine is the significance of these results? They signify victory over old age, nothing less. And what are the consequences of this victory in economic terms? With the population rising and more and more people surviving into old age, our governments and their ministers should be prepared for a dramatic rise in the number of elderly people needing medical care and, with it, the increasing burdens on our health services. And how will they provide for the pensioners, who in Russia in particular are currently paid such a miniscule allowance? How will they support a whole army of people who will live beyond the age of 100? Isn't it perhaps time that we took a serious look at the ways in which we care for our elderly people and, instead of abandoning them to their fate after a certain age, learnt to value them as worthy members of the community, still able to work and make their own contribution to society. Healthy old people need not be a burden – provided our medical services do not give up on them. Many letters in this book from elderly people confirm how they have discovered a renewed energy and appetite for life after treatment by Dr Konovalov, and with it the ability to keep on working.

## The First Signs of Illness Should not be Treated, but the Illness Itself

'Have you ever thought,' asks Dr Konovalov at his healing sessions, 'why, after a stone is extracted from a patient's organ, it forms again some time later? Or you take away a cyst and it reappears in exactly the same place?' He answers his own question: 'It's because the doctors only remove the problem after it has manifested itself; they take away the pain, but the illness itself remains there, inside the patient.'

Right now, literally thousands of patients come to Dr Konovalov's centre every day. For fourteen years non-stop he has been treating diseases which all the medical reference books list as incurable. He not only gives people back their lives, but makes their lives considerably more active ones. Thousands of patient testimonies are crammed with feelings impossible to describe. For years on end these people had suffered from all sorts of medical problems and had often endured constant, unrelenting pain. Most of them had come to accept that pain was a way of life. They had also become reconciled to the fact that the doctors were at a loss to make them better and that medicine had not yet discovered ways of treating their complaints.

After attending Dr Konovalov's healing sessions people of all ages discover life anew – a life that, without pain and the constant reoccurrence of illness, turns out to be entirely different. It may be difficult for a healthy person to understand this. But who, in our day and age, can honestly be called healthy? We have all become so inured to our own physical ailments that so long as they don't bother us we are prepared to consider ourselves healthy. It's often some time before kidney stones move; osteochondrosis at first doesn't bother us much; stomach problems, to tell the truth, give us trouble from time to time, but we live in the modern world, which means that we make everyday use of a huge range of painkilling drugs and proprietary medicines that we see advertised in magazines and on the television. Or at least, we continue to do so until the doctors finally diagnose us with something more serious – an ulcer? – cancer? But when will that be? In ten years' time? In a year? A month? Here is Dr Konovalov's view:

*'If you have been examined and diagnosed as having some kind of disease, it doesn't mean that you have suddenly and only recently contracted it. It is more than likely that you've lived with this disease for many years, possibly since your early childhood, and that it is only now that it has manifested itself clinically, that the pain has started, a tumour has appeared or your skin has erupted.'*

## The Scientific Principles at the Heart of All the Doctor's Work

Dr Konovalov not only uses his own original techniques in treating diseases, he also makes full use of his innovatory theories about their causes and their treatment. He continues carefully to study the medical literature on new methods of treatment and thoroughly appraises all new currents of opinion; he makes a point of investigating new medical preparations and technologies as they appear, but he resolutely avoids reading books on bioenergetics or any other esoteric medical or scientific doctrines. Dr Konovalov is extremely well versed in the methodologies of both the conventional and alternative schools of medicine. He recently became director of the Peptides Laboratory at the Institute of Bioregulation and Gerontology in St Petersburg, where he heads a team of researchers who are investigating conventional medical ways of dealing with the problems of ageing. Dr Konovalov's passion for research has attracted to his team other outstanding researchers in the fields of physics, biochemistry and genetics.

*'I am a practitioner,' he says. 'I am a scientist, and I can't be convinced of something that exists only in hypothetical form, which I cannot see with my own eyes and verify in practice. Because of this, from the moment I knew that I possessed the ability to channel energy and utilize it in the healing process, I took the decision not to read any esoteric books, in order to preserve the integrity of the experiment. None of the theoretical knowledge about both disease and the system of the universe which, bit by bit, I describe during my healing sessions has come to me from books. I have grown accustomed to constantly checking and double-checking everything that I do, because a medical man cannot make mistakes; the doctor's responsibility for his mistakes is too great; it might mean the cost of a human life.*

Although Dr Konovalov doesn't read everything that is written and published about the biological makeup of the human being, about the organization of the universe and about the human soul, his extensive theories, embracing the formation of the universe and explaining the causes of various diseases, are in some respects similar to other, universally held doctrines. But in other, significant ways they are highly idiosyncratic.

His theories contain few sweeping statements and vague assertions; they explain much that till now has remained a puzzle for us. And they explain it at the scientific level. Even in this, Dr Konovalov continues to remain a sober-minded scientist, testing everything in his own practice and taking into account the achievements and discoveries of contemporary medicine. It is just that his way of thinking is more far-reaching and extremely revolutionary, particularly his views on what the real causes of illness are. These are the subject of our next chapter.

# CHAPTER 16

# THE TRUE CAUSES OF PHYSICAL ILLNESS

## Overcoming Conventional Medical Logic

When drafting one of his many books, Dr Konovalov wrote the following:

'I have chosen my own path in seeking out the origins of disease and the ways in which it acts on the sick organism. From the very outset, I knew it would be a most arduous and difficult journey. This is because I lacked any texts, monographs or books on the subject. I was confronted by the great abyss of the unknown and I had to feel my way along the path towards knowledge. I had many things to overcome along the way, first and foremost the logic of an ordinary person and that of a conventional physician. And it was very, very difficult. It's a logic that is always with you. It weighs you down, oppresses you, and doesn't allow you to think freely. Changing to another way of thinking only seems a vague possibility; but it only seems that way to someone who has never done it. For there's nothing simpler, day in day out, than to read and assimilate well-argued material written by others and then show off one's encyclopedic knowledge: "This author's written such and such, and that one something else" … "What, you mean you haven't read it?" "But what do you think about it?"

Dear friends and colleagues, where are your ideas? Are you telling me this knowledge is original to you? You're making a serious mistake. This is somebody else's knowledge which you have conscientiously studied, memorized and applied in your everyday lives. Yes, it is necessary. Knowledge is essential; without it there's no progress, no forward movement, no evolution in human thought. But the time will come, the moment when you too must move ahead, when you will have to open your own door into the unknown, when even you won't be able to take things on because they are quite different from established, familiar knowledge. You need to feel that this knowledge is the true and right one. And, in consequence, practice is sure to bear this out.'

An echo of such ideas and experiences can be found in the English philosopher Francis Bacon's seventeenth-century treatise on science, *The Great Instauration:*

'Even those who have been determined to try for themselves, to add their support to learning, and to enlarge its limits, have not dared entirely to desert received opinions, nor to seek the springhead of things. But they think they have done a great thing if they intersperse and contribute something of their own, prudently considering that by their assent they can save their modesty, and by their contributions their liberty.'

These words were written 400 years ago, but to this day, they still accurately reflect the 'advancement' of traditional science. What new knowledge can really be brought to science if one relies only on those truths known to it today? What do a multitude of theses add to science? Have their authors edged one inch further along the path to knowledge? Or have they simply added a few new cosmetic touches to an already well-worn theory?

## Where Modern Science Came to a Halt

*'Modern conventional medicine based on the newest chemical, biochemical, physical and technological discoveries has, to a degree and with considerable sophistication, penetrated to the heart of disease. But there is still a whole range of things which it hasn't got to the root of and where its actions have not been able to effect a complete recovery. This failure has been officially acknowledged in scientific medicine by the institutionalization of the concept of the so-called chronic – that is permanent – disease, in the treatment of which the sick person can only count on support for their bodily suffering and the occasional relief of pain.*

*The crux of the current impasse in traditional medical science lies in the limited view it takes of the human being as fundamentally a physical body. In which case, overcoming chronic disease is possible only if a fundamentally new source of information about how disease takes root and develops is drawn upon. And this source is linked to a whole range of the newest ideas about the existence of a special energy, either manifested at cellular level or absorbed by the organism from the surrounding environment – the cosmos itself.'*

With these views in mind Dr Konovalov was able to reject traditional medical ways of thinking and turn towards what he considered to be 'the unique source of things'. Through his practical work he was able to bring together his own unique concept of what exactly constitutes disease and good health, leading in turn to a wider view of the general system of the universe.

## The Living Human Organism as Part of the Cosmic Ocean

The living, human organism is an accumulation of trillions of cells, organs and physiological systems which function to a clearly defined rhythm. It is a consolidated energy system holding within it the energy potential of every single cell – those hundreds of thousands and millions of energy channels which pass through the physical body much as they do the celestial one.

It is Dr Konovalov's view that this living organism is an energy body that exists independently within the much larger celestial body – itself another vast, biological field. The healthy biological rhythm of the workings of the cells, of the body's systems and organs – indeed of the entire organism as a whole – constitutes a sophisticated vibrating mechanism. In turn, the highly sensitive pulsation at the gene level of the nucleus of every cell in the human body is in synchronization with the yet unseen and unmeasured pulse of the cosmos as a whole.

A more detailed explanation of the biorhythms linking the working of the organism – both as a whole and through each one of its individual cells – with the rhythm of the universe will be found in future books by Dr Konovalov. At present, his doctrines are most fully laid out in *The Path to Health* and *Man and the Universe*, both of which books will eventually become available in English editions. It might be useful, at this point, to look at how notions about energy, biorhythms, the biological field and its links with the cosmic ocean have been known to mankind since ancient times – a time when the human intellect was as yet untrammelled by the cumulative effects of civilization and the irreconcilability of different religions.

Unable, as yet, to reject the existence of the innate natural forces of biological energy, scientists have failed to unravel its inner secrets; nor have they been able to measure it by technological means. They are yet to explain to us how it came into being, or define its potential and teach people how to make use of it. The most famous physicists and chemists, psychologists, biologists, physicians and mathematicians are currently engaged in researching this question. But the further they delve, the more obvious it becomes that the solution will not be found in the near future, nor possibly even in the millennia to come. It is difficult to imagine the possible consequences of people learning to direct their thoughts, realize their dreams, eradicate disease, and postpone old age till they are over 100, by learning to channel this energy. The ideal would be to bring about a paradise on earth, but right now humanity is by no means ready for such a thing.

## The Lost Paradise

There's a very apposite Russian proverb – 'Oh to be in heaven but our sins won't allow it' – best paraphrased in English as: 'We would if we could, but we can't!' The human race manages to turn everything that at first seems a beneficial scientific discovery into a means of its own destruction. It is impossible to predict what catastrophic consequences might follow if it were to be revealed how the biological energy might be channelled: the consequences of the atomic bomb at Hiroshima, Japan, in 1945, or the Chernobyl nuclear disaster of 1986, would pale into insignificance in comparison. For this reason, the earth's information field remains 'closed' to 'under-developed' human beings who might try to misuse its information. (How else can one describe people so consumed with the desire not only to annihilate others but themselves, inevitably, as well?) Contact with the secret knowledge contained within the information field of the cosmos is allowed only to those, such as the doctor, who have been chosen or initiated, who have been called upon to extend the parameters of our knowledge about the universe, the cosmos and the human soul. But so far none of those who have been initiated has yet revealed all their many secrets to humanity. This is why as Dr Konovalov gradually passes on this knowledge to his pupils – and there are many who have been following him since he first started who find it impossible to tear themselves from the new path opened up to them – he never reveals everything that he knows. The reason he does not do so is because, first of all, knowledge of the world is infinite and, second, because to take on this knowledge brings with it a huge responsibility – towards the universe and towards humanity – to make proper use of it. The doctor's mission is to help the human race to reach the next stage in its development, to become well both in body and in mind and move closer to a state of harmony and higher truth.

It is no accident that Dr Konovalov began his work in 1990, at the height of the political change in Russia known as *perestroika* followed, a year later, by the collapse of the old communist regime. This was a time when people had begun to let go of the things that had previously dominated their lives – material possessions and the pursuit of money, as well as the violence and tyranny that had been spreading across society at such an alarming speed. Since time immemorial it has been said that when worldwide, universal greed rears its ugly head, then somewhere the lamp of goodness will once more start burning equally as brightly and offer people a source of support and hope in such terrible times. No matter how long this struggle may last, the human race and the world as a whole will survive until goodness has once more conquered evil.

## How Chronic Disease Manifests Itself

Dr Konovalov's view is that chronic disease develops in the following ways:

- When the biorhythm of a single one of the cells is disrupted;
- When one or several of the body's energy channels become 'blocked';
- When a bio-field is weakened.

If illness is triggered by a change in the cell, it will induce disease in various organs as well as the physiological systems of the body. Blockages to the energy channels lead to the appearance and development of diseases of the brain and spinal column, of the subsidiary motor systems and of the arteries. They also lead to the appearance of cysts, polyps and various other growths. Blockages to the energy channels deprive the particular zone of the organism linked to them of essential nutrients and quickly weaken and extinguish all its physiological functions. The most obvious examples of such a process are: arthrosis, arthritis, osteochondrosis of various sections of the spine, multiple sclerosis, syringomyelia, and stones in the gall bladder and kidneys. The weakening of the 'ethereal field', as Dr Konovalov terms it, leads to cancerous formations, systemic disease of the connective tissues, and the lowering if not total destruction of the optimum levels of the body's immune system. In short: in circumstances such as this precious energy simply 'escapes' from the sick body.

Thus, if you have a liver problem, it doesn't mean there's a disorder in the biorhythm of one of your liver cells, it means that a disease brought on by a disorder in the cell's rhythm has found a weak spot in your body and homed in on it. In cases such as this conventional medical treatment will be directed at the afflicted organ, although the seat of the illness will not actually be located in the organ that is causing the person pain – because that is not the root of the problem. And so, in the conventional medical way of things, the treatment directed at a particular organ only deals superficially with the symptoms of the disease, thus allowing it to become a chronic one. And what makes matters even worse, when this happens, is if the doctors resort to surgical intervention. For the seat of the disease is located somewhere else, inside one of the body's cells, and will simply work its way out and find another, different weak spot in the organism. This hypothesis is constantly borne out in the doctor's practice.

A woman of fifty writes how, after a hysterectomy and the removal of her ovaries, she began suffering from fibroadenomatosis of both breasts. Both breasts were removed soon after. Immediately after this, the lymph glands throughout her entire body became swollen. In his practice, the doctor encounters many similar examples.

### From case history 1014763 (born 1952)

'... On 28 March 1997 I had an operation on my thyroid – a resection of the isthmus of the thyroid gland.

Before the operation, the right lobe measured 18 x 19 x 38 mm. The left was 30 x 34 x 52 mm, with nodes that were 25 x 20 mm, 11 x 8mm and 8 x 7 mm in the isthmus.

On 24 July 1997, four months after the operation, an ultrasound showed that the right lobe had become enlarged to 48 x 18 x 16, and the left to 45 x 25 x 22 mm, and there was a node now measuring 39 x 25 x 20 mm. The doctor explained to me that this new node had appeared because of the stress of the operation – and she told me I'd have to have another one.

At that time, I'd already been bleeding from my uterus for six months because of the myoma there. Between December and July I had had three D&C procedures.

During the first treatment programme the bleeding stopped. My mood and sense of well-being improved. My gastrointestinal tract began to function better too. ...

During this, my 8th treatment programme, I went to see my gynaecologist. This was the third year he'd been treating me. After examining me he said how amazed he was at the changes in my uterus. The myoma (of 4–5 weeks) hadn't got any bigger – rather the opposite. My uterus had "calmed down" because the inflammation had disappeared. Previously, they'd suggested an operation to deal with the myoma of the uterus, but after he'd examined my breasts, the doctor said that everything was normal. His reaction, when I told him I'd been going to Dr Konovalov's healing sessions, was a very positive one.'

*(In October 2001 everything had cleared up. Condition stable)*

## The Body's Energy System

A person's energy system reaches beyond the bounds of their physical body, yet is still connected to the body by the major, median and minor channels which penetrate into every organ, every cell of the body. The interconnections between these channels take the form of large 'nodes or knots' which function as energy accumulators. The major one is that located near the heart and Dr Konovalov has named it 'the cup of the heart'. The organism's energy levels are replenished the moment that we make the transition from full consciousness into sleep. The energy now enters the 'cup of the heart' and spreads throughout the body's other systems and organs. This is why the heart's basic function, along with the mechanical circulation of the blood, is to transmit this energy to all parts of the physical body as well as what Dr Konovalov calls the 'sensitive body'.

The normal functioning of the energy channels – in other words the whole range of a person's energy systems – depends on a great deal of subjective and objective conditions. The subjective ones would include inherited predispositions to illness, acute contagious infections, different types of trauma, injuries, hypothermia, surgical intervention, alcohol addiction (as well as dependency on drugs), stress and personal lifestyle – including one's actions and feelings at a particular time – and the degree of personal and spiritual awareness that a person has attained. Objective conditions relate to the world we live in: radiation levels, the state of the atmosphere, the spread of civilization, the destruction of our natural ecology – including its information fields.

# CHAPTER 17

# DR KONOVALOV'S TREATMENT METHOD

Dr Konovalov's practice is based on his ability to control and direct sensitive energies by creating a special 'dome' during his healing sessions, in which he concentrates the energy drawn from every corner of the hall, and which exceeds in intensity the usual bioenergy levels of our surroundings. 'Is it really that simple?' you ask. Of course not. This book provides only an outline of the theories and essence of Dr Konovalov's treatment method; he will expand on the details in future books. Every patient, depending on the extent of damage sustained by their biological field, soaks up this invigorating energy into all their cells, like a sponge. It takes time for a person's energy channels to be cleansed and, of course, such a complex process cannot be completed in one session. So, in recent years, after having studied thousands of case histories, Dr Konovalov has worked out a clearly defined course of treatment.

Today, Dr Konovalov now conducts sessions in three halls simultaneously: two of them are for healing; the third is for preventive treatment. The difference between them is that the healing sessions deal with detailed, recorded case histories – with patients suffering from a particular disease – whereas the other one doesn't. Here, Sergey Sergeevich works by intuition or, more precisely, makes use of the extraordinary extra-sensory abilities that he possesses. Even in the preventive-treatment hall, however, they do make use of a questionnaire for patients taking up a specific course of treatment.

## The Patient's Questionnaire

The patient's questionnaire is an extremely important, fundamental part of the treatment method and for this reason I'd like to dwell in more detail on why it was adopted and explain its significance.

When Dr Konovalov first took up healing practice at the hospital, he always drew on a patient's case history during the diagnostic period. With time, patients who had recovered began bringing their friends and relatives who needed treatment to the healing sessions. The number of people in this small hall increased with every day. The doctor remembers how 'There were twenty people at the first session, but when I came for the second, there were already forty, and by the third, there were sixty.' Word about him spread amazingly fast, so much so that they couldn't fit everybody into the limited space available. It was then that Sergey Sergeevich began asking patients to note down how they felt during the healing sessions. As a natural researcher, he wanted to ascertain to what extent a person's personal characteristics – their profession, the diagnosis of their problem and other factors – had an effect on their intake of the energy and the speed at which they recovered. After a while and having analysed the questionnaires, he realized that even if a person had had absolutely no sensory reaction during the sessions, they still got better.

*'I understood that any new direction or line of investigation could only be acknowledged in situations where the statistics were strictly verified. Even then, I foresaw that this was only the beginning and that it would not be long before my healing sessions would be attended by thousands of people at a time. And so there had to be a clearly defined method of documentation which would allow me to prove to myself, first and foremost, that everything I was doing then, as well as everything that I would do in the future, was not a whim or mere fantasy, but grounded in present-day reality and that of the days to come. Yes, I was including healing sessions in the list of recommended treatment in my patients' case histories, but this did not reflect the main purpose and content of my sessions with them. And then the patient's questionnaire was introduced. At first it fulfilled the function of a simple, statistical document – in essence, the history of a particular complaint. But, later on, it became a very important element in my interaction with the patient; it became the pivot, the focal point of the healing sessions and an additional source of knowledge, which till then I had lacked, about the real, true essence of a person, of human relations and all their crises, sorrows and joys. Today I call it the patient's personal testimonial.'*

What does the doctor most want to know about a patient and their case history?

1. *Their full name, date of birth, profession, address, telephone number, and the major diagnoses made by their doctor*
   This information is essential, primarily for statistical purposes. Statistical data allow the doctor to establish which diseases respond best to treatment using the sensitive energies. (Today the list of such diseases is large and growing all the time.) The data serve also as the basis for ongoing research, because Dr Konovalov is never satisfied with his achievements and is constantly working to find ways of speeding up the healing process and optimizing it.

2. *The patient's physical complaints*
   In this part of the questionnaire the patient should hold nothing back. Everything is important to the doctor, even things that seem utterly insignificant. For example, patients often consider their chronic rhinitis or other ailments to be insignificant because they have simply got used to them.

3. *A description of how the patient feels during the healing sessions*
   This information is essential to the doctor in establishing his energy diagnosis. As has already been pointed out, a clinical diagnosis (and many patients come to the doctor with a whole 'arsenal' of diagnoses – as a rule between 30 and 40 of them) does not necessarily reflect the true nature of what someone is suffering from. Based on how patients describe themselves in the questionnaires, Dr Konovalov gets a clearer picture of their problem. He then devises individual treatment programmes for them, based on his assessment of where their problem lies, which are then put into practice during the second, diagnostic period of treatment.

4. *The confessional part of the questionnaire: a revelation of the inner self*
   Each of the treatment halls can seat up to 2,000 patients and every day Dr Konovalov studies hundreds of patients' questionnaires. After they've handed theirs in, a patient receives individual attention at the next

healing session. This means that during the session, the doctor singles out a small group of patients whilst working on a particular part of the body. Many are puzzled as to why they are asked to stand up – if, for example, the doctor is working on the intestines and digestive tract – when actually their problem is with the kidneys. This is because Dr Konovalov makes a clear distinction between the clinical diagnosis and what he terms the 'energy diagnosis'.

A huge amount of work and effort is demanded of the doctor in his treatment of individual patients and in making an energy diagnosis. His working day begins at five in the morning. He reads and analyses the latest patient questionnaires, many of which are 8–10 pages long. Then he goes to the morning healing session, which lasts for two hours. When he returns, he allows himself a few minutes of rest and then once again sets to work on case histories; then after that there's the evening session. When he comes home he has a 15-minute break and then gets back down to the questionnaires. On a good day, Dr Konovalov finishes work at midnight. It is only such superhuman abilities which have made him able to sustain such a colossal workload over so many years.

The questionnaires that form the basis of the patients' case histories often become confessional in tone because in them patients describe their whole lives and the many life changes they have gone through since their treatment commenced. A life cannot, of course, be described in a single hour; it may take many years, which is why the questionnaires are looked upon as a kind of confessional. Many patients admit to never having been able to make their confession in church, that they've never done this kind of thing, even with those closest to them. So why on earth should they pour out their life stories to the doctor? It's difficult to explain in words. Every person who comes to the hall is offered so much love, warmth and understanding that they are able to cross the usual boundaries separating doctor and patient. They feel that people care about them and love them; they feel wanted. Many experience this feeling for the first time in their lives. And the doctor's great faith in his patients is reciprocated by their unequivocal faith in him, so much so that they often have greater trust in him than they do in their own father or mother, their husband, wife, or children.

## How Long Does Treatment Last?

The treatment programmes, as well as those aimed at preventive treatment, each consist of a series of ten healing sessions, which are conducted on a regular basis, with brief breaks, throughout the year. But one can never predict how many treatment programmes a particular person will need to attend in order to be rid of a specific disease. Practice has shown that this depends very much on the individual, subjective response of the patient. It's often the case that a person will make a complete recovery from several complaints during a single treatment programme: for example, kidney stones dissolve, skin infections clear up, the gastro-intestinal tract starts working normally again, or pain brought on by osteochondrosis recedes.

The length of time needed for treatment depends also on the goals that patients set for themselves. If they are intent on being rid only of those specific problems that cause them the most discomfort, then as soon as they are diagnosed as having recovered, they stop coming for treatment. But every year the number of patients who keep up their treatment for some time, over a period of several years, increases. These patients, once having become acquainted with the model of health advocated by Dr Konovalov, seek complete recovery of their health. Sergey Sergeevich himself always cautions those patients whose clinical symptoms of disease disappear too quickly. Many years of practice have shown that a rapid recovery from the physical signs of disease does not necessarily indicate that the person's body is back to full health. If that person stops coming for treatment, then in time the disease may recur, because the real seat of the problem has not been totally eradicated. In this way, those patients who have been through an extended course of treatment not only get better, they also maintain their good health for many years after. This can be said with absolute confidence, because Dr Konovalov's Humanitarian Rehabilitation Centre retains its links with patients who have recovered by monitoring their state of health for many years afterwards. This is the major objective of the centre's section for ongoing, dynamic observation, which can confirm, after many years' experience, that if a patient makes a full recovery then the disease does not return.

People who come expecting a miracle are often put off when they find out that it's not a matter of simply attending one session but of going through several treatment programmes, perhaps over the course of an entire year. Just think about it: eight treatment programmes (each consisting of ten two-hour healing sessions) in a year is the total equivalent of about seven days. And what hospital today is capable of curing the serious or chronic complaints of the kind that the doctor deals with in the space of seven days!

Today, there is particularly graphic evidence that, after a year's treatment, people of 75, 80 and even 85 make good recoveries. After three to five years of treatment programmes an awful lot has changed for them. Their supposedly 'healthy' peers, who laughed at the method of treatment for which they had opted, have long since died, whilst they have now recovered their health and feel far better than before. They knew this would be the case because Dr Konovalov had predicted it during the healing sessions. But he also had cautioned them, as follows:

*'My dear patients, over the next ten years you will have to endure great tragedy and face up to many of life's dramas. Your contemporaries will pass away while you will continue to grow stronger and feel better and better. You must start preparing for this.'*

# CHAPTER 18

# THE STAGES OF TREATMENT

As soon as they begin making contact, through Dr Konovalov, with the healing energy of the cosmos – or the 'energy of creation', as he terms it – which provides the organism with the power it lacks in order to mobilize itself and fight disease, patients must enter a series of treatment periods.

## Taking in the Energy: 'The Period of Imagined Well-being'

This is the time when the energy is actively taken into the body. After the first few healing sessions nearly all patients have a very pleasant sense of having absorbed new strength and energy, as one does after a good night's sleep. They describe their first encounter with Dr Konovalov's methods in very similar ways: 'I didn't walk home after the first session, I flew along, as though on wings'; 'After the very first session I felt significantly better.'

The restoration of a person's energy balance is the equivalent of a month's holiday by the seaside. Patients often describe the state in which they find themselves during the first healing sessions as being akin to one of peace and tranquillity. In clinical terms, this manifests itself in an increase in vitality, improvement in mood, normal sleep patterns, and the disappearance of painful symptoms aggravated by dependency on conventional medication, and so on. Dr Konovalov calls this the 'period of imagined well-being', being of the opinion that it is comparable to the effect of traditional palliatives, such as hormones, tranquillizers, etc. When patients first come to the clinic he warns them not to jump to conclusions, build up their hopes, or count on an easy victory. Disease is a very crafty adversary and every patient needs to go through the full diagnostic period.

For the majority (60–70 per cent) of patients, the period during which they take in energy lasts for 7–10 days, the equivalent of 2–3 healing sessions, although for patients with weakened bio-fields – who make up about 5–8 per cent – this can take months.

## The Diagnostic Period

Various kinds of sensation are triggered during the second period of treatment – sensations linked to the passage of the energy through the body and the commencement of recovery in the diseased cells. Some patients find that the external symptoms of their disease get worse and sometimes other latent problems, for which there might not have been clinical signs for several years, come to the surface: 'Even my operation scar began to ache – and I had that fifteen years ago.' Patients describe their feelings variously as a prickling or burning sensation, a sense of inner heat or vibration, and so on. Sensations such as these most commonly accompany procedures aimed at specific organs or systems of the body. Slight pain even occurs in between healing sessions. But these symptoms never become unbearable and do not signify that a disease is developing in some other part of the organism. None of the following are aggravated during the diagnostic period: stenocardic pain, arrhythmia and extrasystolia, stones in the gall bladder or kidneys, nor does blood pressure go up.

These sensations last from 3–5 to 7–10 days and then disappear without trace. If, however, they cause the patient too much distress a method has now been established for bringing them under control. This is done by means of what is called the 'healing leaflet', in conjunction with use of the energized water and continuing contact with the doctor. In the overwhelming majority of cases, people patiently endure any 'intensification' of their diseases during the diagnostic period because they understand how vitally important it is for the body that their diseased cells return to their normal biorhythm at this time. Besides, they know that any pain they experience can easily be eased with the help of the leaflet. In all this time there has never been a case where a patient has had to be hospitalized as a result of entering the diagnostic period.

## The Treatment Period

It is essential that the diagnostic period is followed by a treatment period. By this time the organism has soaked up the energy; the energy channels are now opening up and beginning to work normally and the organs and body systems are functioning normally as well. During this period the physiological defence and healing mechanisms transmitted to the body by nature are coming into operation. For 1 per cent of patients this period lasts 5–20 days, for 2–3 per cent 30–35 days, and for the remainder 2–6 months or more, though in all cases this is in regard to the disappearance of all symptoms and not simply the most obvious ones.

## The Recovery Period

During this fourth period, the patient gains the much-needed psychological reassurance of their own recovery. Its duration is closely tied to the patient's lifestyle. The criteria for recovery are as follows: no complaints of sickness by the patient, no clinical signs of disease after three years of observation, and no physical irregularities detected by traditional diagnostic investigation. It is only then that the clinical diagnosis of a disease can finally be crossed off a patient's chart.

*'Recovery depends first and foremost on the patients themselves, on their sense of purpose, on their wanting to get help to recover and their willingness to attend healing sessions. If patients accept that their disease will not be eliminated at a stroke, at one sitting, and that it might take months if not years, if they believe in the doctor's abilities as well as in those of their own organism, then they will be well again.'*

In the next part of this book I will describe the various methods that Dr Konovalov has devised for patients to continue with their own self-healing and the maintenance of good health when they are not attending the treatment centre. It also provides readers of the English edition with details of the all-important link-up sessions for those who do not live in St Petersburg – or even in Russia.

# PART III
# HEALING AND ENERGIZING PROCEDURES

# CHAPTER 19

# THE HEALING LEAFLET AND EXERCISES THAT CAN BE DONE AT HOME

This part of the book sets out to describe as fully as possible some of the exercises and procedures devised by Dr Konovalov that patients follow during healing sessions at the centre in St Petersburg. All of these exercises can be done by patients, wherever they live, in their own homes. They were originally created as a means of supporting those Russian patients attending the medical and preventive-medical halls in St Petersburg, but the doctor encourages all his readers to do them. Although patients who, for whatever reason, cannot attend the healing sessions do not obtain the same results as those attending in person, the doctor's years of practice, backed up by the testimonials sent in by patients across Russia, has shown that treatment in the home can nevertheless be highly effective.

Every procedure, and every recommendation that the doctor makes, is the result of many years' experience. Practice has taught him a great deal. Just like a plant biologist, who comes across something that has taken root in a seed bed, begins experimenting with it and tries to create a new hybrid, so the doctor is constantly engaged in his own selection process, trying to ensure that his treatment of patients is quicker, more effective and utterly reliable.

## How the Healing Leaflet Came About

Today, Dr Konovalov's patients successfully work with a range of biomaterials, all of which came into use by accident – much as did his use, for example, of the water from the hospital ward, described in Chapter 11. If the patient in question had been told at the time that the water had healing properties, his recovery would have been put down to some kind of self-hypnosis. However, he spilt the water on to his hand quite by accident and then forgot about it. He only remembered when he woke up the next morning and noticed with amazement that the ulcers on his arm had gone.

It was the same with the healing leaflet, which about 98 per cent of patients now successfully use. Once, during a healing session when he was still at the hospital, Dr Konovalov noticed a newspaper lying on a table. Someone in the hall where he conducted his healing sessions had obviously been reading it and had left it behind. Sergey Sergeevich had been standing near the table and several times had brushed against the paper with his hand. No one would have paid this the least attention if it hadn't been for one of the patients having a pain in the small of his back that evening. He was walking up and down the corridors, unable to keep in one position for long. He tried sitting down, first here, then there, then in an armchair, then on an upright chair, in an attempt to ease the pain – if only for a moment. As he moved from place to place, he sat down on the chair standing by the table with the newspaper on it and a few minutes later the pain stopped.

He didn't, of course, make anything of this. The pain went – and he thanked God it had. This kind of thing often happens of its own accord. The next day when his backache returned and he started walking up and down the corridors again, from one place to another, the patient once more found himself at the spot where the pain had stopped the previous day. Once more, he sat down on the same chair and straight away felt the pain go. But he hadn't the faintest idea why it had done so.

However, when the pain started again and he went straight back to the 'miracle' chair, he had a definite feeling of warmth and tried to see where it was coming from. When he turned round he noticed the newspaper, and put two and two together. He put the newspaper inside his clothes near his painful back and went back to the ward where, not long after, he bumped into Dr Konovalov.

The doctor was intrigued by what had happened, although at first he was sceptical when the patient told him that 'there was heat coming out of the newspaper'. He brought another, ordinary newspaper and placed it against the patient's back. This, of course, didn't make the pain go away and the patient didn't get the warm sensation either. This meant that the newspaper that had been in the hall during the healing session had received some kind of energy charge and now possessed different properties. In order to define what these were, patients at first tore newspapers into sections and the doctor charged them with energy by placing his hands on them during healing sessions. Then the patients would ease their pain at night using these and the specially charged water instead of sleeping pills. In time, Sergey Sergeevich realized that it was possible to transmit energy to practically anything. But it was a few years before the leaflet was put to practical use.

Dr Konovalov decided to do an experiment. During healing sessions he asked patients to tell him the kind of things they'd like to see in the leaflet. At first, he'd planned to include images of St Petersburg, for example the Peter and Paul Fortress or other scenic views. But having asked around, it turned out that the majority of patients wanted to see a photograph of the doctor himself on the front of the leaflet. Dr Konovalov was rather taken aback by this, but he nevertheless went with the majority view. It was clear that this made it easier for people to stay tuned in to him when at home or taking part in link-up sessions, as well as with the energy transmitted by him. 'People look at me with ordinary eyes,' he says, 'they look at the stage and the first thing they see is me. They don't see the huge power that is also there.'

## The Experimental Use of the Healing Leaflet

The leaflet plays a crucial role in harnessing the energy of creation, in establishing contact with the doctor and in conducting treatment at home. For the doctor is able to call up his para-psychological abilities to transmit the energy of creation to the pages of the leaflet.

Experiments with the use of the specially energized leaflet began. In their questionnaires, patients began to describe its various possible uses: it helped stop pain, as well as attacks brought on by a variety of things. Many patients were pensioners, which meant that they were also keen gardeners and allotment-keepers. They were using the leaflet to 'charge' their seeds before planting and hung the leaflets in their greenhouses. They took great pleasure in describing how their allotments produced bumper crops. But this was not enough proof for Dr Konovalov. 'The evidence from a hundred patients is nothing. It doesn't prove anything. The verification of scientific hypotheses demands a long period of experimentation; everything must be checked and double-checked.' So Dr Konovalov's leaflet was tested further – much more so than medication often is at clinics. But he was not finally convinced of the leaflet's effects until thousands of patients had sent in specific details about them, although he had for some time been convinced that the leaflet was helping about 40 per cent of his patients. The latest poll among patients has now shown that the leaflet's effectiveness is significantly higher.

## When to Use the Healing Leaflet

The leaflet is used as part of treatment at home for the following purposes:

1. *To prepare the specially charged water*
   A container holding not more than a quarter of a litre (9 fluid ounces) of water is placed over the doctor's photograph on the front of the leaflet. The water is charged and is ready for use after 20–30 minutes. If the water is left overnight, the charge it receives will be equivalent to that received during healing sessions at the centre in St Petersburg.
   You're probably already aware, from the questionnaires cited in this book, that the specially charged water has a positive, therapeutic effect on the digestive system, improves sleep, normalizes blood pressure and dissolves kidney stones. It is used for washing, for bathing infected skin and as drops for conditions affecting the eyes, ears and nose. It can be used for watering house plants and also be given to sick animals.

Charged water can be taken daily, half a glass before mealtimes.

*From case history 1014037 (born 1932)*
'I'll tell you now about the effects of the charged water. In the summer I was working at a children's holiday camp. A young 18-year-old worker had been carrying a container of bleach which had spilt and gone all over his feet. The container was metal and he had been wearing sandals. Two of his toes had been cut to the bone. They took him to hospital, where his feet were treated and bandaged. I took him a glass of the charged water and said he should keep dabbing the water on his bandages without undoing them. When he went to have his bandages changed the next day everybody was taken aback. The toes had healed and only a small scar was barely discernible. The water

also helped other people who'd had accidents, or burns or bites. All those of us whom you have helped by means of the water thank you, doctor.'

### From a case history (born 1973)

'Something truly amazing has happened during this treatment programme. The problem I came to you with about two years ago, and which I took several pages to describe in your previous questionnaire, has gone. Practically all the warts on my fingers have disappeared. I noticed it by chance. I was working on the teeth of one of my regular patients when I glanced at my fingers and noticed that something was different. Goodness gracious! My hands no longer looked terrible and knobbly like bark. They were normal. The biggest and most noticeable warts had begun to disappear. I'm looking at my fingers right now: there was a huge wart on my right little finger only a week ago – but now there's only a tiny spot. I've already been out and had a manicure. It's really funny, my kidneys were troubling me before this, and yet I was as happy as a kid that the warts had disappeared.

I want to say that I was very sceptical about dabbing the warts with the water specially charged for treating skin complaints. I really didn't believe in it. But then, one day my mother and I charged some water for using on the face. First mother dabbed at her own wart and it "dissolved", so I tried it a couple of times. My husband looked at my hands and said: "Give me some too and I'll put it on the wart I have." He tried to find it, first on one hand and then the other, and then said, "Well that's down to Sergey Sergeevich too." Now I just sleep on the leaflet and drink the charged water. Thank you.'

### From case history 1005632 (born 1952)

'My mother's right ear was inflamed. Poultices and medicines didn't help, rather the reverse, for it started discharging pus. So then I started pressing the leaflet to her ear and bathing it with the water. The discharge stopped and a week later mother's hearing was better, yet she hadn't been able to hear well out of that ear for a long time. She began to sleep better too.'

*January 1994*

2. *During morning and evening energizing exercises (for the treatment and prevention of disease)*

    After waking up in the morning you must stand on the leaflet to do this. Now raise your arms above your head and stand for 5–7 minutes, reciting the prayer from the leaflet either in your head or out loud. Afterwards, drink half a glass of charged water and do the energizing exercises.

    Repeat this procedure in the evening along with the evening prayer: 'Dear Lord. I have given my heart to you and you alone. There is no power on earth that can break the bond that unites us. All the powers of evil will depart and become impotent when faced with the love and strength of my heart and yours. Amen.'

3. *For normalizing the energizing state during sleep*

    With this in mind, the leaflet (or several, although it must be an odd number) should be placed under the mattress along the line where the spine normally rests (in other words, along the path of the divine channel), with the photograph facing upwards.

4. *For pain relief*

    The photograph on the front of the healing leaflet, which the doctor has invested with a special energizing impulse, is used for this. The open leaflet is placed with the photograph against the seat of the pain, burn, bruise or cut and so on, for an unlimited length of time.

5. *In order to create a positive energizing state*

    The leaflet's photograph possesses a variety of energizing levels, which creates a therapeutic energizing environment in the home. The photo should be hung on a wall (perhaps in a frame) facing into the room, whenever people are in the room.

    Case histories from thousands of patients confirm that the therapeutic energizing force field has a particularly marked effect on a person's sense of well-being; it also helps improve personal relationships, be they between family members or co-workers.

    The use of the leaflet among chickens and other domestic livestock almost doubles their productivity levels and gives them a greater resistance to low temperatures. When the leaflet is hung up in allotments, orchards and in greenhouses, productivity increases, and in places where they are stored, fruits retain their quality and the length of time they can be stored increases; seeds too retain their germinating capacity for longer.

## The Protective Power of the Leaflet

The protective power of the leaflet is manifested in different, extreme situations, at times of heightened physical, psychological and spiritual stress. Leaflets are often taken into events such as exams, competitions, tests, business and other important personal meetings, and so on. In all these situations the leaflet has to be on the person's body. Many patients have found that, for them, it works within a radius of about five metres (about fifteen and a half feet) of where they are in a room. So, if there is not one, but several leaflets in a room, then their effect is intensified the more that gap is reduced in size.

The Healing Leaflet™ can be obtained at Dr Konovalov's sessions held at the Humanitarian Rehabilitation Centre in St Petersburg. If you live outside Russia, you can obtain it by checking the Creation Publishing website at: www.creationpublishing.co.uk or sending an email to: info@creationpublishing.co.uk

## A Warning

The leaflet has absolutely no effect when someone has evil intentions, or is negative or insincere in what they are doing, when they haven't thought things through, or are not totally committed spiritually. The energy of creation cannot be made to work to selfish, material ends. It will only work for you if your intentions are honest, unselfish and altruistic.

*From case history 1017046 (born 1949)*
'My husband became paralysed three years ago. Since then he has not parted with the leaflet. He's now quite a lot better – manages to do a few things for himself, washes himself in the bath, prepares his food, reads, and even fixes things for a bit of extra money. His right side was paralysed as the

result of a brain haemorrhage. And it's quite an achievement that he can do these things. I thank you on his behalf. He is a great believer in you.

I also treat my mother with your leaflets. She fell from a window at work and has lost her coordination, her memory's poor and she suffers from depression. Now she can move around better and has become more active.'

*8 October 2000, St Petersburg*

*From case history 1014319 (born 1921)*
'I have known you for a long time and have been undergoing external treatment for about five years. Our acquaintance came about when I saw you, in a white doctor's coat and hat, on a television programme. You made a considerable impression, heightened by my anxiety about my wife, who was practically unable to get out of bed any more. We grasped on to you, as though reaching for a lifeline, as the one hope left to us. Later, in the autumn, my wife began attending your treatment sessions. And our life was transformed. We began living in a state of constant amazement, in constant expectation of a miracle. From session to session we gained a sense of peace and had faith. And now, thank God, for the last five years my wife has continued her treatment with you and is able to do a little around the house, within her own modest limitations.

After every session we talk a great deal about your instructions and the treatment. Your leaflets can be found left open in cupboards and on window sills. You are the guardian of our home, our closest friend. We have talked about you and handed round your leaflets, with all the necessary explanations, to our children, grandchildren and friends. I myself won't be separated from them, day or night, even when I go out. This is how I became one of your external patients. I make use of the water from the treatment centre, which has been specially energized to treat my inflammation of the bladder. ... I use the leaflet for all kinds of pain: in the chest, in the stomach, in my joints, for cuts and burns, and have never once been disappointed in my expectations. ...

Dear Sergey Sergeevich, on the 21st of October I came to my first live session. My first impression coincided a great deal with the conclusions I had already come to. I knew that you sometimes play your own musical compositions whilst healing patients. While I was listening I remembered how, years ago, my wife and I used to go to concerts by the Bolshoy and the Maly Philharmonia Orchestras, to hear Vladimir Ashkenazy and Bella Davidovich play. It was exactly the same atmosphere: a large group of attentive people, a feeling of elation, celebration and expectation, and the music. And then, when you began speaking, my soul reached out to you ...

During the 5th treatment programme, it was with considerable emotion that I listened to what you said about good and the need to be tolerant towards the people around us, about how essential spiritual transformation is before the body can begin its physical recovery. I understand how difficult this is, that such a state of being can only be acquired on the brink of repentance and self-cleansing, almost in the religious sense of overcoming self-centredness, temptation and everything that is demeaning. How good it is that you have spoken about this. And how appropriate were the beautiful prayers with which you sent us on our way.

The tales told by patients coming to the microphone were amazing. I was struck by the story of one woman who for eleven years had been fighting for the life of her child, condemned since birth with a terrible, incurable disease. And here was the result: her child was alive and well, thanks to the mother's faith and your uplifting work. Is this not a miracle? How many other inconsolable mothers' lives have been lit up by such hope and faith? I too wanted to go up to the microphone and say how I had been receiving external treatment from you for almost five years now, and that I was now already 76, with several aggravating conditions, and I had never thought that I would live this long and could not have done so without your assistance. I'm glad that I was able to see you, to hear you, to be a witness and a participant in the miracle-working medicine of the future.'

*(In October 2001 condition stable)*

### From case history 1013085 (born 1922)
'When I am at the treatment centre I feel well and I sleep. The headaches have gone. My kidney had felt as though it was encased in a hard shell – but now it doesn't. I feel cheerful and have begun to sleep better at night. A miracle has happened. My sister was dying, she hadn't eaten for a whole month, her days seemed numbered. I took her the water for healing the eyes, because she couldn't see out of one eye and had had an operation

on the other. And what do you think? She recovered and even put on weight. And, after twenty years, she began to be able to see out of the blind eye again. On 15th March she saw her own hand for the first time. Thank you very much.'

### From case history 1010764 (born 1945)

'Because of my work I can't get to your healing sessions, so my mother comes for me. To tell the truth I didn't believe in these sessions until I sprained my ankle at work. It began to swell up, there and then, before my eyes, and the pain was so awful that I couldn't walk. They took me home by car, and I was going to see the doctor, but my mother told me to wait until morning and tie the leaflet to my ankle. I slept through the night and, by the morning, it was like a miracle. The swelling had gone down, my ankle wasn't hurting at all and there was only a small bruise left.

The next day was a holiday and I went out dancing and forgot all about my ankle.

Since then, I've started drinking the water my mother brings home from healing sessions. I had kidney stones, but the ultrasound now shows that they have gone. They've crumbled away and have been expelled. Now, if anything hurts, I immediately tie the leaflet to me. The other day I was cooking some meat in the oven for a special occasion and accidentally took hold of the hot iron handle. Straight away, I poured the energizing water over my hand, wrapped it in a towel and soaked everything in the water. The pain stopped immediately and I didn't even have a blister.

I used to have a terrible, fibrous scar on my spine from a burn. Every morning and every evening I dab it with your water: it has become softer and smoother and if you run your hand down my back you can't feel it, whereas before it protruded by half a centimetre [¼"]. My fibromyoma has also dissolved. Thank you very much, dear Sergey Sergeevich. God give you strength and health in your wonderful work.'

*(In October 2001 condition stable. Feels well)*

# CHAPTER 20

# PROCEDURES FOR WORKING WITH THE SENSITIVE-BODY SYSTEM

Each exercise procedure devised by Dr Konovalov is a system of movements directed at re-establishing the healthy working of what he terms 'the sensitive-body system'; many similar exercises to these are carried out at the healing sessions at the centre in St Petersburg. They are constantly being modified and new ones being devised, thus reflecting the *ongoing development* of the doctor's treatment methods. For those following these instructions at home, all energizing procedures are performed either sitting or standing on the healing leaflet.

## Finding the Location of the Divine Channel

We must begin by locating that part of the body defined by Dr Konovalov as the 'divine channel' – the body's major energy channel, which passes down through the spinal column. In order to do this, the doctor asks you to stand with your arms raised, to spread them fairly well apart and then slowly begin to draw your palms together with the arms straight until you feel resistance building between them which makes pressing the palms together a strain. As soon as this happens, stop and do not make any attempt to overcome this feeling of resistance, no matter how weak or strong it is. The distance beyond which your palms can move no further towards each other defines the width of your *divine channel.*

Everybody taking part in this procedure in the centre in St Petersburg can usually perform it with ease. You may not be able to get it right on your own, in which case, simply note that the divine channel is usually about 20 centimetres (7–8 inches) wide.

## Opening Up the Sensitive-Body System

You are now ready to begin the exercises that work with the sensitive-body system. For simplicity, the *divine channel* will henceforth be referred to by the initials DC.

Standing on the healing leaflet, raise your arms above your head to the width of your DC. Bend your elbows, bringing your hands together above your head. Now slowly draw your hands down, separating them at waist level and placing your palms on the sides of your thighs (*Fig. 1*). This is to open up the sensitive-body system at the beginning of the exercise sequence and it is also used to close it at the end.

The movements made during energizing procedures differ from ordinary physical exercises in that they must be done very slowly, without straining. This is particularly important with regard to elderly patients. You need to be in a good frame of mind to do them properly. And they'll do you no good if you do them when you don't want to.

Fig. 1

## Energizing Exercises for Restoring the Sensitive-Body System

Described below are the exercises devised by Dr Konovalov and performed by his patients at the beginning of healing sessions at the centre. They are aimed at restoring the sensitive-body system and at penetrating the body's energy channels. Patients can do these exercises at home as well, whether or not they are receiving external treatment, as can readers and patients all over the world. Wherever you live, you can take part in the weekly link-up sessions, which will be described in Chapter 21.

Each of the following movements should last about thirty seconds.
1. Bend your head forward and then back to normal position.
2. Bend you head backwards and then back to normal position.
3. Turn your head to the right and then back to normal position.
4. Turn your head to the left and then back to normal position.
5. Rotate your head slowly in a circle to the right and then back to normal position.
6. Rotate your head in a circle to the left and then back to normal position.
7. Rotate both shoulders forwards.
8. Rotate both shoulders backwards.
9. Raise your arms above your head; rotate your wrists in a circle, clockwise and then anti-clockwise.
10. With your arms as in the previous position above your head, stretch and bend your fingers.
11. Let your arms fall to your sides and then slap them gently against your thighs a few times.
12. Stretch with your arms raised above your head.
13. Lean forwards with your arms still raised above your head.
14. With your arms down, gently slap them against your legs. Shake your arms, hands and fingers.
15. Standing in the same position, rock your feet from heel to toe and back.
16. Twist your body first to one side and then to the other.
17. Raise your arms above your head to the count of three, clap them together and allow them to flop down onto your thighs.

## The 'Energy Umbrella'

1. Raise your arms as high as you can above your head; link your hands with the palms one on top of the other and facing down. *(Fig. 2)*
2. Keeping the palms in this position and without bending your arms at the elbows, begin to lower them very slowly in front of you.

Fig. 2

3. Stop when you reach eye level.
4. Bending at the elbows, pull your arms in close to your eyes for a few seconds, and then go back to position 3.
5. Lower your arms till they are in front of your chest. Bring them slowly in towards your chest and then stretch them back out again.
6. Lower your arms again till they are in front of your abdomen. Bring them slowly in towards your abdomen and then stretch them back out again.
7. Continue lowering your hands, separate them and then drop your arms along each side of your body.
8. Repeat steps 1 and 2, this time stopping when your arms reach the level of your heart. *(Fig. 4)*

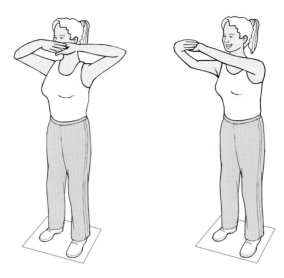

Fig. 3

Fig. 4

9.  Pull your arms in towards your heart for a few seconds, and then return to position 6. *(Fig. 5)*

**Fig. 5**

10. Repeat steps 5, and then steps 1 and 2. *(Fig. 6)*
11. Stop moving your arms when you reach the level of the cup of the sun (the solar plexus or pit of the stomach), bring your arms close towards your body, turn the palms face down and then allow your arms to drop by your sides. *(Fig. 7)*
12. Use the exercise for opening up the sensitive-body system *(Fig. 1)* and to close it down again.

### From a case history

'On 23 October 1999, I began reading your first book (I automatically put the second one, closed, beneath my pillow). I read a couple of pages and then went to sleep. I placed the book beside me, on the bed. I have known you, from a distance, for a long time now. Five years ago, without knowing it, I slept with a copy of the healing leaflet near me. Suddenly, during the night, I started doing exercises to stretch the spine, first with my legs, then with

Fig. 6

Fig. 7

my arms, as though I were trying to shake something off me. I ran my hands down my legs (and so on, over the whole of my body). ... I'd never done exercises like this in my life. I'd been doing this for half an hour, because my landlady has a luminous alarm clock. The noise I was making woke her up. And then she told me about the healing leaflet which had been lying near me (she is one of your patients).

And so, after I had placed the book alongside me in the bed, I lay down and began doing the exercises again. The energy stretched my body like a bowstring. My arms, which were at my sides, suddenly opened out of their own accord; my fingers spread outwards, staying that way till they felt numb. And then they pressed hard against each other until it hurt. My legs tensed and stretched. I remained in this rigid position for a few minutes. I began to lose all sense of my body and could no longer feel the tension. Suddenly my arms slowly raised themselves upwards (at that time I had not yet read and had no knowledge of your exercises). They lifted up, taking the blanket with them. They went back over my head until they touched the wall and remained in a relaxed and semi-bent position. Then my arms dropped to the side of my body, the fingers contracted tightly into a fist until it hurt, and for two to three minutes stayed like that. And then everything went limp. My arms continued with the exercises. The palms of my hands took hold, first of my left breast, massaging it from top to bottom as if they were pulling something out of it, and then did the same with the right one. After that I slept well. All of this happened without any effort on my part. It was as though I was watching from outside my body. This is no fantasy, nor is it the delirious ravings of a sick person. As a result of this, on 24 October, that is, the following morning, I lay down at 11.30 and slept for four hours. I slept well that night, whereas before I had always slept badly because the whole of my back ached. But this disappeared, as well as a sharp pain in the phalanx of my toenail, which was swollen. The hope of recovery had made itself known to me. I am coming to you for treatment. Thank you.'

*28 November 1999, St Petersburg*

## Unconventional Forms of Contact
## between the Doctor and His Patients

Examples of para-psychological contact between Dr Konovalov and his patients don't arise very often, but they are so interesting that they should be mentioned. In their questionnaires, many patients talk about how they first became 'acquainted' with the doctor. For example, one woman patient, remembered how, at a particularly difficult time in her life when she felt she had nothing to look forward to, she was sitting on the edge of a cliff and in her despair prayed to God to help her. And at that moment she had a strange vision – in the shape of a person she didn't know – and a voice inside said 'He will help you.' At the time she had no idea who this man was, where he lived, or what his profession was. But when the patient came to St Petersburg and went to Dr Konovalov's healing sessions, she was amazed to find that the doctor was the very same man she had seen on the cliff-top. 'Sergey Sergeevich,' she wrote in her questionnaire, 'I know you already, I've seen you.' Other patients described how in difficult moments in their lives they had heard a voice saying to them 'Go to Dr Konovalov, he will help you' – and this despite the fact that they had not heard about him till then and knew nothing of his healing methods or his success rate with patients.

It is Dr Konovalov's belief that

*'Facts such as these confirm the presence of the unifying information field of the living universe, which "speaks" to people, and guides them when they open themselves to it, whether it is in sorrow or in joy. However, people rarely turn to it when things are going well for them.'*

It is precisely this unity of the living universe with people everywhere that has made possible the development of the link-up sessions for patients all around the world. These are the subject of our next chapter.

# CHAPTER 21

# LINK-UP SESSIONS:

## HOW DR KONOVALOV BRINGS HELP TO PEOPLE ALL OVER THE WORLD

### A Message of Hope for Sick People Everywhere

Dr Konovalov lives and works in St Petersburg, Russia, but just because you live in another country and are not able to come to see the doctor in person, don't be hasty in dismissing this book or the message it carries. First of all, it isn't simply a book about recovering from ill health, it also brings with it a wealth of information that will warm your heart and fill you with hope. It will illuminate your soul with the light of the doctor's great love for people everywhere. For his is the kind of love without which none of us can survive, which we all unconsciously search for in our everyday lives but which we cannot find because, in the modern world we live in, there is practically no room left for it.

Russia is a vast country. Many of Dr Konovalov's patients do not live in St Petersburg and cannot attend his healing sessions there, and so he has already had considerable experience in treating people from a distance. To do so, he uses specially energized materials: the healing leaflet described in Chapter 19, which is charged with energy during the healing sessions or sprinkled with the specially charged water.

If you cannot attend sessions in St Petersburg then self-treatment in the home can still prove to be highly beneficial to you. Try it. Dr Konovalov's many years of practice, supported by patients' questionnaires and letters, all testify to the fact that this treatment exceeds the results of conventional medicine.

## How Link-Up Sessions Were First Devised

Link-up sessions between Dr Konovalov and his patients worldwide are held all the year round, every Sunday, from 21.00 to 21.30, St Petersburg time: 18.00–18.30 London time. You can check the Creation Publishing website, at www.creationpublishing.co.uk for a full list of local times. The original purpose of these sessions was for Russian patients attending the centre to maintain the proper functioning of their sensitive-body systems that they had established during treatment. As such it is a form of para-psychological contact, not specifically with the doctor, but with the energy which he is able to tap into – and patients can tap into this energy wherever they live in the world.

As with all the doctor's other energizing procedures, treatment by link-up session came about in its own unique way. Since the time he held his very first healing sessions, Dr Konovalov has often come across extraordinary things in the questionnaires sent back by patients. These tell how people have called on the doctor's help in difficult times – when their illness has got worse and the pain severe, or when they've had personal problems, trouble at work, or have been depressed. In other words, they've called for the doctor's help in times of trouble – either out loud or in their heads – after which they have received help in the most wonderful of ways: the pain has gone away, a crisis has passed leaving no trace, and their lives have fallen back into place again.

Sergey Sergeevich didn't pay much attention to such accounts when he first read them. It was perfectly possible that dozens of patients could exaggerate, fantasize, or take something that was coincidence as an indication that their unspoken appeal for help had been heard. But when he began to get thousands of descriptions of the same thing he started giving serious thought to what exactly was happening and whether there was some way in which this could be made to work in accelerating the recovery rate of patients. He understood, of course, that patients who were turning to him were actually calling up the power which had been partially incarnated in him. He carefully analysed all the relevant cases for some considerable time before coming to an astonishing conclusion that *the patient is able to call upon that part of the energy of creation, of which Dr Konovalov is the conduit, by exerting their own will and mental powers.*

Dr Konovalov concluded that if this really was the case, then some form of treatment ought also to be possible. In order to verify this theory, during healing sessions, he told his patients that an experimental 'link-up' session was being set up and asked all those who decided to take part to write down the details of what they experienced. A time was decided upon and the necessary preparations made for patients to take part.

Dr Konovalov conducted this external healing session in his own home, at the appointed time, summoning up the energy of creation and transmitting it out across the city. Everybody was stunned by the results it produced. Details sent in by patients indicated that their reactions were very similar to those normally experienced by patients at the centre during live healing sessions: pain disappeared, people felt better in themselves and had a sense of renewed energy. Since then, practically all of Dr Konovalov's patients take part in link-up sessions, not just as part of the immediate recovery process, but as a preventive measure that they maintain after their treatment is completed.

Sometimes, when the patients of the doctor travelled abroad, they'd continue to take part in link-up sessions rather than interrupting their treatment. Soon letters started arriving from Europe, America, Australia, telling the doctor about the successes achieved by these his 'external patients' on the path to recovery, about how they felt during the sessions, and how deeply indebted they were to the doctor for introducing this new form of treatment. In order to take part in link-up sessions at the correct St Petersburg time, patients who were abroad often had to get up in the middle of the night, but the results always made it all worthwhile.

## Taking Part in Link-up Sessions

It goes without saying that anybody reading this book will want to know whether they too can benefit from taking part in the link-up sessions and whether by doing so this will assist their recovery. Dr Konovalov himself feels that he still hasn't received sufficient data on this, even though thousands of patients write and tell him this is indeed the case. For there are many more people who take part in link-up sessions who don't write in and tell him how they felt at the time or how their health is now. It's possible that they simply don't want to distract the doctor from his many other patients, not realizing that their details might make an important contribution to the basis of a new treatment method. And so, if readers do decide to join in link-up sessions, then it is really important they let us know how they felt during them and keep Dr Konovalov informed of any improvements in their health afterwards. Patients can email the details to Creation Publishing at info@creationpublishing.co.uk or contact the website.

In so far as the treatment method by link-up sessions has yet to be thoroughly tested and approved for patients who have never attended live sessions, it is best that they have a copy of the healing leaflet with them when taking part. It is essential to note that patients under psychiatric treatment, or with psychological problems, should not take part in link-up sessions. It is often that case that patients are unaware of such a predisposition and it's important that they take note of their reactions during the session. If you should hear voices, especially if they are trying to make you do things, then you must immediately stop taking part in the session.

## Preparing for the Session

Just before the session starts it is important that you take yourself off into a quiet room. No external noises should disturb you; put on some calming music, preferably classical, if necessary, and imagine yourself at the doctor's centre in St Petersburg, Russia. Even if you have never been to the city, you're sure to have seen images of it. If not, try to get hold of a book with photographs of St Petersburg in it, especially of the Peter-Paul Cathedral, which is located within the Peter-Paul Fortress. The fortress as a whole is a specific point of orientation; the Human Rehabilitation Centre where Dr Konovalov holds his healing sessions is situated nearby, and the cathedral itself is the spiritual heart of St Petersburg, for it is where most of Russian tsars – including the last tsar, Nicholas II, and his family – are buried.

Having prepared yourself for the session, you must now read the 'Prayer for the Beginning of the Link-up Healing Session':

'Dear Lord, I give my heart to you and you alone.

There is no power on earth that can break the bonds that unite us, you and I.

All evil forces will be rendered impotent and helpless when confronted by the united power of my heart and yours. Thy will be done. Amen.'

You should then conjure up an image of the doctor's face. If you wish, you may address him out loud with the request: 'Be with me, Sergey Sergeevich' (or 'Give me strength', or 'Lord, heal me with the doctor's help' – or something similar). Once you have tapped into the power of the energy of creation, close your eyes and sit quietly, thinking of something pleasant: images of nature, your childhood, happy events in your life.

Do not attempt to stir up any kind of inner sensations or try and listen to your body by holding your breath, in the hope that you will feel something out of the ordinary.

As has already been stated, sick people get better even if sometimes they have absolutely no sensations of any kind during the session. But if you do experience an onrush of feeling, don't try and stop it. Don't count the minutes, and don't set the alarm clock for when the time is up. You can take part in a link-up session for as long as you feel it necessary. You can sit there for 20 or 40 minutes – it makes no difference. What's more important is that you are not distracted by trying to keep track of the time.

Start in a standing position. Open the leaflet, put it down on the floor and stand on it. Raise your arms up to the width of the divine channel (roughly 20 centimetres or 7–8 inches), link your palms above your head and slowly, slowly drop your arms in front of you in line with your spine (in this way you will open up your sensitive-body system). Then place your hands over your heart, sit down, relax and close your eyes.

Then make the following movements:

1. Bring your hands in front of you with the palms linked, as shown in Figure 8. Elbows down, arms relaxed. This movement is best done with eyes closed.

2. Now slowly bring your palms together and listen to your inner sensations. You may sense a growing resistance between your palms, as though something is preventing them from coming together. Or you may, for example, experience a sense of heat or tingling in part of your body or your internal organs. These sensations vary considerably from person to person, so you must listen carefully to your body. As soon as you feel any of them, stop trying to bring your palms together. Sit quietly for a moment.

   *Variation:* If you do not sense any change, go straight to movement 8.

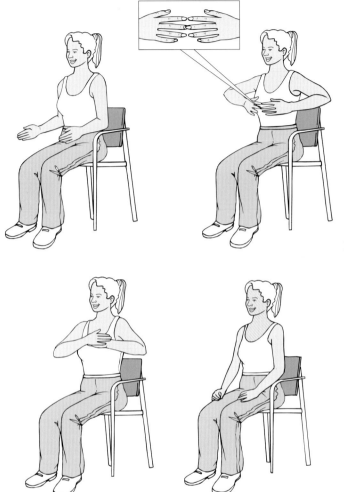

Fig. 8

Fig. 9

3.  Now bring your hands towards each other so that the fingers join to form an arch, as in Figure 8, on a level with the cup of the heart. Don't worry if the sensations alter.

4.  Now imagine that you hold in your hands a golden, shining ball of energy. It's there, inside your hands. The intensity of feeling may increase when you do this. The body's temperature may also go up.

5. Now lead these beams of energy away from your heart and down the arteries of your whole body. You don't need to know anatomy or the circulation system to do this. It's enough to know that the veins, arteries and capillaries extend into every part of the body. In this way you can imagine the energy penetrating into and enveloping your entire body, as it is moved through it by the beating of the heart. Carry on imagining the energy moving through your body for another five minutes.

6. Open your eyes. Draw your palms in towards your heart and place them one on top of the other, but without touching your body.

7. Now slowly bring your arms down. When they are below your stomach separate them and place them on your knees. Try to relax as much as possible. Don't rush – even in your thought processes. Sit in this position for 1–2 minutes (*Fig. 9*).

8. Now drop your arms down and then raise them up, as shown in Figure 10, at the width of the divine channel. Say out loud: 'Lord, help me recover with the doctor's help.' After this, slowly join your hands over your head and then slowly lower them in front of you and lay them over your heart.

9. Sit with your eyes closed for 10–15 minutes. Whilst doing so, mentally direct the energy at that organ which is causing you the most distress.

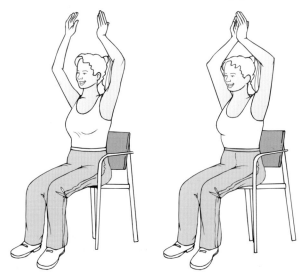

Fig. 10

If you suffer from:
- Tumours – mentally 'burn' them;
- Kidney stones or gallstones – mentally 'dissolve' them;
- Chronic inflammations – mentally 'accelerate' the activity of the lymphatic system and 'destroy' the disease-bearing micro-organisms;
- Infections or allergic reactions – mentally 'wash' the allergens out of your blood and your lymphatic system, and 'send them away' from your body, across the intercellular spaces.

In conclusion, raise your hands above you once more, press your palms together and slowly lower them in front of you – in this way, you are now closing down the sensitive-body system (*Fig. 10*).

After this, recite the following prayer:

'Dear Lord, make me a channel of your peace,
May I sow love where there is hatred,
May I forgive when others injure me,
May I unite where there is discord,
May I speak the truth where confusion prevails,
May I shine a light where darkness reigns,
May I give joy where sorrow dwells.

Dear Lord, grant that I may seek to console rather than be consoled,
To understand rather than strive to be understood,
To love rather than to strive to be loved.
For in giving we receive,
In forgiving we are forgiven,
And in dying we are born again.
And if we die trusting in you, Lord,
Then we shall be born again to eternal life.
Amen.'

At the end of the session it is recommended that you drink half a glass of the specially charged water.

# CHAPTER 22

# THE ENERGY DIAGNOSIS AND HOW THE ENERGY OF CREATION AIDS RECOVERY

'Today, things begin working for the individual patient from the moment I read their questionnaire,' says Dr Konovalov. 'The information is transmitted through me into the planet's information field and, from there, to the power which works with me.' This is how patients' are 'recorded' in what Dr Konovalov refers to as the universe's information banks.

## The Energy Diagnosis and the Information-Energy Map

*'After that I begin to look at the patient's problems. What exactly is it that is hurting, what they are most worried about, what is affecting them spiritually, what troubles them as a person? All this information in turn acts on the power that I am able to channel in working with that patient.'*

After carefully studying the physical reactions of the patient during treatment at several healing sessions, Dr Konovalov makes an individual energy diagnosis for them.'

*'The clinical diagnosis has no particular interest for me. I then enter the patient's name in the information-energy record card.* (This card has patients grouped together according to their energy diagnoses). *The energy diagnosis reflects the true reason for the patient's illness, which is why there are not as many energy diagnoses as there are clinical ones. In fact, there's really only one and this forms the basis of further treatment.'*

For example, a patient comes with a range of 15–20 diagnoses to be treated but, basically, is really troubled by only one – fibromyoma of the womb. Why? – because she's bleeding, because they want her to have an operation, and because she's scared. And because of this, she's under the impression that her cancer is the main problem. But the energy diagnosis, which pinpoints the real cause of all her problems, the most visible manifestation of which is the cancer, actually relates to the displacement of the third and fourth vertebrae, which happened when she was a child, and which caused a severe malfunction in the artery of the divine channel, which led to the formation of the fibromyoma (tumour).

*'At one of the healing sessions I ask patients in the hall who have handed in their questionnaires to stand up. Their energy diagnosis will dictate the way in which I work with them. What's special about such individual treatment is that it lasts for the whole treatment programme, until such time as we obtain a result. This is especially the case with cancer patients, for whom it is essential to have uninterrupted healing contact, with the energy being directed specifically at them. I carry the energy maps with me all the time, so that its influence is never interrupted.'*

Treatment is not always fast, nor is it without pain. Sometimes it is hard to get rid of certain diseases; and sometimes the treatment process will need an awful lot of time. During this period patients experience a whole range of feelings, but their faith and their tenacity lead eventually to excellent results. And what never ceases to amaze them is the human body's ability to fight back, and to recover from disease.

## How the Lymphatic System Fights Infection through the Power of the Energy of Creation

Dr Konovalov often reminds his patients that he alone does not set the healing process in motion; he does not heal with his own energy alone, but by enlisting the energy that is in every living person. The healing process takes place thanks to the inner power and reserves of the human organism, which nature has so constructed that it is capable of dealing with all kinds of infection. The lymphatic system is there to prevent viruses from penetrating the human organism; it acts as a natural barrier which attacks and destroys every kind of invading virus as soon as it appears. But nowadays this essential system in the human body barely functions as it used to, say, thousands of years ago, when the first human beings appeared on earth. The energy of creation which gave birth to our universe had a different density then: it was at its full complement. However, over the centuries, many millions of human lives have since been lost through countless wars, repressive regimes and the widespread increase in violence. Millions of energy structures – human souls – have been sacrificed to a whole range of unnatural occurrences unforeseen by nature, and their unexpected 'loss' in turn has disturbed the equilibrium of those energizing layers nearest to the earth. For this reason, nowadays, people are unable to summon up the human organism's natural power in helping them to recover from ill health. And a whole range of therapies and methodologies – of meditation, acupuncture and other energizing procedures – have provided us merely with a surrogate for the true energy of creation. The doctor's gift is to enable the human organism once more to soak up the full power of this energy.

## Mastering the Energy – The First Experiments

The doctor's first experiments with the energy brought many surprises. For example, it sometimes happened that a prearranged session had to be cancelled for some reason. The patients would be disappointed, but for Sergey Sergeevich it was absolute torture to have to do this: his whole body would feel weighed down with a terrible heaviness; it would be difficult for him to stand, let alone go out of the house or do anything. For two hours (the time the healing session would have lasted) he would feel utterly depressed and drained. And then the feeling would subside, the heaviness would go as suddenly as it had appeared.

After several of these strange attacks Dr Konovalov finally realized that the energy that he had planned on summoning up for the healing session had come to him anyway, even though the session had been cancelled. At that time he had only just started his practice and did not yet have complete control over what happened to his body. Unpredictable things occurred several times when he was conducting sessions at the Kozitsky Palace of Culture in St Petersburg: the energy, breaking free from the doctor's control, gathered itself into a huge, shining globe and began to hurtle round in the air. There, right in front of the eyes of astonished patients, it would smash the bulbs of the overhead projectors.

## Challenging the Highest Laws

When the first cancer patient appeared among those who came to see the doctor, the energy seemed not to want to obey him. The doctor attempted to summon it up but there was no response. He tried to do so over and over again, but the result was exactly the same as before. Doctors with extrasensory powers who witnessed these attempts tried to talk the doctor out of carrying on: 'Don't do it. It's very frightening. Don't do it!' And indeed it certainly was very frightening to challenge the highest laws and natural forces which were trying to prevent the doctor from healing sick people. But Sergey Sergeevich would not give up. He tried again and again; he prayed and asked God's help, and in the end his desire to help his patients, no matter what, turned out to be stronger than all the barriers and limitations put up against him. The energy began to come to him.

There aren't many cancer patients at sessions – about 1 per cent. But they are, however, the doctor's greatest problem and preoccupation. Having not yet got to the definitive root of what causes cancer, he urges patients not to abandon their current medical treatment and to make use of every available modern-day means offered to them. That is, not to refuse *any* of the medication prescribed by their doctors, to attend healing sessions, to make use of the healing leaflet, the specially charged water, and to do the energizing exercises. In general, Dr Konovalov urges patients not to scorn any reasonable means that might help them conquer this terrible disease.

*From case history 1000055 (born in 1941)*
'Under urographic examination a defect of the control mechanism in the left side of the bladder was detected, which caused very frequent urges to urinate. ... It was then that I began attending your healing sessions. Two weeks later, a controlled examination revealed that everything was fine ... it's hard to believe.

The doctors started to say that maybe there had been a mistake in the original diagnosis, but I knew and I hadn't forgotten the discomfort of what I'd been going through for two years. And suddenly, it all went away and everything was normal. I am indebted to you.'

*(In October 2001 condition stable)*

*From case history 1004919 (born 3 November 1926)*
'I have bilateral fibroma of the breasts. I am registered as a patient at the

Oncological Institute. After your healing sessions, somehow or other, everything seems to have disappeared.'

*1996*
*(By October 2001 the disease had not recurred)*

**From case history 1013285 (born 10 April 1946)**
'Every time I start to write to you, feelings of indescribable gratitude and a deep sense of spiritual emotion well up in me, towards you, my most revered physician. This is my 24th treatment programme and I now find it hard to describe how I feel during the healing sessions. To listen to you, learn from you, and feel myself a participant in a unique experience have all become a necessity, an integral part of my life. It is hope that brings every one of us to the hall and we are anxious to turn it into reality. But, as I myself came to understand, the achievements gained will not be permanent until hope has been transformed into faith. Yes, you offer us protection so that we don't fall back again, but we need also to learn how to protect ourselves from within. But lack of will power, irritability, depression, intolerance, an inflated sense of self – all of these things often lead to poor results (and this includes me). Now I've discovered a sense of inner protection thanks to your sessions, and with it belief in the divine power of the universe, in the potential of my own organism and in your wonder-working gifts.

You've been treating me now for four years. During this time my general state of health and how I feel about myself have significantly improved. My bowels work normally, the "dragging" gastric pains have stopped, the tachycardia has disappeared, I don't have any headaches, my osteochondrosis hardly bothers me, and the pains in the small of my back have stopped. In all this time I haven't had any colds, and the frequent attacks of bronchitis and tracheitis are now in the past.

As for my major problem – breast cancer – there is a noticeable improvement. Although they tell you at the centre that cancer can be cured, it isn't till you sense it personally that you really experience a turnaround in your attitude to yourself and the possibility of recovery through you. Two months ago the tumour had gone down by 20 per cent. I was at the Oncological Institute today and the rate of regression was now 30 per cent, the tumour is forming scar tissue, and the small nodules are dispersing.

Sergey Sergeevich, no words of thanks that I have written here can ever express my feelings. Today my eyes shine with joy, and my heart and mind are full of thanks to God and to the universe. I have the deepest respect and love for you, and your professional integrity as doctor, healer and a wonderful human being.'

*(In October 2002 condition stable)*

### From case history 1011582 (born 1935)

'You have been treating me since 1992. I'm now on my 29th treatment programme. I have cancer in my right breast. They hadn't operated; they said they couldn't because of the swelling. Between the start of 1993 and the end of 1994 I had three lots of radiotherapy, and then three of chemotherapy. I have a lot to be happy about: the results are good. I had a scan (including one of my entire skeleton) and everything was OK. Yet an acquaintance, who was in the next bed to me in hospital, didn't want to go to your sessions and she died a year ago. My leukocyte count has gone up from three to six. And in addition to all this, the osteochondrosis has gone, the coronary heart disease and haemorrhoids have disappeared, the circulation has improved in my feet and I've stopped getting cramp in them. I had an ultrasound and there's only one stone left in my gall bladder – 1.7 in size. The second one, which was 0.9 has disappeared, dissolved. I now feel very well.'

*(In March 2000 condition stable)*

# CHAPTER 23

# THE DYNAMICS OF TREATMENT:

## THREE TYPICAL CASE HISTORIES

### The Usual Statistics Looked At
### Within Unusual Parameters

There are several unique aspects to the patient questionnaires that Dr Konovalov collates at his centre in St Petersburg. On the one hand, as in any medical establishment that prides itself on its reputation, the centre maintains an archive and a computer centre for preserving an accurate, authenticated account of the clinical diagnoses of the illnesses of every patient attending the doctor's treatment programmes and then gathering statistical information from the patient's questionnaires. A whole book could be published containing all of this material; in fact, there's enough for dozens of doctoral dissertations. On the other hand – and this is where Dr Konovalov's approach differs – the statistics are arrived at according to a set of parameters that are not made use of in conventional medico-scientific institutions. For in conventional medicine a clinical diagnosis is only based on the external manifestation of one specific medical condition, whereas 10, 20 or even 30 different diagnoses can often be the external manifestation of a single condition. So the real single statistical unit, if one can call it that, is in fact the individual patient. This means that even the most ordinary of colds has characteristics that are peculiar to each individual patient. Dr Konovalov's objective is the complete recovery of the patient, irrespective of age, the number of diagnoses made, or how long they have suffered from their conditions. 'Is such a goal possible?' you ask. Yes, and thousands of the doctor's patients have already attained it. The case histories that follow describe the often long and difficult path that the patient and Dr Konovalov must travel along together in order to reach that goal.

## The Typical Case of an Elderly Person

This female patient was born in 1922. Most doctors would immediately say: 'So what do you want me to do? She's a woman of 77 [at the time of writing]. She has all the physiological symptoms for a woman of her age.'

Dr Konovalov pays no attention to age. He is only interested in a patient's age in so far as it is registered on the computer, for statistical purposes, along with other information on an individual patient's history.

*From case history 1002383 (born in 1922)*
'I had barely crossed the threshold of the doctor's divine temple when everything in me began to change. I came to the healing session with a temperature of 38.4°C; that night, after the session, I slept well and in the morning my temperature was 37.2°C, and by the evening it was back to normal. I was amazed at how quickly and imperceptibly my temperature went down, without any medicine, but just with the help of the water, the leaflet and the doctor himself. ... I have an ailment that is as old as I am. This is disease of the nasopharynx, inherited from my father. I've been familiar with ointments and drops for the nose since I was a few months old. Trachoma, endless bouts of angina, all kinds of colds and flu – I've had them all. I'd lost my sense of smell too and nobody could help me. ... But now I'm getting better .... In the 1950s, there were another 200 patients like me under Doctor Grobstein. We all used to go to the institute for blood transfusions, and breathe in oxygen, ozone, etc. Professor Voyachek himself said that the disease was incurable. But what do I see now? When I look at the mucous membrane of my throat in the mirror, convinced that it will be totally pale, dry and lifeless, I see that it is pinkish-red and moist and is gradually recovering. This is such a victory, doctor!

In February 1944, when we were on a military assignment, another radio operator and I fell through some ice up to our waists. ... Our sheepskin jackets, thick felt boots, padded trousers, etc., were all immediately heavy with water. The frost did its work, boxing us in with ice, our matches were soaked, we couldn't get them to light. ... We were half alive by the time they got us to a fire; we'd been in these wet things for two days and since that time I've been plagued by nephritis, cystitis, lots of boils, rheumatism, and my feet have always been cold – from progressive, degenerative, arteriosclerosis of the lower extremities. Since the war my skin has kept coming up in goose bumps and I always have to keep my head covered, even bound up tightly. I also have fits of vomiting. I'd even gone and got myself a walking stick because my legs were in such a bad state. And on top of that, I have chronic cholecystitis, chronic pancreatitis and my bowels don't work well. Now my gastro-intestinal tract is back to normal too, and my stomach has gone down (it was swollen). Since 1941 I have been plagued with insomnia but now everything's fine. I am very pleased with the results.'

## How Diseases Disappear Without Being Noticed

From this, her first questionnaire, it was clear that the patient, as she went through the form describing her basic ailments, started remembering other things: oh yes, her stomach had been swollen and now it was back to normal. She came to the healing sessions primarily for her major problem, which was the pain in her feet. She had already got herself a stick, in anticipation of the illness getting progressively worse. But on coming to see Dr Konovalov, she was absolutely amazed to discover that other problems, about which she hadn't even thought of getting help, were also getting better. This was confirmed at the leading scientific centre in the country; one of the best specialists had told her so. And he wasn't mistaken, he wasn't fooling her. It's simply that modern-day medicine doesn't know how best to treat such diseases.

So, although the woman started feeling considerably better she didn't stop going to the healing sessions, unlike other patients who, overjoyed that their health is on the mend, don't make the time to see their recovery through to completion. They don't wait to get to the bottom of what is really making them ill and in so doing end up not protecting themselves from going down with new and different diseases.

Let's see how our patient progressed.

*Continuation of case history 1002383*
'I'm coming to the end of my 27th treatment programme, which means I can now talk of a 90 per cent recovery. Of course, there is still something

left for you, my body and the energy to work on, but this needs time and my regular attendance at sessions. But the most important things have been accomplished: many of my illnesses have gone. For example: progressive endarteritis, a cyst on the left leg, haemorrhoids, osteochondrosis, radiculitis, chronic pneumonia, headaches, high blood pressure, a weak heart, chronic tonsillitis, paradontosis. My sleep has also settled down, my gastro-intestinal tract is working well, and I feel healed in spirit too. Sergey Sergeevich, at long last two of the toes on my right foot have got their circulation back and have stopped hurting. What joy! And there's been even more success and happiness: the angina which had tormented me till now has gone and my glands have gone down. They had given me no peace, were always filling up with pus which every so often I had to drain out myself. I'd taken so many antibiotics for this that I'd had a temperature all the time. After putting my spine right during the healing sessions, my cervical vertebrae have righted themselves too ... A huge thank you to you for making me better, for all the goodness and kindness that you do for us.'

## Recovery in Less Than a Month

By this time the patient, having attended 27 treatment programmes, had spent, in all, about 540 hours at the treatment centre – the equivalent of 22.5 days. But where else in the world might a patient be cured, in less than a month, of such a catalogue of 'incurable' diseases? How? And by whom? Has there ever been a time when such wonderful things have been achieved? And just look at the number of this person's case history – 1002383. This alone will help you understand that it is no one-off, no miracle. It's impossible to take in such a huge number stories of recovery; it serves only to underline the fact that we have never before encountered something like this.

The patient's final questionnaire was handed in on 17 December 1998:

'In the morning, when I went into the bathroom, I could smell the soap and the toothpaste, and when I turned on the tap I could even smell the rustiness of the water, which had been standing all night in the rusty pipes. Dear God, my dreams are coming true! Where can I write about this? Who can I share it with? Only you, Sergey Sergeevich, can understand my delight, my joy, my happiness. If someone had asked me at that moment what was most precious to me – my sense of smell, or wealth – I wouldn't have hesitated in replying: my sense of smell – that is real riches. In fact, to tell the truth, I've lived my whole life without it. And another miracle has happened. My hearing has never been very good either. My poor hearing had made it difficult for me to study and live in general. Using my eyes helped; I'd follow someone's lips as they talked. When I came for my first healing session, all I could think about was my feet, and I thought only they could be treated. Not understanding or knowing anything, I made mistakes. Gradually, little by little, my diseases started clearing up – and there were so many of them. Things in my sick body got better with every healing session. And I became more and more convinced that there wasn't a disease that you and the energy of creation could not overcome. I thank God, and I thank you, dear Sergey Sergeevich, and bow down before you. It's so hard for an uneducated person such as me to fill in this form. It'd be easier for me pile up a great stack of chopped-up firewood than express my thoughts and feelings on paper.'

The patient attended sessions over the course of three years. She began her treatment when she was already over seventy. Today she has almost completely recovered her health. She is healthy thanks to Dr Konovalov, his energy and her own faith and dogged determination to get well. In October 2001, her condition was better.

## Case Histories Typical of Any Clinic, In Any Town, In Any Country

This second case history is not just typical of recorded cases found at Dr Konovalov's centre, but of any clinic in any town. It is typical of the catalogue of complaints with which a patient comes for treatment. But in terms of the results achieved, no other clinic compares with Dr Konovalov's centre.

*From case history 1008383 (born in 1942)*
'I'm attending my 6th treatment programme. The myoma in my womb has disappeared. The stones I've been passing through my bowels are getting smaller and smaller. At first they were as big as dried beans, but now they are the size of a match head. My liver doesn't bother me now, my

haemorrhoids and the varicose vein running down my left shin have gone, and the frequent migraine-like pains in my head too. My chronic bronchitis has almost cleared up – I don't cough up very much now and not often. I can't feel the osteochondrosis, the corns on my feet have nearly gone, the skin on my face has got smoother. ... I don't want what I say to sound like flattery, but having seen healing sessions on TV done by other people as a kind of well-rehearsed performance, I am an even greater admirer of your simplicity (with a capital S), your tact, and your sense of proportion. ...

I've drawn up a list of all the things affecting my health over the 10 treatment programmes, and am putting it in the questionnaire: I haven't had a single occurrence of the spasms of the blood vessels in the brain – migraine – for the last year; my blood pressure had been erratic for the last 31 years but now it's normal. For more than 40 years I've had patches of greasy seborrhoea on my face, in my ears and on my scalp. The skin on my face is significantly better – it's clearer and not so greasy. The stones I've had in my gall-bladder (30 years) don't hurt; there are no stones and mucus either (according to the ultrasound); there's no sign of the haemorrhoids I've had for 34 years. As for the fibromyoma of my womb which had numerous nodes – the largest being 4.2 x 3.9 (more than 25 years) – there's no myoma now and only one nodule of 1.5 x 1 left (according to the ultrasound). I've been offered an operation for my prolapsed womb for eight years now, but it's back in place (according to the ultrasound); as for the diabetes and things linked to it (more than 12 years) – when I was attending healing sessions my sugar levels went back to normal; in between sessions they went up again, but I'm not sticking to a diet. The chronic bronchitis (more than 25 years) has significantly improved; I've not been aware of my osteonchondrosis (more than 20 years) during the time I've been undergoing treatment. The congestion (3 to 4 years) has all gone; the umbilical hernia (more than 15 years) can't be seen; the pain in the right knee joint (more than 10 years) – there's no pain now; the varicose vein in my right leg (about 4 years) has gone down, the leg is smooth; my bowels weren't working well – constipation for 5–6 days at a time – now everything's working normally; I no longer have mastopatia of the mammary glands (about 18 years); the papillomas on my face and body (about 15 years) have gone.

## Recovery from Physical Disease Brings With It a Renewal of the Spirit

In her subsequent questionnaires the patient was no longer talking about her ailments, because they'd all gone. She was now on the brink of an inner transformation; she had turned to the Gospels and had begun to think about her life and her future.

'I'm coming to the end of my 27th treatment programme. ... For a long time I've not been able to understand the commandment to 'Love God'. I had come to the conclusion that God could not possibly want our love because he had created us and we are smaller than insects to him. ... In 'God's Law' it is written that God is love. But these were just words to me and didn't touch my heart. Then when I started coming to your healing sessions, I was bowled over by the miracle of what you were doing, by the miracle that someone like you existed, and it's only now that I understand what a wonder it is that knowing each of us, with all our faults and inadequacies, you nevertheless love us and do everything you can to help us. I've long known that to love humanity as a whole is a very simple thing; it's easy to love like that and practically all of us can do it. But it's very difficult to love each individual person. If you love us so, then it means that you need our love too, and our understanding. It couldn't be otherwise. So now I've come to understand that the Lord God needs our love as much as we need his ... please accept my deepest love and my boundless respect for you.'

Later, the patient reported back again:

'Sergey Sergeevich, I've now completed four years' treatment with you. This is my 31st treatment programme. When I look back, I can say only one thing – that everything that I have today, I have because of you. I'm not just talking about my health, which you have given back to me, but my whole life too. I came to you in November 1994 (it's now November 1998), full of rage at the world, only I didn't realize it at the time, and if you had said this to me I wouldn't have believed you and would even have taken offence.

Now I know exactly what my problems are – they're to do with me, although understanding what the problems are and coming to grips with them is not one and the same thing. So there's only one solution – to try and become a better person. ... My gratitude to you for all you have done is so huge that I can't measure it. I admire your self-sacrifice and would like to stay in touch with you for ever.'

*(In October 2001 her condition was good)*

## Treatment Becomes a Testament of Faith

Very often a patient with a catalogue of complaints that cannot be successfully treated finds that the doctors give up on them, leaving them to feel lonely and abandoned. Those with the courage to take up the fight against their ill health with Dr Konovalov's help very often have their lives transformed and discover a new sense of faith and hope for the future.

*From case history 1014778 (born in 1956)*
'This is my fifth treatment programme. I started feeling unwell quite suddenly: headache, vomiting, fever, discomfort, and bleeding from my uterus. I go to the hospital and they only ask one question: "Could you be pregnant?" And that's the sum total of my treatment. I got the tablets from the chemists, and treated myself.

But it got worse and worse. My spine ached, I couldn't sit down, my coccyx hurt so much. But at the hospital it was the same old thing: "either you fell and hurt yourself, or it's osteochondrosis." So what point was there in going to doctors? I kept on applying heat to the parts that hurt, massaged them with oil, used suppositories, and so on. But nothing got better. And then my kidneys began to fail; I had stones and attacks of colic, cystitis, my knee joints began to ache, I couldn't climb stairs – the pain was terrible. I couldn't coordinate my movements and was afraid to go out without somebody helping me. Then a tumour appeared in my chest. They did an ultrasound – and found a fibromyoma of 14 weeks; my thyroid gland was, in the words of the doctor, "shot through with holes" as though a moth had been at it, but what exactly the problem was, he didn't know. They said they'd have to do a blood test. By then, I was no longer able to go to work. So they admitted me to the First Medical Institute for an operation. Thankfully, it turned out to be a cyst. They examined me while I was there, and one astute assistant professor remarked: "It can't be radiculitis that's making your spine hurt like that. Let's do another X-ray of your spine.

They've only taken one half of her chest."...

They did the X-rays and were shocked: they found a tumour, 3 x 5 x 3.5 cm large, on my iliac bone. The sent me to the Institute of Cancer's scientific research department. They examined me, advised I use a walking stick, take tablets and use suppositories. They told me to come back in six months to be examined again. And that was it. Can you imagine how I felt? I prayed to God to take me to his bosom: I didn't have the strength to do it for myself. It was absolute hell. Life was passing me by and there was I, standing by the roadside, like a broken down, homeless, abandoned dog that nobody wanted. I was writhing in agony from the pain and my life was an absolute torment. I stopped seeing people, didn't want to have anything to do with anyone, and lay, listless, in my bed for days on end. My children quietly turned their backs on me. They lived under the same roof with me like disgruntled flatmates. I was beginning to go mad with the isolation and my sense of hopelessness.

It was then that a lady doctor recommended I sign up to see "Doctor Konovalov". I heard her out with a wry smile but paid no attention to it. But some inner voice kept saying to me: "Just try it, maybe it will help?" Time passed and I still hadn't got round to seeing you. I remember I was lying in bed, and suddenly leapt up, got dressed and went to the hall where your healing sessions were being held. This was 18 January 1998. I went to the box office and asked for a ticket for Dr Konovalov. The cashier looked at me and said: "Let's see if your luck's in – morning or evening?" I thought for a moment and said "Morning." "You're in luck", she said, "ten minutes ago someone who can't attend the morning session returned a ticket." The 19th January was a public holiday – Epiphany. And that's how we met, my dear doctor. That is how I came to you. As soon as you started playing your music, I began to weep, quietly at first, and then barely able to suppress the tears and the sobs. Then the healing session began, and I remember how something like a lilac-coloured cloud encircled me and entered my body. I was frightened and then it went from me.

During the first treatment programme I had very severe pains in my back. I couldn't sit and you were talking about some kind of cells, the sensitive-body system, and so on. I wanted to get up and leave; to be honest, your voice even irritated me. The initial sessions were an absolute torment for me. What kind of nightmare is this, I thought, what have I got myself into, why am I doing this? But an inner voice kept on saying: "Don't be in a rush, be patient." And this is how I got through the first treatment programme.

During the second one my spine suddenly straightened itself out during one of the procedures, so much so that I could hardly stay on my feet. At home, between the 2nd and 3rd programmes, my stomach and bowels went back into position; I didn't understand what was happening and once more got frightened, fool that I was. But during the third treatment programme, after the fourth or fifth healing session, I became aware that I could sit without being in pain and could even lean back in the chair. I was so happy. In my mind I called out to you: "Look at me, Sergey Sergeevich, I can sit! Can you see – I'm sitting. I haven't been able to do that for three years!" I was scared that I'd actually shout it out loud. I was absolutely overjoyed.

During the 4th treatment programme everything got bad again: all my joints ached, my fingers, my breastbone, I couldn't turn my neck, the place where they'd operated on my chest hurt. But I didn't take a single tablet, didn't see a single doctor. I couldn't sleep, I was crying with the pain, I couldn't turn on my side. But I put up with it all, just as you had told me: "Endure – listen and endure." I was vomiting and running a fever, I felt really awful. During the 5th treatment programme, little by little, it all began to subside. I was so happy.

And now a few words in summary: the pain in my knees has gone, I can run up the stairs, my movements are much better coordinated, the headaches have practically gone, the pains in my heart too. I no longer have cystitis, there are no stones, no colic; my blood pressure is 120 over 80. I've got no dragging pain down below my stomach; the haemorrhoids have shrunk and don't bleed. My feet are warmer, I can bend my spine, and my step has become sprightlier. And many, many other little things have gone away, which, to be honest, I don't even think about now.

But the most important thing, Sergey Sergeevich, is that I've begun to smile again and hum a tune under my breath. And now I want to look nice. Many people tell me I've changed for the better. Things are fine with my children. The youngest says to me, 'Mum, you're a different person. Let me kiss those cherry-red cheeks of yours!" Everyone asks me: "Who is this Konovalov man?" And I tell them: "He's my doctor; he's is treating me and teaching me too." "But what is there for him to teach you? You're a grown woman?" And I tell them: "Life has doled out too many short straws to me; it's time I made up for it."

I get very frightened when I think about what might have happened to me if I had not met you. There's an awful lot I don't understand. But there's one thing I know for sure: it's not diseases that are our problem. It's our state of mind. I'm frightened of going back to the person I was when I first came to you; I don't want to go there, don't want to go back. I have this feeling, as though I am wearing a crystal-white dress, and I'm frightened of making it dirty, so I'm being careful and cautious.

God grant you health and happiness. Thank you.

PS. We must live, we must struggle for life, because all sorts of things are possible. Maybe I haven't been lucky in life, perhaps fate has ordained that I should go through all this, put up with things and by so doing come out of it a better person. But to do this you have to be very, very strong, and the main thing is not to lose heart, not to let go. And this is what you have taught me, Sergey Sergeevich. Nobody in my life has ever said to me "I can take your pain away." Who nowadays could possibly take it into their head to take away somebody else's pain? May your name be blessed, dear doctor.

*With respect, your patient and pupil'*
*November 2000*

# CHAPTER 24

# GENERAL PRACTICAL RECOMMENDATIONS FOR MAINTAINING GOOD HEALTH

My work on the first book had come to an end, but I wasn't feeling happy about things. Surely, I asked myself, if tens of thousands of people had read about the possibility of complete recovery from their physical ailments, this might pose a huge problem for Dr Konovalov. Most of all, I was worried that there'd be huge queues for tickets for the treatment programmes, and that people who'd been attending them for a long time would no longer be able to get in. Even today, without advertising of any kind the tickets sell out the minute they become available. Sergey Sergeevich doesn't think this will be a problem. Why? Because the vast majority of people can't and don't want to take care of themselves. Treatment requires time. One treatment programme lasts a month and they don't want to make a long-term commitment, not just to getting but staying well.

People will say 'I've been coming for a month now but there's still no change', forgetting that a single treatment programme is only about 20 hours, in other words, less than a single day and night. And there are other benefits: once you start treatment you no longer need to take medicine every few hours that will harm your body. The energy has already begun building up inside you and has already initiated the healing process. If you are patient, the results of this will soon become apparent to you.

## Worrying About the Minutes, We Squander Years

Why are we all so preoccupied with the passing of time but not with our health? By setting aside 20 hours of our time over the course of five weeks are we really shortening our lives? What kind of false economy is it to worry about minutes and yet be wasteful about years? 'Laziness,' according to Dr Konovalov, 'is a devil-may-care, irresponsible attitude to one's own well-being. A person thinks that arthrosis, say, is simply going to disappear of its own accord. But with every day, every month, every year, a disease like this carries on undermining a person's health; things go from bad to worse, and all they do is sit there. They take their tablets, go through the motions, and it's the same with many other diseases.' It's the same, too, with Dr Konovalov's sessions. 'People prove how lazy they are by not coming to me. And they find it even easier to justify their not coming by saying that my treatment methods go against conventional practice.'

There are people who are suffering terribly with illness yet who decide it's just too hard for them even to travel a single stop by bus to come for treatment. And there are a lot of people like this even though it goes against all common sense. Meanwhile, there are others who travel into St Petersburg for sessions not just from the outer suburbs but from as far away as the regions of Pskov and Novgorod. People even come from Moscow, hurrying to get back to the capital on the night train after a session, so that they can get to work on time in the morning. It isn't the cost of treatment in Russia that discourages patients – for it is minimal. Yet people still are ready to think up a whole raft of excuses to explain away their cavalier attitude to their own health.

Dr Konovalov sets high standards. He only considers those people his real patients who set themselves the goal of complete recovery. There aren't many of them – perhaps a few thousand in a city of millions. But his heart is always open to them and he devotes all his strength to supporting them on this difficult path.

## Dr Konovalov's Concept of Good Health

This book will provide only pointers towards Dr Konovalov's overall concept of good health. It is a theory that will be described in detail in future books, which will outline for the reader exactly what it is that causes diseases, their origins, the concept of good health and many other things. In the meantime, Dr Konovalov has set out a few general guidelines for living a healthy life.

The most important thing to remember is that when a person first feels pain this does not indicate that a disease has only just taken hold, nor does it when the doctor makes a diagnosis. The roots of disease lie in a person's lifestyle, in the way he or she behaves, and so on.

# 1. Eye disease – the Disease of Our Times

Some of the most common diseases of the modern world are those affecting the eyes: cataracts, glaucoma, progressive short-sightedness, degeneration of the optic nerve, and so on. Why has eye disease taken such a hold in our times? It's because we don't look after our eyes. The twentieth century brought us the widespread use of electric light and, since then, in all the time we've been enthusiastically and naively gazing at this new and convenient source of light new diseases have been springing up.

A hundred or so years ago the human eye was not used to harsh electric lighting, and was acclimatized only to the natural light of the sun and the light of candles or gas lamps. Daily activity would stop when the sun went down, and eyes would be rested. But today we find ourselves under the glare of electric lights practically twenty-four hours a day. A sudden flash of artificial light, especially if a lamp is turned on in the darkness (when you wake early in the morning or get up for the toilet in the night) can immediately cause a microscopic burn to the retina. With time, this damage gets worse, and in some people causes macular dystrophy, dystrophy of the retina, dystrophy of the optic nerve, cataracts, and so on. Sitting in front of the television for hours on end can have the same effect, as can working long hours at a computer without a protective screen, or reading by a table lamp. The retina receives by far the most damage, however, from a sudden flash of light in darkness.

## How to protect your eyes
In order to minimize this effect and avoid micro-burns to the retina, close your eyes before turning on a light. And after you have switched it on, keep your eyes closed for a few seconds longer (count to ten). The light filters through your eyelids and your eyes will get used to it more gradually. When you open your eyes they should already be used to the light. Better still is to have small night lights in your home, enough to light your way if you get up in the night for the toilet, for example, or go to the kitchen to get some water.

## 2. How too Much Intake of information Leads to Health Problems

Nowadays, over the course of a single day, people take in huge amounts of information – as much as they would once have absorbed in a lifetime. But the human brain has not enlarged correspondingly in size to allow for this; neither have the number of nerve receptors increased over the centuries. It is possible that during the next millennium the human brain will go through some physiological changes as a way of adapting to this increased intake in information. But this is yet to happen, and right now the 'information cocktail' that we ingest daily contains only about 2 per cent of useful or essential information. The remainder simply overburdens our brain.

What is curious is that this information overload is of no use – either to us or to our bodies – and yet day in day out, out of habit, we subject ourselves to all this additional stress. We get up in the morning and straight away turn on the TV or the radio, unleashing a flood of information on ourselves. We're usually getting ready for work at this time and having the TV on is only background noise. At the underground station or on the way to the bus or train, we buy a newspaper or pick up the free magazines that are usually available there. To while away the journey to work we bury ourselves in reading matter, once more taking in unnecessary information and overloading our brains. Work for most of us is computer-linked, and this is yet another major information burden. And on the way home – it's back to the book or newspaper, and once we're indoors the TV goes on again. It is therefore not surprising, in view of such a huge overload to the brain, that many people complain of sleeping badly, of feeling stressed out about nothing in particular, of asthma attacks and lots of other complaints. But they are all caused by the information overload to which modern-day people are subjected. And this has its effect not just on the individual, but on their children too, leading to chronic illnesses and disability.

### How best to absorb information

The advice Dr Konovalov gives for dealing with this information overload is actually very simple and easy to carry out. Your response may be a sceptical one, but just stop and think about how much you worry about your own welfare and the health of your children.

First of all, Sergey Sergeevich advises us to define our goals and think about what it is we really want out of life. You don't have to set a lifetime goal, but merely think of something you want to achieve in the next 5–10 years. Once you've set one for yourself, don't deviate from it and waste time on things that are aimless and unproductive.

It's much better to switch on some music when you get up in the morning. It doesn't matter what kind – classical or pop. The main thing is that it reflects your mood. Music that fits a person's inner mood can have either a calming or an enlivening effect. And either way, it helps a person achieve harmony and a state of balance.

Don't sit and read newspapers on the way to work by public transport; don't start loading your brain with unnecessary information, don't take in negative information, of which there is far more than there is positive in today's newspapers. Journalism today is a hostage to advertising. Many articles are written merely to serve advertisers and, by reading them, you are not listening to an independent journalist but to another form of advertising, only dressed up differently. Instead of reading – just rest. Close your eyes and relax.

When you come home, the first thing you should do is unwind. Put on some of your favourite music again or watch a TV programme that is soothing. The murder and violence on our TVs, day and night, on every channel, have a subconscious effect on us, no matter how resistant we think we are to them. Absorbing this kind of information, people can, for no particular reason, suddenly become aggressive. Day after day, people get used to seeing mass murder, terrorism and violence on their TV screens; and it's a habit that couples who are just starting a family together can pass on to their children.

An evening stroll has a wonderful effect on a person, taking away the stress brought on by this excessive intake of information. If you don't want to go for a walk then sit for a while by an open window, and listen to some calming music. A moment's tranquillity is far more beneficial than switching on the TV.

## 3.   Healthy Eating: Listening to Your Body

Eating healthily is to eat when you want to. Listen to your body. If you want to eat – eat; if you don't – then don't. We're talking here, of course, only about people who are healthy. This advice should not be followed by those who are sick, who need to eat at fixed times in order to cope with their condition – for example, those suffering with diabetes.

If it's time for your lunch-break at work and you don't feel hungry, you don't have to go to the canteen or eat your lunch just because it's lunch time. It's better to take something back with you and eat it when you feel like it. If you want to eat five times or even ten times a day, then go ahead. If you wake up hungry in the night then eat something. But don't make yourself eat when you don't want to – for example, in the morning, when people often don't feel hungry; there's no need to eat simply because it's a long time till lunch.

Some people eat because they think that their stomach needs to have something to digest. This is wrong. If you don't want to eat there's nothing wrong, so long as you don't chew gum, because the act of chewing makes the gastro-intestinal tract start working. You mustn't do this.

Many people are interested in which food products are good for them and which harmful, in learning how to cook them and in which order to eat them. Dr Konovalov does not stick to any strict rules in this respect and advises his patients to do the same. As far as he's concerned there are lots of ways of obtaining nourishment. A limited diet is harmful but a varied one doesn't mean that someone has to load their organism down with set amounts of foodstuffs from a long list of products. Today you may want an apple, tomorrow a pear; today a carrot salad, tomorrow a green one, and so on.

As far as meat is concerned, consumption again depends on desire. If you want meat today then eat it; if you don't feel like it tomorrow then you don't have to have it.

People who are overweight should remember that all the advice given here is for people whose weight is normal. Excessive weight (and by this I don't mean a couple of pounds but 40–60 lbs) is a sign of a dysfunction of one of the body's systems. During treatment programmes, there are some patients whose weight has been 300 lbs (22 stone) and over, who have lost 130–160 lbs (9–11 stone) without going on any special diets.

Women who are worried about being overweight sometimes eat very little. But as soon as they do eat something, everything they consume is immediately absorbed by the body. They try and eat as seldom as possible, but Dr Konovalov advises such patients to eat as often as they can, approximately once every half hour, but only in very small and varied portions.

In general, there's no need to eat several courses at dinner, including dessert. It is very hard for the body to digest such a huge intake in one go. If you really want to have a four-course meal, then take a break between each course, of up to half an hour. This way you can have, say, a salad for the first course, then half an hour later (or two hours – whatever you wish) have the second course, and so on. A regular intake by the stomach of huge amounts of food leads to obesity and problems with the working of the gastro-intestinal tract.

After having a large meal or a sit-down feast of some kind, don't then rush to take any of the products that are widely advertised as aiding digestion. And if your pancreas can't produce enough enzymes to digest all this don't take anything either, otherwise things will just get worse as you go on. The pancreas will stop producing the enzymes needed for the body to function properly. Taking such preparations on a regular basis will only impair the proper functioning of the liver and pancreas and you will thus find yourself using them more and more as time goes on.

## 4.   Good Planning: the Basis of Your Future Health

Dr Konovalov has further recommendations relating to how you plan your day. However, they aren't the usual kind of plans and you will only come to understand in full how they function in your everyday life, and what goes on during such planning sessions, from the doctor's future books.

In the morning, we are usually rudely woken by the noise of our alarm clock; we rush to get ready, wash, have breakfast and head off to work. It's rare, at times like this, for us to find a moment for ourselves, or think about our lives – our real lives – rather than our hair, our shoes, how we look and how hungry we feel, even though we'd all agree that such things are no less important.

In order to find time, of which we never have enough, Dr Konovalov recommends that we set the alarm 3–5 minutes earlier than usual. And the alarm itself should not be too loud. Once you've woken up, don't rush to get on with things by leaping straight out of bed, but allow yourself a moment to snuggle down under the covers – the physical state we're in first thing in the morning is suited to this. And then slowly wake up and rouse yourself. (If you're one of the doctor's patients then summon up the energy of creation, and follow it mentally down through all your organs and your body's systems. This will take about 20–30 seconds.) After that think about the day ahead, from the first moment (when you get up) and in every detail: how you get up, take a shower, go to the kitchen, have breakfast, make your bed, leave the house, start the car (or take public transport), and make your way to work. Visualize the things you will have to do at work, or the list of tasks which you need to get through that day, how you come to the end of the working day, where you go next, which shops you go into, the way home, and what you do when you get in. You must allow all these events, one by one, up to the moment when you are back in bed again, to pass through your consciousness. In this way you set out a plan of events specific to your own information field which will become part of the general information field of the planet for things that will happen during that day.

You can now get up quietly, do a few of the exercises suggested in this book and say a prayer. You don't need to read some prescribed religious text or repeat the same prayer day after day. People get by today without this. What you do need to do is call upon the universe, the planet (the doctor's patients can call on the energy of creation through him) and ask that the day will go well.

After you have done this, and without hurrying (Dr Konovalov warns that you should never ever hurry), you can get on with what you have to do.

Simple, isn't it? Utterly simple. In fact, it's so simple that the sceptics raise doubts as to the effectiveness of such simple recommendations (which is precisely why they are sceptics). Let's give a personal example. As a psychologist, I've been used, since my student days, to experimenting on myself with all kinds of mental tests and exercises. So I started trying out Dr Konovalov's day plan as soon as he first dictated its details to me. In the evening, before going to sleep, I ran the day that was over through my head and visualized the one to come. In the morning, after turning off the alarm, I imagined the things I had to do that day in even more detail. And there was a lot to do. First of all, I'm working for two publishers at the same time, so I have a lot of writing to do. I had long since set my daily target at around

7–8 page spreads a day. Secondly, I have a family – a husband who works long hours, and two sons, for whom every day I have to prepare meals, wash and sew, and help with their homework. The picture of my daily duties is completed by a dog which dreams of being walked three times a day, and a permanently hungry kitten, which the dog recently found. And there's nobody to share all this with. So I rush round in circles, like a hamster on a wheel, from half past seven and collapse into bed at about one in the morning, and even then, in my sleep, I think about all the little things I should have done.

### Planning your day according to Dr Konovalov's recommendations
When I first tried planning my days according to Dr Konovalov's recommendations, I honestly didn't have a clue how they would help me in concrete terms. I certainly didn't expect instant results. Yet on the very next day, on waking and having visualized my plan for the day ahead, I noticed at precisely 2 o'clock in the afternoon that I had already got through all the things that before would have taken me a whole day. I wrote my eight pages, prepared dinner, did the washing and even tidied the flat. Everything had been done in two hours' less time than usual.

And what's more, I did everything without hurrying, which is also not my usual way. I didn't rush and yet it still took me two hours less. Since then, I take time to make my day plans in the evening and again in the morning. And I now plan to get through twice as much work as before. I don't sit at the computer until ten at night, as before; and yet I manage to write 16 pages of text in four hours during the day. There's enough time left for all my household chores and even to relax and go to bed earlier.

Now, whenever I sit down at the computer, I don't agonize over the creative process. The text takes shape by itself; my fingers fly over the keyboard so quickly that I don't always manage to put in the punctuation. So now I try and draw up more concrete plans tailored to my particular objectives.

I'm convinced that everyone who takes on board Dr Konovalov's recommendations will be able to use them to change their life to suit their own needs. For example, one of my friends, whom I'd told about my successes, when trying to plan her own day, suddenly realized that she really had no need to plan anything, because she had nothing to do, that her life was not as full as she would like it to be. This in itself was a positive result: for now she has taken a serious look at what she is missing out on and the things she can do to fill her life.

## 5. Don't Rush – Trust in Fate

It sometimes happens that just as you're going out of the door you start worrying that you've left the iron or the TV on indoors, that you didn't turn off the gas or have forgotten something. You get anxious. Everyone knows the saying 'there's no turning back'. You mustn't worry. If you do go back to get something you've forgotten, to check the gas or the electricity, then go up to the mirror and take a close look at your reflection for 10–15 seconds. Only do it calmly, without worrying.

As you approach the bus stop, don't run if the bus is moving off. Concentrate your mind on the fact that you'll have to wait for the next one, that you might be late. This isn't your bus! Don't rush to get on it. You've simply left home a bit late. If you go through your morning procedure correctly your bus will arrive on time.

When you're using public transport, standing in a queue, or find yourself in the middle of a large crowd of people, never become confrontational. Don't allow yourself to be provoked, don't get into arguments or rush to defend yourself, and don't react to the rudeness of others. If people push you, and you feel it, even if you think it's deliberate, don't retaliate. Step aside or move away. You can only feel sorry for the person who pushed you. Perhaps he or she is on their own, unhappy, has lost someone near to them, and has no one to take it out on; they've met you by chance (on a bus for example) and take their bad temper out on you. Don't respond whatever you do, or you'll lose your composure, your energy. Don't get into an argument, don't try and justify things to anyone, even those standing close by. You are dissipating your precious energy and no one will give it back to you.

You should never allow yourself to get drawn into the kind of stress that accompanies confrontations on public transport when, for example, people complain out loud about how young people never give up their seats to older people. Joining in such arguments only brings illness and a loss of energy. If you see an old person who is really ill and who is finding it hard to stand on the bus or underground, then go up to a young person who is seated and politely ask them to give up their place. Don't antagonize or be judgmental, just be polite. And if the response is rude don't start laying down the law. Neither public transport nor chance encounters in the street are the right place or time to start trying to re-educate people. You can't change them.

### Never do something you have not planned

Never do anything that you have not decided on and planned yourself. It's often the way that people suddenly ask you to drop everything and do something, go somewhere with them and that they can't do it on their own. You must politely turn them down. If you haven't planned something like this for that particular day, then don't do it. Experience has shown that many unpleasant things, including accidents, happen precisely in this way, when things are done on the spur of the moment. Of course, it's quite likely everything will be fine, that nothing bad will happen. Doing things by chance, is, however, one of the enemies of well-being. Single people often seek out chance encounters; for maybe that way they will meet someone interesting and make a new friend. But even they should not put too much emphasis on chance. Friendships can be made during the course of the day that you yourself have planned that morning, and you can plan every day with the clear intention of meeting up with someone whom you will care about.

### Never imagine that something bad has happened

If you're expecting a friend or relative and they don't arrive on time and are late, never ever start thinking that something awful has happened to them: that they've been mugged, or crashed the car, or other similar dreadful things. For this in itself is a form of planning! Don't get stressed out before an exam and tell yourself you're sure to fail. That's planning things too. Don't use rude and insulting words and phrases. If somebody says them to you then mentally wish this person better health and happiness. Because only someone who is ill or unhappy says things like that. Always keep this thought in mind and remember that that is how it is. Stay calm and don't allow irritation and anger into your heart.

**Don't take any notice of negative predictions about the future**
Don't allow astrologers or psychics to bamboozle you into letting them predict your future. Steer clear of anybody who tries to tell you something bad is going to happen, or that you're not giving out healthy vibes and so on. Don't use the word 'devil'. Exclamatory remarks such as 'what the hell' or 'go to the devil' are a way of calling up negative forces from which no good will come. Saying 'God knows!' is a lot better and safer thing to say. Do not use swear words; don't allow them into your home. And don't say the devil's name out loud or even think it.

**Be sure to wind down at the end of the day**
In the evening, before you go to bed, it's important to take a shower or have a bath in order to wash away the spent energy of the day that's gone. After you've done this, don't dry yourself down, but just put on a thick towelling dressing gown. Don't use a dryer. And don't put the TV on in your bedroom. Before going to bed, make sure you say goodnight to your family.

At the end of every day the doctor's patients go through a special closing down exercise to complete the day that has passed, and you can do it too. Once you've got into bed, close your eyes and run back over all you've done that day, as systematically as you had planned it. Then thank God, your guardian angel, yourself and those you've been with throughout the day. Now allow yourself to be carried forward mentally to the day to come, to the starting point when you will open your eyes in the morning. Allow the whole of the day to come to flow through your mind. Now you can sleep peacefully.

If you do all these recommended things regularly you will arrive at a normal and healthy state of living.

**You are the creator of your own destiny**
In addition to planning your days, you also need to plan your future. If you're planning for example to go on holiday in the summer, or on a business trip in a month's time, then you need to plan this too. Don't leave things to chance and hope that somehow they will sort themselves out. You don't need to make these plans during your morning and evening planning sessions – just be aware of them. Think about when and where you are planning to go and gradually make a mental note of what you need to take

with you, and so on. All of these recommendations will help you avoid making mistakes, will stop unpleasant things happening – precisely the kind of things that frequently go wrong in our lives.

And one more thing: in life, it's natural for things not to go the way a person would like them to. And sometimes, as a result, we don't feel like working or even getting up in the morning. There's no point in wasting your energy by forcing yourself to do something you don't want to do. Simply try and remember always that the coming day is your day. And it's your day in the sense that it will never be repeated. You can't live it over again. Look upon this day as though it was your last, but not in the sense that you won't be here tomorrow, but that the day itself cannot be repeated. In this way, you can start seeing things from a different perspective. Today's terrible weather can then become a pleasant shower of rain, or wet snow, or sleet; and it becomes pleasant because it will never come again.

## 6. Bringing Up Children Begins the Moment They Are Born

During healing sessions, Dr Konovalov frequently addresses the problem of bringing up children. Patients often write telling him that their lives at home with teenagers have become a living hell. And children, even quite young ones, from time to time write telling the doctor they hate their parents; as one young girl once remarked about her mother: 'I want to kill her!'

Sergey Sergeevich explains that bringing up children is an ongoing, daily process, from the moment they are born. And he makes no allowances for parents whose excuse is that the just don't have the time. In his view, such attempts at self-justification do no good. If the child is already grown up and the parents aren't paying him or her enough attention, or showing enough care and consideration, then it's too late to make drastic changes. Having grown up, the child is most likely now to respond to his parents with indifference at best. Doctor Konovalov advises parents never to interfere in the lives of their grown up children, not to lecture them and not to demand things of them simply because they are their parents.

## Do Not Pressurize Children

As far as small children are concerned, they should never ever be pressurized into acting like grownups or behaving in ways that are beyond their mental capacities. This kind of pressure leads to situations where parents and children are at each other's throats. Care, consideration and love are the foundations of good parent–child relations. Children must be made to feel the parent's concern for them, and be confident in their unqualified love, not just at times when they do what parents want them to do, but even when they do things they don't like.

Dr Konovalov asserts that about 85–90 per cent of the child's personality is formed before birth. His information field absorbs everything that his mother experiences during her pregnancy. His development is affected by his emotional background, his relationship with the people around him, and by events within the space his mother inhabits, including those of which she may not even be aware. Further discussion of the child's relationship with its parents and how to bring up healthy children can be found in Part IV.

PART IV

# LOVE, HEALTH
# AND THE FAMILY

CHAPTER 25

# HOW EXTERNAL EVENTS AFFECT OUR HEALTH

'Good health', Dr Konovalov tells his patients, 'is when the cells of the body are indifferent to external events. This is not selfishness, but simply being true to oneself.'

We become healthy when the body's cells pulsate in harmony with each other. And this can only happen when we are not under emotional stress, when we are not harbouring grudges, when we have no repressed feelings of anger, or envy or hatred. Practically all negative feelings and desires have a detrimental effect on a person's sensitive-body system and can even, in time, become the cause of some of the most serious illnesses from which they suffer.

This doesn't mean that we must become cold and unfeeling in order to maintain our health; far from it. It doesn't mean that we should live at other people's expense, imposing on those around us, making use of others merely for our own benefit. This is selfishness, pure and simple, and not loving oneself in the true sense of the phrase.

## The Attainment of Inner Peace

Many of the doctor's patients are well acquainted with that state of being which we might call 'inner peace'. Thanks to the energy of creation, without realizing it they have learned to love themselves and have not allowed feelings of resentment, intolerance and anger into their hearts. They have been feeling their way, adjusting to things as they go along, by intuition, as they move towards an improvement in their physical state and with it an end to many of their illnesses.

But how can people who have never been to see the doctor achieve this? How can we help those few patients who can't get rid of their diseases and get back on the road to health and retain it into old age? It's very simple – by reading this book from start to finish, over and over again. Here, you will find the answers to all your questions.

## Our Problems, Especially Those Relating To Health, Do Not Happen by Chance

Some time, long ago in the past, this earth ceased to be a paradise. We all know why that is and it's the reason that there are so many dark clouds hanging over our present-day lives. People today have so many problems! We create some of these for ourselves and are only too well aware of it. Some of our other problems are also of our own making, only we won't admit it. And then there's the kind that we look upon as 'a bolt from the blue', the kind of unforeseen consequences of a catalogue of events or circumstances. But in a world created by the divine plan of God nothing happens by accident. Maybe you've already realized this. Such 'unforeseen' problems are, perhaps, in some way linked to our karma or destiny, and people think it's more important to deal with them than other problems. The trouble is we cannot predict such things by drawing on our natural, human resources alone.

## When the Sensitive-Body System Is Out of Sync

It is tension that causes problems. But tension doesn't just amount to stress: it's the body's way of responding to everyday things, or to particular events (both good and bad ones), or to the life rhythms that we have created for ourselves. The body gets out of synch – out of its natural rhythm – and negative feelings set up vibrations which disrupt the functioning of the sensitive-body system. This leads to illness, which finds a weak spot in the body and strikes at it. But by the time your doctor is able to give you a diagnosis and confirm that you are indeed suffering from something, the illness has long since been spreading, unchecked, inside your organism. At first it would have been contained in a single cell which, having received an excessive charge of negative energy, had gone on to penetrate the intercellular space in search of a vulnerable organ. And so, a disease diagnosed today may well have been working its way through the body for the last five, 10 or even 20 years.

So how can we learn to cope with the insane lives we lead today and preserve our health?

## Planning Your Health

It stands to reason that the person who plans their day meticulously can easily avoid coming up against unnecessary problems and will not create them for themselves either. A person like this will not rush through life in a distracted state, running up blindly against first one problem, then another; nor will they create problems for those around them. A person who has a specific objective (whether it be a lifetime goal that will take several years or a clearly defined plan for the day ahead) will be a lot less susceptible to the destructive influences of the kind of unexpected things that happen to us.

## Avoiding Arguments Which Damage the Sensitive-Body System

Imagine this typical everyday situation in Russia. An old lady is standing in a queue at the post office or the bank to pay her telephone bill. The queue is long and she is at the very end of it and becoming agitated. It all starts with a simple question about the present rental charges for the government-run telephone service. She asks the people in the queue and they all tell her the same thing: it's gone up twice lately. With every answer she gets, the old woman becomes more agitated. 'Where's the money coming from to pay it?' she asks, 'What about us pensioners?. They must be mad to do this.' She ends up not just criticizing the increase in her bill but also the government, getting into an argument with others in the queue. By the time she gets to the head of the queue, she's taking out her anger at the price increase on the cashier. Frustrated by this, the cashier asks her to let her get on with her job. Someone else then tries to point out that it's not the cashier's fault. But by now an argument has flared up, and the old lady is lining up her 'supporters' and 'opponents' against each other.

If you were to get dragged into such a row and join in, then, by the time you've left the bank, you'd probably find that your heart is beating more rapidly, your blood pressure has gone up and even your cheeks are flushed. Even if this doesn't happen it will still have given rise to a sense of irritation in you.

Dr Konovalov regularly warns his patients never ever to get involved in situations such as this which do not directly concern them or have a bearing on their lives. Despite being aware of the utter futility of their words and actions in such situations, even people who are aware of it can't always resist getting drawn into arguments which will bring harm primarily to the sensitive-body system – and with it, their health.

## Being Angry Dissipates Our Precious Energy Levels

If you took the time to look more closely at the kind of people who initiate arguments such as this, then you'd make a fascinating discovery. For that same old lady who started the scene in the bank eventually leaves it completely unruffled, if not with a sense of satisfaction at what she has done. So what's been going on? Here's Dr Konovalov's view:

*'There are some people in life who feed off the energy of others. They unconsciously provoke quarrels, during which the other person (or persons) get worked up and in so doing unwittingly give out their own energy.*

*It all probably starts quite by chance. Somebody says something unpleasant to someone else, meanwhile remaining not in the least perturbed by it. The person who's been offended gets annoyed, maybe loses their rag and hits them, and in the process expends a large amount of energy. This leaves the attacker drained, whilst the person who has offended them has the reverse reaction and feels energized. And incidents like this stay in the memory of the offender because of the physical reaction he or she has got from them. Sooner or later they will be repeated. The offending person thus gets confirmation of how, by starting arguments, they get an intake of energy from others; with time they turn into a kind of 'energy vampire' who winds people up, goads them and provokes an extreme reaction in them, from which they then suck out the energy. And what is more, people like this are not necessarily strong. They can be weak; they can be women, old people and even children.'*

Schools immediately spring to mind. In every classroom there is sure to be a student who teases the other children: he pulls the girls' hair, runs off with other boys' school bags, and so on. The other pupils – boys and girls – often gang up on kids like this, but it doesn't change their behaviour. The psychologists put it down to being 'a form of attention-seeking'. Such a view has always seemed odd to me. If a person wants the attention of others, do they really want it to be in the form of aggression? It would seem to be the case today that children have simply learned to feed off the energy of others and that they enjoy doing this.

Take another example: a teacher is reprimanding a pupil about something or other. She gets angry, loses her self-control and shouts at him, but all the energy she is transmitting just bounces off him and has no effect. What is happening? The teacher is sending her energy out in all directions and the pupil stands there soaking it up. By the end of the day she will feel like a wrung out dishcloth and he will feel fine. And that's not all. The pupil will now behave in the same way again, in order to take in another charge of energy. He already knows subconsciously that he can get it by driving his teacher mad.

This same exchange of energy happens in families too. You'll probably agree that when people in families have had a row and later sit down and analyse what started it, they'll more often than not agree that it was over something trivial and was about nothing in particular. In other words, there was no need for a row, or what provoked it was so insignificant that it could have been resolved amicably before it happened.

It goes without saying that, in the heat of an argument, it never enters anyone's head that it isn't just normal relations between people that are breaking down at that precise moment but that an exchange of energy is also taking place. The initiator of a quarrel, and particularly quarrels about nothing, has subconsciously been aware that their own energy level is low and tries to compensate for this at the expense of someone else.

Take a close look at people who are known for being argumentative or causing trouble. You'll get the impression that they are impossible to please and the sole pleasure they have in life is in spoiling things for others. How do such situations come about in our daily lives?

Take this example: two women share the same office at work and one of them makes the other one's life a misery by constantly going on at her. She picks on everything she says, criticizes everything she does – from her hairstyle to how she does her job. They often have rows and their other colleagues are dragged into them. Usually, it ends with the person who has done the offending being put in her place. But the trouble is this has absolutely no effect on her. She comes to work the next day and is just the same.

And because this is the way things often are, the people drawn into and upset by quarrels bring on themselves all kinds of illnesses, while the ones who've caused all the trouble are never off sick. Worse still, those who've had to put up with this will think that life's unfair and will come to the conclusion that you only get what you want by being difficult and argumentative. So they lose heart and get depressed and this in itself is the fertile soil in which illnesses take root.

An understanding of human nature might help the participants in little dramas such as these to get a different perspective on things. They'd then see that the person in front of them is encroaching not just on their own personal views or human qualities but on their energy too. They might then suddenly realize the covert motive behind this unexpected attack. And if they do, then they might feel sorry for the person who's upset them, who can't get by, can't survive, without other people's energy, which means, of course, they are, in fact, in our hands and utterly dependent on how we react and behave. Realizing this might be sufficient to stop us reacting angrily and avoid being drawn into situations that provoke negative responses in us.

Try out this experiment for yourself: take a look at people interacting in shops and on public transport and see how rows spring up between them (only for heaven's sake, keep your distance from what is going on!). Assess what's happening from the perspective of your new-found knowledge. What do you see now? An ill-mannered young man will not give up his seat on the underground to an old lady. She starts having a go at him, but he just sits there calmly, drinking a can of beer. The woman is not showing herself in the best light: her face is strained, her eyes are bulging and it looks as though any minute now she's going to hit him. What is happening to her? First, her anger is setting up negative vibrations which are shattering her sensitive-body system and, second, she is losing her energy. What does this mean? It means that she will now find it harder to fight illness, and that her emotional equilibrium will be upset for some time. And now look at the young man. The woman's outburst has played straight into his hands and every now and then he provokes her further with rude remarks. He's completely unruffled, because he's taking in her energy.

Have you ever witnessed situations like this? Then remember what Dr Konovalov says: 'Good health amounts, first and foremost, to knowing how to love oneself.' Do you love yourself or would you at least like to learn how?

Then just think how often you've found yourself in the same situation as the old lady on the underground. Is it really worth not loving yourself and instead allowing yourself to waste your energy and with it your health in such an utterly futile way?

## The Energy of Creation Teaches Us to Be Calm

So what must you do? First of all, in situations such as this you must keep calm. I know that's easier said than done, especially when the source of irritation is not somewhere outside, on the street, but in your own home, in your own family. The doctor's patients have learned how to stay calm because they know they are helped by the energy of creation, which has a way of teaching a person not to react in confrontational situations. But what must other people do? The first thing is to learn to love yourself and to look at the world with different eyes.

## Learning to Love Ourselves is the Foundation of Good Health

The physical universe, in its precise arrangement of planets and stars, and in which no chaos exits, exerts an influence over us with its beauty and grandeur. Sergey Sergeevich tells us that this wonderful work has been created through the power of love. And it's not just the universe. The harmony and beauty which lie at the heart of our planet and every being on it are a testament to the love of the creator for his children. The human race has been created with love in God's own image and is the beautiful pinnacle of his creation. By acknowledging this greatness you can begin to love yourself, by realizing that you too are a part of the cosmos, a child of the planet, and that the human body is not just a physical entity endowed with a preordained number of flaws that exists only in the material world. The human being is the most complicated creation on the planet and in the cosmos and is united with the universe as whole; every step a person takes impacts on the most complex processes going on in the world. This is why it is important that you acknowledge and learn to love this 'new' person you have discovered in yourself, rather than the person you see in the mirror every day and who you think is the real you.

## The World Is Built On Love

The whole world is built on love – that is, both the sensitive world and the material world. Adam and Eve were the first people on earth and the first manifestation of love came with the love of men and women for each other. How often have you heard that romantic phrase – and maybe you've said it yourself – 'We were meant for each other'. If in the past you have considered this to be wishful-thinking, then now, having read Dr Konovalov's book, you are more likely to understand that real love is all part of the programme of things that are to be realized on earth. Are you aware how things happen in this world? First, there's the programme (the plan) and then comes its actual, material realization. And it's the same with love. A man and a woman may not have met yet, but their souls are already primed by the premonition of love to come. (I'm talking, of course, about sensitive people who are receptive to the way they feel and their emotional responses). A premonition of love simply marks the first stage of the realization of a love that has already been programmed. So, when the couple eventually does meet, from the very first look they are sucked into a whirlpool of dizzying feelings. This is how real, earthly love takes root, but before it happens that love has already been born in the sensitive world which people refer to as 'heaven'.

## When Family Life is Loving, and When It is Confrontational

At the present stage of development of civilization people are still striving to make the family the focus of their love. Dr Konovalov feels that this may not be the ideal way of uniting two people, but, at this given moment in human development (in social and economic terms and with regard to our present moral values, the rule of law, etc.), it is fully justified so long as family life does not turn into mutual enslavement.

It is the task of every human being born on this earth to go through a preordained process of development and perfection. If love in the family helps them fulfill this process of development then it will lead to harmony and human happiness, which in turn will contribute to the preservation of health. In other words, in these situations, the family is not a source of unhappiness and does not exert stresses and strains and the kind of negative feelings which are guaranteed fairly quickly to wear down the healthiest of people.

It would be a good thing if every one of us could keep in mind our lofty aspirations towards the people we love, rather than simply looking upon family life as a set of obligations, many of which involve kowtowing to popularly accepted convention and to the clichéd perceptions we have of how people should live. I think you'll agree that in the average family (and even in most harmonious ones by today's standards) you'll hear parents telling their children 'You must go to college' or 'You must get yourself a job.' Parents rarely tell their children what their real duty is on earth – in relation to themselves, the planet, the universe – which is to fulfill their destiny, find their own way, learn to understand themselves and become better people than they are now. It rarely crosses parents' minds to discuss things like this with their children and even fewer bring their children up with this in mind from the moment they are born.

## The Ability to Give Love is a Sign of Good Health

Love always makes a person grow. Its absence or destruction has exactly the same, profound effect on the highest of bodies of the universe. You may remember that Dr Konovalov has said that the love between a man and a woman is created at the primary or – what he terms – 'tonic layer'. And the emotions and feelings of tenderness, without which love is impossible, are related to what the doctor defines as the 'astral-body layer'. When a person is out of step with the universe's information fields they will become callous and unresponsive to love. We've come once more to the question of whether it is worth getting upset when we run up against people who are insensitive, harsh and rude. You probably thought that people such as this deliberately choose to behave as they do. But we now know, as Dr Konovalov has explained, that such people are acting in this way because their information fields have been disrupted. Maybe it's their own fault, but maybe, also, the fault lies with their parents, or even earlier generations. For surely the doctor has told us that if the information fields of the planet have been disrupted, then why should we blame individuals who behave badly? Are they really rude? Or is rudeness something which has spread to practically all members of the human race? Isn't rudeness now the norm in all strata of society? Aren't our television screens propagating bad behaviour, rudeness and violence and infecting every household? Every evening we spend in front of the television wears down a bit more of what's left of our positive feelings, eroding more and more of our good health. And you can see this sickness mainly in how inured we've become to the daily sight of hundreds of deaths on our TV screens. We now have the same response to the 'fake' deaths that take place in TV thrillers as we do to the real-life scenes of death that confront us in daily news broadcasts from around the world.

## How the Human Race Could End up Destroying Itself

The first murder committed on earth is well known to anyone who has at some time opened the Bible. Cain killed his brother Abel and was cursed by God. (Dr Konovalov believes that this was the first powerful disturbance in the energy of creation's fields). In warning people against further acts of madness, the Bible said:

'Whosoever slayeth Cain, vengeance shall be taken on him sevenfold.' (Genesis 4: 15)

The thirst for revenge, or 'resisting evil with violence', is, in fact, the quickest way to self-destruction.

## How Love Maintains the Links
## between Man and the Divine Universe

If we cannot learn to love ourselves we cannot stay healthy. In order to do so you must take part in Dr Konovalov's sessions, or if you live outside Russia and this isn't possible, then you must read and re-read this book with the utmost care and attention. And at that precise moment when you realize with your whole heart and soul how genuine Dr Konovalov is and you give your love to him, then love will, in turn, come to you.

How do we distinguish between people who have learnt to love themselves and the ordinary person? People who love themselves live a life that is not hemmed in by the narrow parameters of the material world. This is because, first of all, they are conscious of their own nature. They strive to develop and become better people; they are courageous and never succumb to laziness or exhaustion in attaining perfection. Aware of their close link to the divine universe they work at maintaining it. How? During the course of the day they thank their guardian angel and ask for his help and support in the knowledge that their angel is an integral part of their being and forms the link between themselves and the energy of creation. Such appeals for help can take the form of a deeply felt prayer, so long as it has not been learned by heart and recited as children do in class at school. But appeals such as this can take many other forms. The important thing is the genuineness of feeling and profound faith with which they are said. Constant interaction with one's guardian angel can give a whole new meaning to one's life and bring with it new perspectives.

In addition, the person who acts in this way doesn't forget to plan their days either and continually endeavours to free their spirit of all feelings of vengefulness, jealousy, envy, irritability, hatred and pride. And that's because all these feelings are linked to the disruption of the information fields. The presence of negative thoughts and feelings in our hearts and minds sets in train their negative effect, and this primarily affects the highest systems of the human body.

## Reading the Doctor's Books is a Form of Healing

People have often discovered their faith thanks to a miracle. The time may well have come for us to contemplate why it is that miracles take place for those who have been initiated. Maybe it's now worth listening to the words people summon up in trying to convey to others the miracles that happen to them. These are people from other cities and other countries who live thousands of miles away from the doctor but nevertheless write to him about the fantastic results they've achieved from the link-up healing sessions and by using the healing leaflet.

*'It's still the same work and still the same treatment. The first book had to tell people about the path I had taken, in order that they could understand and believe. I didn't even believe it myself at first, nor did I understand it. A doctor works in the real world, he is not a fantasist. If the impact of the energy of creation had not been so obvious, so tangible, it would not have produced such striking results, and I would not have believed in it. But it is impossible NOT to believe what you see with your own eyes — the results from data analysis and personal experience.'*

Do you think that treatment is one thing and reading books another? You're mistaken. Treatment is going on all the time. The energy of creation with all its astonishing power is bearing down on you as you read this. And the people who are most sensitive to it are those who greet it with an open mind and are ready to fight for their health without let-up and without finding fault.

If you have even a shadow of doubt, if you still demand explanations, then remember that a human being is not flesh alone. Not just flesh, nor merely a sensitive body. The human body consists of six information fields. These comprise the stabilizing bodies of the first, second and third degree, as well as the mutable body, the tonic body and the astral body. These, and other aspects of Dr Konovalov's philosophy, will be explained in the next books in the series of 'Books That Heal', publication details of which will be announced on the Creation Publishing website.

## The Doctor's Books Provide a Curative Charge to the System

The information fields of Dr Konovalov's healing books, which are written under the influence of the energy of creation, in turn have an effect on the information fields of those who read them. Treatment is ongoing! It is moving to another level. Today thousands and thousands of people talk in their letters about how they have recovered their health thanks to the unique healing action of these books.

Dr Konovalov has written that *'The healthy person is someone whose whole body is in harmony and has been put in order.'* This is simple and comprehensible when we talk of the human being in the abstract. But what if we look at ourselves? We think everything's fine – it's just that we've got an ulcer. Everything's fine, but our arthritis is giving us a lot of pain. Everything's fine – we've got asthma, that's all.

But everything can't be fine if your physical body and your sensitive-body system are out of synch. All the body's systems are inextricably linked, which means that if the information fields are disrupted, so too are the bodies of thought and desire. Illness is more than just a matter of something hurting, being swollen or inflamed, or giving pain. Illness has long since spread into our lives and thoughts, into our desires and the way we see ourselves.

# CHAPTER 26

# DESIRES AND ASPIRATIONS:

## THE KEYS TO GOOD HEALTH

### The Things We Strive for

The human body is a whole world of desires, aspirations and ambitions; they are the highest things we seek in our lives. And our own information field has been created in the same image as the world of desires of the divine universe. Our own body of desires was formed in the same way as other, higher bodies in the depths of the universe. So to ignore our own desires and aspirations or suppress them and substitute them with something else is to do ourselves harm. Of course, in today's world, at a time when the fields of the energy of creation have deteriorated, it's become difficult for people to work out what their real desires are; either that, or the desires themselves turn out to be 'unhealthy', like the people themselves.

So, in our busy lives today, do we always pay sufficient attention to our own needs? Thousands of questionnaires sent in to the doctor talk of how it's only when they start coming to healing sessions that many of his patients begin to think about what it is they really want out of life. It's only at the centre that they've come to realize how rarely they've given this subject any thought and how difficult it is to work out the things that they really want. But Dr Konovalov brings them back to this difficult subject at every session.

The more meaningless a person's life becomes, the more difficult it is for them to pinpoint what they really want. There's a whole difference between the things we want and what we are committed to by present obligations, because they all depend on circumstances – parents, children, work, the environment we live in. This in itself marks the beginning of an understanding of the significance of things. For the person in question may no longer be young and by now may be thinking that there has been no point to their life. Firstly, because they did what their parents told them, they did the same at school, and then they did what society demanded of them, and there was never any time to think about their own desires and aspirations. Or, more likely, they wanted one thing but ended up doing the opposite. For example, a woman wanted to go to drama school but, afraid that she wouldn't be good enough to get in, she became a secretary instead. Or a young man wanted to get married to a beautiful girl he loved but, afraid that she was too good for him, he chose another, not as beautiful and whom he didn't love as much. He doubted himself far too much, and his friends compounded this by telling him to 'play safe'. So he did, and happiness evaded him. He didn't once do what he wanted to do, which means he didn't listen to the voice of the energy of creation, didn't do the things preordained for him, didn't fulfil the destiny for which he had been born.

*'It's easy to put it all down to circumstance,' says Dr Konovalov. 'But what about you? What have you actually done? What have you been striving for? Where have you been going?'*

## When Disease Appears in the Body and the World of Desires

The body's world of desires is an integral part of a person and can also be susceptible to disease. The *absence of desires* is in itself a manifestation of disease. This is because most people's desires come automatically, like their thoughts; their entire destiny is formed in this way. A man sees a new car in a TV advert and wants it; a woman sees a new dress on a friend, and wants one too. The whole of life is like this. Somebody has seen something somewhere, heard someone else saying how good it is and wants it too. But the world of desires is a divine world. And what are we turning it into?

I ask Dr Konovalov: 'So, what if all a person wants are material blessings, will their wishes come true?' He explains:

*'A person who is constantly preoccupied with such things can't concentrate on any single, concrete desire. He wants a lot of things and so his wishes flit from one thing*

*to another. He wants first one thing, then another, then another and is trying to do too many things at once. Such an obsession with material things stops a person concentrating on one important thing. And if a person is ill, then it's not just their physical body which isn't working properly; they don't have the right kind of desires either. They can't have. Unhealthy desires and thoughts are part and parcel of today's morality. Most of us know about the terrible immorality that reigned in ancient Rome: the bloody spectacles that took place in the coliseum, the sex orgies and incest. Many people today consider that we've reached a higher level of civilization, that the present generation is greatly superior, more educated, and that things like this no longer happen. But disease has not gone away. It's simply taken different forms. Many of my patients are living in absolute hell but they don't know it. They've simply got used to it and don't know anything different. Things have got to such a point that they think everything's normal. And they don't think of trying to get away from it, but only of maintaining the status quo.'*

## When Desires Become Distorted

She dreamt of love. What else do you possibly dream of at twenty? Real love; not the kind her mother had with her father who was always drunk – a life of quarrels and beatings. She dreamed of a pure, shining love. It was hard to describe it accurately for she'd never seen it anywhere. So she went from one boyfriend to another, all the time thinking, 'it's not him, or him.' So where was she to find this person with whom she'd be able to live a simple, tranquil life, without ending up in tears, without feeling unhappy, without going mad?

She wanted so much to love, and to sing and dance too. Every twenty-year old girl has a head full of music.

She met him by chance, so it seemed. He loved music too; he wrote beautiful songs about love and she immediately understood: this is him, he's come at last. She didn't want to be parted from him and went everywhere with him. And for the two months they lived together she forgot about other men and everything else in the world.

Then something suddenly went wrong. Did it start maybe with that daft idea of his? He was a person who always did things his own way. He decided to get a rabbit: not a puppy, or a kitten, he wanted something less ordinary. She laughed at first: rabbits aren't like kittens, you can't let them loose in the house, they have to be left to live quietly in their hutch and nibble at grass. But he didn't want to put the rabbit in a hutch; he wanted to teach the rabbit to behave like a kitten, to be obedient and not mess in the house. He didn't want the rabbit to be a rabbit.

And then he started hitting it, and when the creature cried in pain, like a child, she felt the pain too. It was as though he had hit her; yet it didn't cross her mind that he might do something similar to her, that he might try and make her do things. A struggle was going on inside her between her love for him and her horror at what he was doing. And then the little creature lying on the floor stopped moving. She couldn't come to terms with what had happened, and yet she so wanted to be loved.

He bought three more rabbits which, one by one, he tormented and then killed. She wept for days on end and even thought about going back to her mother. But she so wanted ... No, she told herself, he was unhappy, a profoundly unhappy person, even if his behaviour wasn't quite normal. But if she left him, who else would want him? No, she couldn't do it. ... She stayed, and the same things kept happening. She wept over the poor dead creatures but she couldn't leave him. She wanted someone to blame and she found someone. His father had been an unpleasant person. But he was good. Of course he was. It's just that he was a bit strange. ...

And then he tried changing her. And it was almost the same as it had been with the rabbits – a form of torture. But it didn't work with her either, and so he threw her out. But she still went on loving him, and thinking he was a good person. All she could think about was that the man she loved would come back to her. For he was, after all, an extraordinary person, he had such a kind heart. ...

So where in all this was the healthy dose of reality she needed in order to put her life and situation into perspective? All the girl could think of was that the man tormenting her might become a bit more humane – just a little. Let him be a bit more like other people and she'd be thanking God for her extraordinary good fortune.

But disease can worm its way into our thoughts and distort our desires. Nothing's black and white anymore, there's no clear distinction between good and evil. Everything is the same – grey and uniform.

## Unhealthy Desires Lead to Physical Illness

Unhealthy thoughts and desires can trigger the onset of physical illness, and the kind of fatal 'chain of events' that make us think that the whole world is against us. Unhealthy desires bring the kind of people into our lives whom we ought to steer clear of. Unhealthy desires make us chase after hopeless dreams and harbour futile hopes.

We know this only too well but keep on forgetting that there's no smoke without fire. How often do we jump to hasty conclusions about people: 'she's a lovely woman, really wonderful; the only problem is, her husband. He's a heavy drinker, goes after other women, and is always beating her up. But she's such a wonderful person!' It isn't possible for two people to spend their lives together, side by side, and for them not to be affected by the same deficiencies in their information fields. The woman who for so long has put up with her drunken husband and with being beaten and humiliated by him clearly cannot be entirely healthy if she's gone on enduring such a life. And it's not without good reason that the rehabilitation of alcoholics also involves their wives too.

## It's Never Too Late to Heal Our Own Damaged Desires

Here's another question for Dr Konovalov: 'Is it better to treat people before they've sunk too low, while they still have something to hope for? If this is the case, what about people who are already beyond help? For example, here's a typical situation: a woman is trapped in an intolerable situation – her husband drinks, her son is flunking out at school. How can she begin to tackle her problems? How can she get to grips with her situation?'

'Whatever she does, she has to start with herself, even in a situation like this. If she comes to my sessions then she'll get better. She'll start looking at the world through different eyes. She'll react to things differently. It may well happen that things change back home, her family start reacting to the changes in her and, by association, begin changing themselves. The situation at home will stabilize. There are plenty of examples of this in practice. Or it may happen differently: she'll distance herself more and more from the family and this may lead to separation. And she'll make the break herself because she has become a different person and no longer wants to stay in this unhealthy family set-up.'

## How Illness Takes the Meaning Out of Our Lives

The procedure adopted by patients during healing sessions towards realizing their major desires or aspirations is a very beguiling one. 'Is Dr Konovalov some kind of wizard?' patients ask themselves. At first glance, it's hard not to explain the concept of the fulfilment of desires other than as some kind of magic. Such 'magic' can, however, be clearly explained in terms of Dr Konovalov's theories about the energy of creation. So what's going on? How exactly do the information fields of the energy of creation respond to the patients' desires? The answer to this question touches on many aspects of our lives.

## The Pattern of Our Everyday Lives

Let's start by conceding the following: modern-day life is constructed around a mundane and simple pattern. In the morning we have to get up and go to work; we have lunch, then dinner, and in the evening we slump in front of the TV – that's another day over. And it's not just the days that are like this – but months and years on end. People like this become robots. And in order to live in this way, as so many others do, we don't need to think about anything: we simply get up, go out, come home and go to bed. The vast majority of people among whom we live today live their lives in this way.

A sense of indifference about our lives overtakes us. We become comfortable with this kind of uneventful existence and, on occasion, even think we're happy this way. This complacency worms its way into our everyday habits, our thoughts and our feelings. And it takes a crippling hold, especially on those who while away their evenings alone, with a bottle. It is precisely this kind of indifference that most often drives people to drink, because it deprives their lives of all meaning. There's no getting away from the relentless logic of this for those already living on the edge of the volcano – those who get caught up in regular family rows or disagreements leading to fights, or who are struggling for a fair deal at work. A safe, comfortable life is much the same as one that is not – for both soon become a matter of habit if a person's life has no sense of purpose.

# When Life Has No Sense of Purpose

People have got used to exchanging a sense of purpose in life for trivial objectives, things they can't do without, and for striving after material needs. For a while this has no ill effect on them. Not, that is, until illness (the disruption of their information field) takes over a person's life, and turns the successful businessman into a hard drinker; or the mother of a large family into a lonely, embittered old woman who feels she is no longer needed; or a happy young couple into implacable enemies living under the same roof. We call this disease the disease of a life without purpose.

You don't need a doctor to diagnose that your information field is out of synch. You can sound out the symptoms for yourself, in your own body. One of them is a sense of dissatisfaction or boredom. The feeling will be a familiar one if you are finding your duties at work tedious or if doing things at home seem a burden to you. Are you bored when you're on your own with your husband or wife? Is there nothing to talk about? Do you show an interest each other's problems? Or are you more interested in sitting and watching the television all evening?

# 'Well That's Another Day Over'

In their questionnaires, thousands of people refer to Dr Konovalov as their teacher. So what does he have in common with teachers? Remember that 98 per cent of the energy of creation resides in the energy fields, so if a person's energy field is disrupted they will not be able to tap into the energy of creation.

The doctor doesn't just treat people, he is also a teacher. But what he teaches is not drawn from personal experience, as it is with parents, nor does he base what he teaches on educational theory, as they do in schools and universities. His teachings are the voice of the energy of creation, directly addressing people. And his objective is to find the quickest way possible of helping patients get well. Everything that the doctor talks about at healing sessions is important. But people coming to see him for the first time don't always realize this. Making people well again is nothing; it's wresting them from the clutches of a meaningless mechanical existence and one to which they have become so used that they don't even notice how meaningless it is – that is the hardest thing.

They may have a sense of unease. We all know the kind of thing: you feel discontented but don't know why. There's something missing. You want to fill the sense of emptiness you feel inside. But how?

People of course have various ways of dealing with this and one can easily list them. First of all, going to work is such a bore you can't raise the enthusiasm. So how do you set about relieving the monotony? You have run-ins with colleagues, argue with your bosses, try and stick up for your rights and those of others at work. This spices things up a bit. This is how to get rid of pent-up energy and it gives you something to think about; but it does so at the expense of your health. At home boredom can de dissipated in drink. You can find a distraction from the dullness of family life in extramarital affairs. Loneliness can be compensated for by having people round, going to bars and restaurants – depending on what you can afford. This way, things aren't quite so tedious.

But if you take a closer look, then none of these forms of diversion go beyond the bounds of the same old deadening mundanity. Because living your life on the basis of simply getting through each day as quickly as you can is no life at all. It's getting you nowhere. It's not a happy picture, is it? Is this how your life is – is it just as monotonous? Or is it different?

## Building the Harmonious World of the Physical Universe

A robot-like existence is not the only product of our modern-day civilization. Its primary product is the disruption of our information fields, which brings with it disease. And if it hasn't yet manifested itself in people in the form of a diseased organ or the onset of illness, then it's only a matter of time. This is because it has already taken root in those whose lives have no purpose. There is, of course, a certain sense of purpose in earning our daily bread, bringing up our children and getting on with our daily affairs. But I'm talking about the individual here as a creature of the universe, the only one of God's creations endowed with the gift of rational thought, and who has a sense of the global significance of his existence, a sense of fulfilling the mission for which he was sent to earth from the depths of the universe.

In his book *The Road to Health,* where he first laid out his energy-information doctrine, Sergey Sergeevich briefly described how man was created, in conjunction with both the divine and physical universes. Just imagine it for yourself: a stream of 'cocoons' containing the soul and the highest bodies of each person moves out from the depths of the divine universe into the fields of the energy of creation. Remember too that every person is accompanied through life by their guardian angel – an exact copy of the bodies of a person's information fields, the unifying link between man and the fields of the energy of creation.

Can you imagine the forces that came together in the process of bringing each one of us onto this earth? Would the universe really have expended so much energy in creating us, just so that we could merely eat, sleep, reproduce ourselves and then turn to dust once more and fertilize the earth?

There's an obvious answer to this question, as the doctor explains: *'The human being is not just a piece of biological raw material that slots into place in the overall world picture. We are envoys, we have been chosen. We are, if you like, missionaries of a sort. And one of our tasks is to carry on the construction of the harmonious world of the physical universe. Each one of us carries within them a divine spark of God's plan, which we must put in motion and realize on earth. And in order to do this we must listen to the voice of the universe and pay careful attention to it in our daily thoughts and deeds.'*

# CHAPTER 27

# HOW TO DEAL WITH THE DISEASE OF UNFULFILLED DESIRES

## Give Meaning to Your Life: Strengthen Contact with Your Guardian Angel

The 'magic' exerted by Dr Konovalov in helping patients achieve their desires is actually in his encouraging people to find meaning in their lives and in so doing break free of the physical inertia of an existence that is merely a matter of 'living because you've been born'. He helps patients examine their feelings and by so doing make contact, however tentative, with their guardian angel and with the information fields of the energy of creation. He helps them home in on the thing they most want out of life, how to keep it in mind and not lose track of it. It is in this way that a person's world of desires establishes contact with the information fields of the world of the living spirit. As contact with the energy of creation becomes intensified during the treatment programmes, desires are more rapidly fulfilled. 'Please don't fritter away your energies on lots of things,' Dr Konovalov tells his patients, 'concentrate instead on one major desire during the course of each treatment programme. And remember, if I ask you for something – it's not because I need it, it's for you. It's to help you get well.'

'Will it work? Is it really that simple?' you ask. Yes, it is. All you have to do is to stop living on autopilot, think about what you want, keep it in mind and keep striving towards it. It's amazingly simple! But if it really is that simple, then why don't we do it? What's the catch? Why do we need someone with miraculous powers to help us live like ordinary people? Isn't this in itself a disease?

## Commitment and Tenacity
## Are Needed to Conquer Disease

The kind of disease that modern-day medicine is grappling with – that is, disease as an expression of discontent and pain – is only the tip of the iceberg. We cannot conquer it without the active participation and will to win of every single individual. The information fields of the modern world have been disrupted and disease cannot be eradicated if the powers of the energy of creation are reduced. Our common enemy – disease – will never disappear while people go on killing each other. But we may at least be able to banish it from our bodies and create an island of good health in an ocean of bad things. We need to be on our guard, or our little island will once more sink to the bottom.

It is not enough to come to the doctor's healing sessions simply in order to get rid of an ulcer or stones or a tumour as quickly as possible. And it isn't enough either just to set out to restore the body to health. We have to restore the soul to health also and learn how to protect it from disease.

## Taking Responsibility for Our Illnesses

Take a look at how lazy we are! We get ill – we take to our beds and let the doctors take care of us. We let them give us injections, fill us with pills, or even open us up and cut something out. That's what they do. It's their job; so we load all the responsibility for our health on them and quietly lie there in our hospital bed. And every day this inherent laziness of ours gives rise to all kinds of new 'miracle-workers'. Lazy people go to them with their problems because it's so easy. Why try and solve problems on our own? Let an experienced professional run around waving their magic wand over us, or casting spells over a photograph of our errant husband – in short, let someone else do the dirty work for us. Let them reassure us that all our misfortunes are down to the malicious thoughts of a neighbour, the nasty words of someone we don't like at work, or it's in our stars, or the animosity of a rival. In a nutshell, let someone else tell us that all our problems are down to somebody else's bad intentions and that we ourselves are good and untainted.

So, instead of taking a look at herself or trying to patch up a bad atmosphere in the family, a woman might rush off to a psychic. And a husband, rather than working harder at his job, tries something similar in order to get rich.

*'Today, more than anything,' says Dr Konovalov, 'religious practice and our relationship with God have become subordinated to our laziness. The majority of those who go to church do so without thinking, because it's now become fashionable or it's simply habit. They come to church, stay for a while, light a candle and think they have been spiritually cleansed, that they've paid for their sins. People invoke God's name far too easily. "What do you expect, it's fate!" "It's clear God meant it this way." It's easy to blame everything on God in order to justify ourselves. But it is really, really hard to fight against one's own indolence.*

*Why do some patients simply run straight out of the hall? Because we make them work, we make them fight for their own health, struggle with their own laziness and work on themselves. And they're not prepared for this. They've come here to be cured in the way they're used to – by not doing anything, and leaving it all to the doctor.'*

## Remember That Man Is a Not an Insect

We're not talking here about ordinary laziness. Many people might think: well, this can't be about me, I slave away all day at things, like a worker bee, without taking a break. The bee spends its whole day working without giving it a thought; and people too have begun to remind us of insects: they're always buzzing off somewhere, they're late and rush without thinking. Just try stopping them and ask 'Why are you doing this?' and they'll say 'I have to! It's important!' 'But why? Who needs it?' They can't explain.

We're talking in general about the battle we all have with inner, spiritual laziness, about the everyday, conscious work we need to do on our own souls. And that includes those of us who are the doctor's patients. Let's take an honest look at ourselves: how many times have we been too lazy to do our energizing exercises in the morning? How many times have we missed a link-up healing session? We all dream of becoming healthy and yet lack the will to do such little things for ourselves. And it's because of this that Dr Konovalov doesn't look upon everybody attending his sessions as being supportive of his work, as being genuine patients.

## The Patients in Whom Dr Konovalov Has Confidence

*'The patients I have 100 per cent confidence in are those who have come to me with terminal diseases and who have wrested their lives, literally, from the brink of beyond.'*

People who have really endured the nightmare of approaching and inevitable death, when the doctors cannot look them in the eye, and when their strength fades with every day; people who have endured the despair of seeing no hope of a miracle and who, thanks to the doctor, have finally pulled through, out of the darkest recesses of their disease and regained their health and a normal life – people such as these never, ever forget what they have experienced. It is they who know, better than all of us, what life – a healthy life – is really worth. They are the ones who aren't too lazy to do their energizing exercises, to charge the water with the healing leaflets, to take part in link-up sessions on Sundays, to keep in mind all the doctor's recommendations.

*'People aren't lazy while pain is tormenting them and making them work. I worry most about those who make a quick recovery, because they really haven't understood the true sense of what has been happening and have gone straight back to the way of life that was the cause of their disease in the first place.'*

Patients such as this often write in: 'I've got back into my old routine really quickly', without realizing that having quickly got rid of, for example, their ulcer or their osteochondrosis, they've simply gone back to a life without pain, without this one, specific complaint, and so therefore, in this one, single respect, their lives are more comfortable. But the way of life that brought disease on them in the first place cannot be called normal.

Patients like this go away and, spiritually, go back onto auto-pilot, lulled back into their old, habitual laziness. When will they realize this? When will the penny drop? Unfortunately, Dr Konovalov believes they will only do so when something bad happens in their lives again: a major upset, an accident, a disaster or some terrible worry. And this is when they'll remember; they'll rush back and start doing something about it again. But until then – and especially if their life is more or less OK – they'll go with the flow. It's curious how things turn out: on the one hand, we all strive towards a calm and contented lifestyle; but on the other, it's lives like this that lull us into a state of spiritual inertia. But, of course, the onset of pain and things going wrong are the quickest way of bringing a person to their senses and putting their spiritual side to work.

## The Road to Health is a Hard One

Whenever patients come up onto the stage to talk about their successful treatment and how their spiritual lives have been transformed they often speak in such terms. Not long ago, one patient exclaimed: 'I came to you, Sergey Sergeevich, with a whole catalogue of illnesses. There were so many of them! But I didn't want them all to disappear at once, at the same time, because that would have seemed unnatural somehow. I simply hoped that they might go gradually, one after the other.' And the woman's instincts were right. One by one the doctors eliminated each diagnosis from the list, and one by one the diseases that had been jabbing away at her like sharp needles went away. It's important to the doctor that everyone sitting in the treatment hall at the centre understands that the road to health isn't easy. It's hard work. And there's nobody else who can do the work for you. It's down to you.

So why are we so lazy? Is that really how the universe created us? Even those Russian readers who have read the doctor's previous book are aware that he didn't describe the mystery of our creation in it in any detail. Such things need to be learned and understood a little at a time. It is hard for us to take in all at once the wisdom that Dr Konovalov has revealed and is yet to reveal to us. We need to get used to it, and the doctor allows time for this. Even now, Dr Konovalov feels that we are still not ready to know everything, but nevertheless he has explained, in so far as this is possible today, how human laziness developed.

'Nature created everything to be dependent on it,' explains the doctor. 'It created the human body in an ideal form.' Later on came the evolution of the consciousness, the evolution of the highest bodies – the body of desires, the body of thoughts, and so on. However, at a certain stage there was an artificial intrusion (which I won't explain right now) into the natural evolution of the human race. In essence, human beings turned into consumers, and this brought upon them the kind of devastating spiritual laziness that we are now struggling against in order to save people from disease. This laziness is a far more terrible adversary than cirrhosis of the liver or cancer. But yet as soon as we launch an assault on it, then diseases too begin to retreat.

## Nobody Else Will Do It for You

So now, let's summarize. Every time that something goes wrong, when you feel overwhelmed with problems, when awful things pile up on you, don't go rushing to blame someone else.

*Here is a summary of the things to bear in mind, as we come to the end of this section:*

- Remind yourself: 'I am a creature of the universe. I am its child and its envoy, which means that the root of all my problems and sorrows lies in me, as also does the root of all my happiness. For this reason, and in order to put right my problems and illnesses, to overcome all obstacles, and change the world around me, I must start all over again – with myself. That is, I must start with the reasons why I am the way I am.'

- Don't forget you have the biomaterials at your disposal: the healing leaflet, the charged water. You can take part in link-up sessions or even come to St Petersburg for treatment. You can do the energizing exercises and other things recommended by Dr Konovalov.

- Fight against your own laziness. Remember that human beings were born to create; don't turn into a consumer. This way lies the desensitization of the spirit, which in turn gives rise to the real nightmares of illness, anxiety, boredom and a sense of futility.

- Set yourself a goal and keep it in mind, using the biomaterials and doing the energizing exercises. No matter how difficult or even how dangerous the situation is in which you find yourself, the energy of creation will help you win through.

- If you've written yourself off, then that means you've become enslaved by your own spiritual laziness. You've allowed yourself to become a 'biological robot' and have made yourself vulnerable to any number of merciless diseases. Even if your life is hell, you can still change things. The main thing is not to give in. In order to win through and get well again, set yourself a goal and follow the doctor's methods. Gradually, your contact with the energy of creation will begin to make things happen in your life that will help you make changes in your personal life and, in turn, to the situation in which you find yourself.

- If you have already set out on the path to good health, don't expect quick results. Even if you experience a distinct improvement after a month of using the healing leaflet and the charged water, even if after a week your thrombosis or your tumour miraculously disappears, or your stomach starts working properly (there are so many examples), remember: this is not the end of the battle, but only the beginning. Quick and easy successes are a real test! If you accept your successes too easily and stop working at things, you're sure to slide back down the slippery slope to illness again.
- The same applies to the fulfillment of our desires, and the achievement of goals. In any given situation, a quick and easy success is a kind of fool's gold and it may, in the end, bring you worse experiences than going through fire and water. Just imagine when you wake up tomorrow that all your wishes (every single one of them) have come true. How would you feel? You'd certainly be ecstatic, in seventh heaven for a while, but then you'd realize that there was nothing left to look forward to. No more things worth striving for. It's a feeling of utter desolation. Would you like to experience it? No? Then don't hurry things. Everything has its time.

## When Things Are Easy We're Being Tested

Easily-gained successes are a test. If you're able to stay focused, even when you've achieved the most fantastic things, if you can stay on course, then there'll be other achievements. But if you can't, then this will be your first and last success.

Enduring success only comes when a colossal amount of work has been invested in achieving it, after many years of work without giving in to exhaustion. Then it is deserved. And the person who has deserved it is made stronger by their effort; they will not become complacent and not be seduced even by the loudest words of praise.

So don't be in a hurry to ask too much from life at once. Remember what Dr Konovalov says: *'Nobody else will do it for you.'*

# CHAPTER 28

# WHAT MAKES WOMEN HAPPY:

## THE HEALING POWER OF LOVE

### Love Creates Harmonious Relations in Families

A family that is happy in all respects is a rarity nowadays. So let's take a look at the ingredients that go to making up happy families.

First of all, there's love. We've talked a little about it already. It stands to reason that the families that are rock-solid and harmonious are those built on genuine feelings, that is, families where a couple are united not just by earthly ties but by heavenly ones too. In other words, a couple's love should have come from heaven and will have been predetermined by the 'programme' of the universe. So there's no point expecting happiness from a marriage that came about purely because it seemed the right time to get married or because the sex was good.

We are often warned that love doesn't last forever, that you have to have shared interests and points of view and similar attitudes. But that is not so. First of all, people who say this are confusing love with physical attraction. Love is an emotion that can be amazingly long-lasting and enduring. If real love unites a man and a woman then they will always care about each other, even if they don't share the same views or opinions or interests. Here's what Dr Konovalov has written on the subject:

*'Love: so much has been said about it, and yet, at the same time, there's so much that remains unsaid and can never be said. Love is eternal like the universe itself. How can it be expressed in words, poetry, paintings, music or dance?*

*How can it be described if it is a feeling that cannot be put into words? One can only experience it or, better still, one has to live with it. For without love life loses all meaning and when we don't feel love then we aren't real human beings, because it's part of being human and it's given to us by God. When people say "there's no such thing as love", I feel sorry for them. For it means they've never experienced it and God grant that they might know it at some time in their lives. Love isn't just passion; it isn't just sex; it isn't just the coming together of two bodies. Love is the union of two people's hearts and souls. Love is the union of angels. And it is when they come together, intertwined, intermingled each with the other, and conjure up this truly incredible, divine, exhilarating, consuming feeling that passes through and penetrates every part of the body and soul of a person – those feelings that are not consciously controlled, which cannot be controlled or concealed or inhibited by an effort of will – then this is LOVE! And if you have experienced love, if it lives in you, then you are a lucky person. You have not been born and lived in vain, and I know that, because of this, you are incapable of doing evil.'*

Today, in our modern world, they're trying to marginalize real love. It's not that they tell us it doesn't exist; it's just that we're shown love as a mad, almost bestial passion that takes a hold on people, along with cigarettes and alcohol. It's depicted as mere sexual passion – often just for one night – as something that doesn't commit people to anything. And whilst it's clear that love without passion isn't real love, that doesn't mean that passion should be confused with love.

For passion means attraction and the arousal of the body. And love is the attraction of two angelic structures for each other. 'Love is made in heaven.' Indeed it is, for love quite often appears when we neither want nor are looking for it. It comes upon us suddenly, for no rhyme or reason. A feeling will unexpectedly take hold of you when you meet a person, even though only yesterday, or the day before, or for a whole year you've not been bothered by such feelings. And then suddenly you find yourself thinking about the other person and this brings a kind of nervous expectancy and heightened feelings. This wave of intoxicating feeling then takes more and more of a hold on you and you suddenly realize the next time you see this person that you can't look them in the eye, can't get the words out properly.

And just a touch from this person can fill you with unexpected feelings and make you shudder with emotion. A single glance can make you tremble and your heart start pounding .... I could go on with this description, but there's not enough space in one book, or even a hundred. Every person who has been in love has their own particular memories of the emotions they experienced – both good and bad.

When love comes to us at a young age and it is reciprocated, then this is a wonderful thing for both partners. Such happiness must be valued; it must not only be nurtured but also be built upon, developed and cherished. Love will not go away; it is the coming together of angels for the whole of an earthly lifetime. Whatever you may do, whatever you may try to forget, you will, all the same, return to that person. But love doesn't always bring happiness, even when we're young, even when it happens for the first time and stirs our hearts and emotions. For two people to be united in love, they must show respect, that most honest of human feelings, for each other.

## The Feelings that Sustain Love

The main feeling that sustains love over a long period of time is respect. In order to preserve it in this way, men and women must remember that each individual is unique and cannot be created over again. And so, first and foremost, we must not attempt to turn the person we love into someone else or make them fit into some kind of preconceived image of a loved one or partner that we had in our head before we met them. We must love the person as they are and respect their individuality and uniqueness.

'A family built on love where there is no respect between husband and wife can't be a happy one. "I love you, darling! I love you so much, but we can't live together, we wouldn't last a day together married." Yes, this is how it is, and it happens quite often. What can be done? How can we carry on? There's no quick answer to this question. There's no general advice or recommendations that one can give. There has to be a strictly individual approach to each specific problem and, with it, a very cautious, well thought-out, honest response.

When there is love but no respect or even the desire to respect the other person, then each of them is on their own: in their work, their interests and their friends. Such people can hardly create a family under such circumstances. They aren't ready for it. This means that you can't create a family with another person if there is only respect between you and no love, if the family is built on your pity for the person who loves you, or if you allow someone to love you out of pity. This makes for unhappy families. For even in its first stages, such a marriage lacks honesty. It's possible to preserve the outward appearance of love; you can try and arouse love in yourself by imagining passion, you can kid yourself that it's love. But you mustn't lie or deceive yourself.

*Stop now. There'll be children, and they can tell when things aren't right; you can't fool them. The family must not be founded on suffering.'*

## The 'Programmes' of Love Can Be Several

We are not obliged to love just one single person in the world in order to create a family. The divine plan preordains for each of us not just one but several 'programmes' of love. It may be that when the energy of creation was in its original normal state, when the earth's information fields had not yet been disrupted, when human beings were still healthy – in other words, when all the higher bodies were in harmony –- that all these 'programmes' might have been realizable. Perhaps people might have been able to love not once, or twice, making use of every new feeling in their ongoing development and perfection. But today, unfortunately, that isn't possible. How many tragedies arise when a husband or wife falls in love with someone else? It ends in heartbreak, jealousy, attempted suicide (that's the greatest sin), and pain. When they find themselves in situations like this people today cannot break out of the prison of illness.

Maybe you'll disagree with me and say that 'love triangles' always were and will be the greatest tragedy for people. And you'll cite the whole of world literature, which is built on such romantic tragedy, in order to support what you say. But let's get back to what Dr Konovalov has to say.

## The World is a Creation Based on Love

From the very beginning, the world was built on harmony. Love is a feeling that was first born in the sensitive world and then found its realization, for men and women, in the physical world. The world is a creation, built on love. But it's unlikely that even the highest of divine plans would set out to make people miserable by allowing them to suffer unrequited love, or deprive one or other partner of love, or make someone love two people at once and agonize over not being able to choose between them. Doesn't it strike you that all these things happen because the information fields of the energy of creation have been disrupted? Is it possible that, having become unsettled, the information fields give rise to unrequited love where, under normal conditions, a programme of love would begin and come to an end (or, more accurately, would change) simultaneously for men and women?

Trying to guess how wonderful the world might be if the field of the energy of creation were once more back to normal would evoke nothing but a deep sense of regret in us. So let's go back to the problems of our present-day reality and hear the doctor's advice on how best to deal with various life situations in order to preserve the relative health that we do have.

The main thing is that we should not restrict ourselves in love, for love can come not just in the form that leads to marriage, but also in the various forms of friendship, affection and respect that we have for other people. You can just imagine the kind of feelings Sergey Sergeevich himself arouses in many patients. It's no secret that people often tell him that they love him. 'There's nothing terrible about this,' he says. 'It's love, and that's the finest feeling. I love all of you too. And it doesn't matter that we'll never be together, will never touch each other. It's just another kind of love. Nevertheless, it's still real love.' And the real love people feel for the doctor bears fruit: patients recover from the most life-threatening diseases and the most terrifying diagnoses. In fact, it's difficult to imagine how you could not love the man who had given you back your life.

## If Love Has Come to You Then Thank God

If love comes to you when you have a family, if you feel love is there, then there has indeed been love. If love suddenly seizes you and has such a grip on you that everything else around you pales into insignificance, and there's no longer a warm atmosphere at home; if you are drawn to this other person you love, and who has no idea that he or she has aroused these feelings in you, and, what's more, if this person is the husband or wife of your best friend – then what can you do? How do you deal with it?

*From case history no. 1016351 (born in 1962)*
'Today is my last healing session. You said we could write to you if we felt the need to do so ... As it happens, nobody but me can tell you the things that preoccupy me at present. You're my lifeline and I've been clutching at you like straws for the last few weeks. I started coming to see you not long ago – this is my second treatment programme. I'm 37 and have a lot of

health problems. I once wrote to you that all my problems stem from my "happy" childhood. My father was an alcoholic, and when he was drunk he enjoyed taking it out on everyone. We had no kind of life – no happiness, no peace. All we had was constant fear. So everything started when I was a child; people say "all sickness is down to nerves" and mine were stretched to breaking point.

I was 25 when my father died in prison, and my first daughter was born. My husband was very good, but I started being irritable, demanding, always dissatisfied with something. Everything seemed to be all right in my life and yet there was something wrong with me spiritually. What was I living for?

I just didn't know how to change my life. In the past I'd enjoyed drawing, knitting, sewing; I'm good at doing things with my hands and made all my own clothes. But now, I didn't want to do anything. The illnesses started building up: neurodermitis, a non-toxic goitre, gastritis, a disorder in the circulation of my blood, something wrong with my kidneys and, last of all, rheumathoid polyarthritis, which particularly scared me, especially after I'd read about it in the medical literature. I was seized by absolute terror and panic and I almost gave up the ghost. A friend who was a doctor got me out of this state. Two years passed and I felt OK. It was my legs that made me come to you. I've enjoyed coming to healing sessions. I understand and take on board everything you say and I try to work on myself. But, all the same, I was coming to you not because of my physical problems. This wasn't what was making me come to you – it was my emotions. I had been so taken aback when suddenly during a session you had started talking about love! This was something I hadn't expected.

Sergey Sergeevich, you're the only person close to me to whom I feel able to write, because I can't keep things to myself any more. In the past I used to confide in my friends and my mother. But now I feel that if I were to tell someone something about myself then it would suddenly disappear, as though I'd been imagining it. And even though the feeling torments me, I don't want – not for anything in the world – to have to give up feeling the way I do with the person I love – even if only for a few moments of happiness at a time.

Sergey Sergeevich, I've fallen in love, despite being married and having two children. He's married and has children too. When I fell in love before,

I was always the one to make the first move and my feelings were always returned. But I can't find the words to describe the emotions I'm going through right now. I feel as though I'm not alive – I'm just going with the flow: my thoughts are with him, every minute of the day. I yearn for him, and the feeling is so strong that I can't do a thing with myself. Is it really possible to be like this, in such a state? At times I feel as though I won't be able to endure it and I get frightened. How can I keep going? What can I do? I've never ever had feelings like this for a man before. I can be at home and, quite out of the blue, I can suddenly feel that if I were to go out of the house I'd bump into him. And it happens that way! Or I go to the shops for three hours and my legs take me to the very same train he travels on. And there are many more such coincidences.

Dear Sergey Sergeevich, you once said that before people on earth fall in love with each other, the emotions they go through have already been preordained in heaven. But how can I live with the emotional burden of spending my life counting the days and minutes, when my heart yearns for him, and I am praying I might see his face if nothing else, touch his hands, look into his eyes! It's even worse because our families are friendly, his wife is like a best friend to me. I love her very much and respect her as a good, kind person who is responsive to other people's problems. And then there's my husband – there aren't many like him, he loves me, we've been married for fourteen years. What can I do? What's the answer to this question?

If only things could be this simple: you love, so why not live together and be happy; but you aren't young, you have families, children, there's nowhere to get away to, and you can't get away from yourself either. Sergey Sergeevich, I feel uncomfortable about writing to you and taking up your time when there are so many people with far worse problems who come and are waiting for your help. I keep on thinking that I must gather up all my willpower, stop and burn my bridges, yet at the same time this feeling of love, which I hadn't known before, is so strong, it torments me so, but is also so wonderful, that I really can't put it into words. Why has heaven sent us the ability to feel both happiness and unhappiness at the same time? What's the answer?'

Sergey Sergeevich responded to this woman and others like her who had got caught up in very complicated situations:

*'Love is sweet it is exciting, and it is bitter and your tears and suffering must be*

*done in private. Nobody can help you but yourself. For nobody will understand what's going on inside you and wouldn't dare to take this feeling away from you. And would you want it to be taken from you anyway? That's unlikely, because it always takes you by surprise the first time. There can't be a first love, and then a second, and then a third. In life there is only one love and you'll only understand it when it comes to you.*

*What do you do in a situation where there's a family, a husband who loves you, and children, without whom life lacks true meaning and happiness? What do you do when the person you love is your friend's husband? Or, as often happens, not your friend's husband but a man who also has a family?*

*I say this: thank God that this wonderful feeling has come, that love has come to you!'*

## When Love Should Be Abandoned

Dr Konovalov is of the view, however, that there are certain times when it is best to abandon love. In situations where a married couple has lived together happily for ten years or more, a break in their relationship – when one of them leaves home – can lead to serious disruption and the onset of illness. And, what's more, this doesn't just affect the one who has been left, but also the one who leaves, as well as the children, if there are any. Serious disruptions occur in the information fields and in the sensitive-body system which make it possible for various diseases to develop. I'm not referring here, of course, to situations where a couple have fought like cat and dog for ten years or so. In this instance a divorce can only make things better for both of them. But what if the family was all right till then …?

How are we to resist love if it never gives us any warning of its arrival? If you've been married a long time and have always valued your 'other half' then you can do it. Love very, very rarely comes quite that 'suddenly', like a bolt from the blue. It can develop into the full-blown thing rather quickly, but even this still needs time. Having noticed that you have this feeling, you can stop it from growing; you can close down the information channels, stop meeting the person or limit your contact with them. This will work during the first stage. In the vast majority of cases, it's a matter of how much the person does or doesn't want these new feelings to develop. And, of course, only a person with a sense of responsibility and who loves their family is capable of doing this.

## Heavy Drinking: the Enemy of Love

In the modern-day family there are many bones of contention. One of them, and it is one which destroys the love between many couples, is heavy drinking. Dr Konovalov advises that you pay attention to it the minute it starts in your family. If your husband hits the bottle in the first year of your married life, and it turns out that he'd been drinking before, then the chances of building a happy life with such a person are practically nil. He's not going to give up drinking, so don't hope for a miracle. And no kind of therapies or preventative measures are going to help. If something as powerful as love did not stop him drinking then nothing else will.

Of course, in life there are exceptions to every rule and miracles do happen. But as a rule, wives (and sometimes husbands) hoping for a miracle will, to put it mildly, lose out in the end. Living with a drunk, your youth passes, the children – if there are any – end up sickly and sometimes mentally disadvantaged; the nervous system weakens with every day and diseases manifest themselves. And, in the end, the husband – the drinker – and not the long-suffering wife, breaks the bonds of marriage and leaves, and the wife is left on her own. 'How many years I wasted on him!' she sobs. And was it worth it? You could have predicted things would turn out this way.

If the man in question began drinking straight after the wedding, had drunk before, and some of his family were drinkers too, then the prospects won't be good. It's pointless waiting and hoping for a miracle in situations like this. The bitter experience of thousands of women bears testimony to this, women who, in their questionnaires, have told the doctor what happened to them. Hopefully their experience may help those who are just about to enter married life and can't make a decision about whether or not they should do so in situations like this If you don't want to destroy yourself then don't hesitate for a moment; leave this person. Otherwise he will end up leaving you; only it will happen a lot later on, when your life has already long since been ruined.

If a husband (and sometimes even a wife) who had never previously displayed a particular interest in alcohol suddenly starts drinking, especially if this happens after ten or more years of marriage, then it is a cry for help. In this situation under no circumstances turn your back on them, nag or have a go at them or blame them. Remember, something's happened. Something in your life together has gone wrong, cracks have appeared somewhere and your relationship is in need of a radical overhaul. Try to engage your husband in conversation, showing that you care but without being too overt about it. Make him understand that you love him, that you'll support him. Encourage him to get into a dialogue with you and discuss his (or both of your) general problems and feelings. But don't try and hurry things along. If you can't get into a discussion the first time and your husband comes home the next day 'under the influence', then don't make a scene. This will ruin everything. Give yourself – and him – time. And remember that it's always easier to break up a relationship than to save it. You can destroy love. But is it worth it, having run up against problems, straight away to run from love and destroy something created by divine nature?

Of course, every person is different in terms of their personal strengths of character. It isn't possible to help all people with one simple remedy. But some useful conclusions can be drawn as general guidance.

It is material things that make a woman stay with a husband she no longer loves and who is periodically drunk and treats her badly. Perhaps she doesn't have a job and her husband's salary is the family's only source of income; or it's just she has nowhere else to go – she can't just go out on the street with her children. Such a woman has been forced into a corner and there's no ray of hope in her life. Many women find themselves in this difficult situation. And so many things depend on money: she has to bring up her children, pay the rent on a flat or house. Such economic problems, for women everywhere, seem insoluble. What can they do? The first thing is to find ways of raising your own morale. Everything you'll learn from the doctor's books about the makeup of human beings, about relationships and learning to love yourself, will help you. You are sure to find love in your life. This doesn't mean that you're sure to get married again and that next time around you'll have a happy family. But you're sure to love again if you don't shut it out. And this love may be a support to you and give you hope in life.

Some people might consider such advice to be wrong, immoral even. But where's the immorality when someone finds themselves in a desperate situation? Who is there to help them? Society? The state? No. They can only help themselves. Some religious sects deem it immoral to resort to medical intervention. Even if the child of parents who profess such beliefs has appendicitis, they'd rather bury that child than take them to the hospital. Isn't this horrifying? Yes, it certainly is. But they put down their cruelty to the fact that 'It's what God wants.' When it comes to a person's health, subservience to moral values can be taken too far. It's stupid to talk about morals when a human being – the crown of creation – is dying. Love and health are the highest forms of morality.

In the family it is essential never to forget the first law of human relations: begin with yourself! By regulating and improving our own information field, we can exert an influence over our relationships with those around us and, first and foremost, of course, with those closest to us – the members of our own family. We must not forget this. If you become more relaxed, more composed spiritually and rid your thoughts of feelings of hatred, pride and antagonism, then the vibrations from your sensitive body and your higher bodies will change, which means the interactions between them and the higher bodies of the people in your household will change as well.

Hundreds of questionnaires testify to what happens to patients whose husbands or sons have overcome dependency on alcohol. Not long ago, at one of the healing sessions, the doctor's patients heard a woman patient tell her own story of how, with the help of the energy of creation, she saved her son from drug addiction. And they did it on their own. We know, of course, that you can't talk a hardened drinker into coming to the doctor's sessions, where he knows they'll help him kick this pernicious habit. In the overwhelming majority of cases, people like this don't want to kick their habits.

But those close to us do get better. They do so because the information field of one of the members of their family changes or recovers, which means the many ties binding families together are renewed, made over again. This only happens, of course, in those families where the wife (or the mother) hasn't lost heart or abandoned her feelings of love. More particularly, it happens where a woman's love has not been consumed by the fire of simmering hatred that is stoked up every time she sees her husband hitting the bottle.

# CHAPTER 29

# THE INFORMATION TIES THAT BIND FAMILIES TOGETHER

## The Child's Natural Link to Its Parents

The ties that bind parents and their children together are far deeper than one might imagine at first glance. For, apart from the genetic links that ensure a child has similar facial and bodily characteristics or the same personality traits as its parents, there are the information-energy ties as well.

At the moment of a child's conception, the guardian angels of the mother and father draw the cocoon of the child-to-be into their information field. During pregnancy, the child and the mother are encircled by an all-encompassing information-energy field. And, as they grow up, after the child has been born, the information fields of the parents have an influence over the child's field and, with it, its health and development.

When mothers tell doctors at the well-baby clinic their worries about their child's health, they are seldom aware that the child's illness – unless of course it's something slight like a cold – has not come about by chance but is the end result of the influence on the child of the information fields of its parents, if not of the whole family. Children are especially receptive to the energy of creation. This can clearly be seen in practice when, a few hours after treatment, a cold or a persistent cough which has plagued the child for several days disappears; or when, after a few treatment programmes, encephalitis and even cancer recede.

## If You Want to Make Your Child
## Better Then Heal Yourself

In particularly serious cases of child illness, and also in cases where the disease is hard to eradicate, it's worth paying particular attention to the health of the parents. The treatment of children with serious conditions begins with the treatment of the grandparents, as well as the mother and father. For they too carry diseases in their own information fields, and it's difficult for a child to deal with disease on their own, if they live in a family where the overall information-energy climate is not conducive to recovery.

In order that a child – especially one suffering from a serious condition – may get well, it is essential to completely overhaul the whole family's energy-information field. Dr Konovalov's patients are well aware of this, but I'll now explain it to readers who are encountering the idea for the first time. It is essential that parents should have an overwhelming desire to help their child get better and a willingness to do everything in their power to achieve this. For this reason, it's important in serious cases, especially life-threatening ones, that the whole family comes to the doctor's healing sessions. Mother, father and grandparents must channel all their energies towards helping the child. In this way, they augment the power of the energy of creation many times over by drawing on both their own energy potential and their individual body of desires.

There are times when young parents who've lost a child come to see the doctor. They are compelled to do so by a great and superior wisdom of which they aren't aware at the time. If a child in the family has died and the parents are thinking about having another one, then they must rid themselves of the spectre of death by rebuilding their own energy-information fields and establishing a positive energy background in their family. If not, their new-born child will be threatened by exactly the same danger that had carried off the previous one.

## Learning the Lessons of History

The energy-information ties in a particular family are carried down through the generations in very specific detail. As we know little about our own, individual ancestry, then let's take a look at history.

It's well known that numerous inherited diseases have been handed down through royal houses. Haemophilia – the inability of the blood to clot – is one such disease. The Tsarevich Alexis, the only son and heir of the last tsar of Russia, Nicholas II, suffered from the disease, which his mother Alexandra had inherited from her mother, Princess Alice, who in turn had inherited it from her mother Queen Victoria, who was a carrier of the disease. It was Queen Victoria's female children who unwittingly transmitted the disease into the royal houses of Europe. Looking at the photographs of the tsar's family, you'll be hard pressed to find any in which the little boy is smiling. This crippling disorder undermined his strength from an early age. The expressions of suffering on his face in photographs don't deceive: the boy frequently cried or whined and was temperamental because of the pain he was suffering. Bruises, which ordinary children rarely pay any attention to, could mean death for the tsarevich, for they could cause uncontrollable, internal bleeding. For this reason, from his early childhood he was very restricted in the games he could play, because so many of them, for him, could be life-threatening.

It has never occurred to anyone to examine similar historical patterns on the basis of Dr Konovalov's theory of the information-energy fields, but if you look closely at certain historical facts then you will see how right the doctor is when he asserts that diseases in children are linked to the disruption of the information-energy fields of their parents.

You may have heard or read about Nicholas II's weakness of character, a weakness manifested in his capitulation and signing of his own abdication manifesto after the Russian Revolution in 1917. All Russians are aware of the fact that it was the tsarevich's haemophilia that gave rise to the hold over the tsar's family, and later over Russia itself, that was exerted by the priest Grigory Rasputin, a man who undoubtedly had extraordinary, paranormal gifts but who was utterly immoral. The disruption of the information field brings with it a distortion of reality and, with it, disasters and disease. In the case of Russia, it was world war, two revolutions (in 1905 and 1917) and eventually execution of the royal family – in a hail of bullets in the cellar of the Ipatiev House in Ekaterinburg – that brought an end to the house of Romanov. However, such a violent end also cut short the ongoing progression of the family's karmic loading of misfortune and Romanov descendants today are not blighted by haemophilia.

It's clear that the story of any ruling dynasty is closely bound up in blood ties. The murder of one's siblings in the struggle for the throne, the waging of bloody wars in the quest for increased personal power, the murder of political opponents and heretics – all these things give rise to numerous diseases that are the curse of many royal houses. Murder is a great sin and cannot be left unpunished.

The protracted Wars of the Roses (1455–85) in England threw the country into an orgy of blood-letting that carried off nearly a quarter of the population. The bloody exploits of the Russian aristocratic elite during the reign of Tsar Ivan the Terrible also significantly reduced the population of Russia. And don't the roots of the madness that haunt kings lie in the kind of bloody banquets portrayed by Shakespeare – in plays such as *Titus Andronicus* and *Macbeth* – in the ranks of God's punishment? Among the 'royal' diseases of the English court were the madness of King George III and Henry VI and the leprosy of Henry I. Even Queen Elizabeth I, who did so much to make England a great power, towards the end of her life became deranged and wandered the halls of her palace with a drawn sword.

In Russia the struggle for power was exceptionally bloody and there were no fewer 'mad' rulers. Even monarchs such as Ivan the Terrible, Peter the Great and Catherine the Great – all of whom did so much for the state – suffered from one kind of psychiatric disorder or another.

## Murder Does Not Serve Human Evolution

Murder never goes unpunished. There's no praying for forgiveness. And anyone who counts on this is fooling themselves. As far as the universe is concerned, the murderer is redundant material, of no use to the evolution process. His soul (the information field) will be washed away in the fields of the energy of creation and will then pass through hell, having passed through the fields of the mutable layer. Such a person will never appear on earth for a second time.

Moreover, the murderer transfers the entire burden of his sin – and murder is the worst sin of all – onto his descendants. Sometimes the serious illnesses of small children are the result of precisely such inherited information links, which exert a hold over families down through several generations. In this instance, I'm not talking, of course, about soldiers who are obliged, by their oath of allegiance, to kill on instructions from their government or ruler. We're talking here about murders which people commit of their own accord, without any mitigating circumstances which might lessen the severity of their fate. The truest and bitterest remorse on the part of the perpetrator will not save them from punishment, and the total destruction of their information-energy cocoon may well have some influence over the fate of their children and grandchildren.

In the great works of William Shakespeare the faces of madness and murder are, as a rule, one and the same. It might now be an opportune moment to consider why they are so similar. The main thing would appear to be what causes them – the disruption of a person's information field and, with it, the onset of disease. We already know that a human being's information-energy field is an open system, directly linked to the fields of the energy of creation. A constant influx of energy, of which 98 per cent consists of information fields, allows the person to live an active and rational way of life. However, the information fields of someone suffering from psychological problems work like a malfunctioning receiver which, because it can't be tuned in to the right frequency, receives only snatches of other people's conversations and transmits a mishmash of sounds, reverberations and noises. The sick person is either 'tuned in' to somebody else's frequency or wanders helplessly through the chaos of fragments coming from someone else's sound waves. He thus only catches fragments of other people's thoughts, his own thoughts wandering into alien information fields. This is where the voices he hears in his head come from, as do general disorders in mental and physical behaviour.

The murderer is also sick in terms of the information-energy theory. The disruption of the information fields interrupts his link to the cosmic energy, which in turn has a dehumanizing effect.

# CHAPTER 30

# THE DISEASES HIDDEN
# IN OUR PAST

## The Deep-Seated Wounds of Childhood

I'm returning once more to historic facts, but not in order to underline some aspect of the doctor's information-energy theory, rather to illustrate more graphically for the reader what the doctor has to say with regard to present-day morality – the disease of a society which we consider to be civilized.

To do this, let's go back again to various things – historical and creative – that happened 300 years ago and which we know about from books.

Tsar Peter the Great's father died when he was only about four years old. Exile, the spearing to death of his teacher Matveev by palace guards in front of the ten-year-old boy's eyes, the attempts of his sister to get rid of political rivals, the constant threats to Peter's life – even researchers who truly admire his talents and acknowledge his genius would not fail to concede that Peter the Great's experiences as a child left an indelible mark on the development of his personality. Fits of rage, nervous tics and unbridled cruelty were all part and parcel of his makeup until the last hours of his life.

Many of the doctor's patients also carry within themselves deep, suppurating wounds that they've had since childhood. You think times have changed, that children are treated differently now, that a child cannot become a toy in the hands of grown-ups or an unbalanced person? Then listen and understand: it's possible that the diseases from which we all suffer are hidden in our past.

'She was resentful towards people, towards God – the whole world in fact. And what is more she had had to endure some terrible things. Her parents had been shot when she was only two. This happened in the 1920s, but ever since then she had tried *hard to forget them. But everything reminded her: the staff at the orphanage, the teachers at school and her lecturers at technical college. Everywhere, whenever she had to fill out forms, she was reminded of them. It was such a difficult time for everybody. But she held a grudge not against the times but the people: her older brother, for not rescuing her from what had happened to her; the man who had made her pregnant. Where was the love in that? Everybody lied to her. He'd had his way with her down a dark alley just the once, and then had even forgotten her name. But she had not been able to hide her pregnant belly. ...*

*Then she plucked up the courage to go and see his mother, not because she loved her son but because she was just a girl, and how could she bring up the child that was growing inside her on her own? And so she even bore a grudge against her unborn child. The man's mother felt sorry for the orphan, took her into their home, and tried to talk some sense into her wayward son. She did, and he married her.*

*But they spent their whole married life fighting like cat and dog. There was no end to the extramarital affairs, rows, and beatings. Nine children were born of this "love", but only five of them survived...*

*Everything about her life wore her down: the dislocations of her childhood, her unhappy marriage, the unwanted children. But most of all, she hated that first daughter, the one for whose sake she had been forced to become the drudge of a man she didn't love. There was no more room left in her heart to hate anyone else and she was looking for a way out. ...*

*And then the Second World War broke out. She found herself caught in the middle of the battle at Kursk, the bombardment and the shooting of partisans. The flames of war hardened her heart even more. And now her husband found someone else. Her heart turned to stone.*

*Whose fault was all this? Somebody must be to blame? Her husband made no bones about his affair and she couldn't get away from this blinding hatred. There seemed no way out. And there, under her feet, was her five-year-old daughter. ... What was going on in her mind? It's hard to tell; all she wanted was to take out everything she had suffered on that innocent little girl. And this time she beat her with particular ferocity. She rained blows on the child's body with her boots, causing her terrible pain. "Cry, go on! I'll hit you until you do!" But the little girl didn't want to cry; in the five years of her short life she had grown used to her mother's cruelty. But, right now, fear and pain compelled her to go and hide, to escape her mother's taunts.*

*Returning home after seeing his lover, the girl's father found her by following the tracks left by her blood. They led to underneath the bed, where the girl had hidden herself. He was shocked by what he saw and soon it was the mother's turn for a beating.*

*Life dragged on in a round of endless rows and beatings. The husband was drinking more often, and she was regularly provoking him into confrontations. He was unfaithful to her, and she to him – with his own brother, and in front of the children.*

*By the time her daughter was fifteen, the mother couldn't beat her any more. The girl was now as tall as she and could give as good as she got. It was then that she started telling all and sundry that her eldest daughter was having sexual relations with her father. Not everybody believed this disgusting lie but the girl was only a step away from doing away with herself ...'*

This story has not been made up. It was told to Dr Konovalov by that very same young girl who'd been beaten by her mother. She grew up, and is now nearly 60. But she still carries the events of 50 years ago deep inside her wounded soul. The physical pain has long gone but the emotional pain has never left her. The relentless presence of this pain caused damage to her sensitive-body system and the consequent outflow of energy has contributed to the development of numerous health problems. But in order to cure her of her physical ills the doctor must first help her overcome her emotional torment and erase the memory of the tracks of her own blood which still oppresses her from her distant past – a past she cannot forget.

## When Wisdom Comes

It is, of course, impossible to wipe out all this past history during the course of just one or two treatment programmes. It's the product of 50 years of someone's life. During all those years it has eaten away at that person's heart, constantly reminding her of its existence and dragging her down into the abyss of illness. Dr Konovalov does not practice hypnosis; he doesn't deliberately set out to make the patient forget their childhood so that they can wake up one fine day without any recollection of it. He considers that to do so would be unnatural and would serve no useful purpose for the patient. It's impossible to deprive someone of their memories without harming them in the process. But there is a different way it can be done. You can teach them to have a different attitude to memories. And then the pain can be replaced with wisdom.

There's a special procedure for this during healing sessions. Everything, of course, takes place against the background of the high concentration of the energy of creation in the hall and the particular influence that the doctor has over it. If you are able to attend healing sessions, then during such moments try and concentrate on the one thing that is troubling you the most and giving you no peace. Then slowly turn things round in your head, mentally erasing these experiences from your life. They won't bother you any more. The patient may need to be taken through this procedure more than once before their emotional wounds are healed. You can also try this yourself during link-up healing sessions.

## What To Do When Your Situation Seems Hopeless

Naturally enough, the process of healing emotional wounds works better with patients who are no longer in contact with the source of their suffering, or in close proximity to the person who has brought them so much grief and who constantly drives them to the edge, humiliates, insults or oppresses them. But what about those who, after receiving the healing action of the energy of creation, have to go straight back home and endure more wounds to their spirit. What can they do?

How difficult it is to heal the child who, after coming to healing sessions, goes back home with its mother or grandmother, back to a drunkard of a father who is capable at any moment of losing his rag, of hitting a five-year-old round the head, or smashing something on the floor, or beating up the child's mother. If everything is still the same at home then no amount of energy will help. Nothing will help. Of course, the woman who has managed to take her child away from their domestic hell and bring him or her to healing sessions wants things to change in their lives as quickly as possible; she wants a miracle to happen like it does for other people who go on to the stage and talk about their successes. She wants her child to stop suffering, her husband to stop drinking; she wants there to be peace and quiet at home, she doesn't want to have to live every minute in fear, she wants the ache inside her to go away. The desire for happiness, good health and domestic harmony is a wonderful thing, and the desire to achieve this as quickly as possible is also totally understandable. But sickness, especially if it is chronic and of long duration, never disappears overnight. Why?

## The Danger of Getting Used to Being Ill

People get used to being ill and adapt to dealing with their symptoms – that is, they become passive and even indulge their illnesses. This is the same not just with physical disease but also with regard to our lifestyle and the way we think. Moreover, illnesses of the sprit and of the body become inseparable, one from the other, due to the distortion of the information fields.

It's very easy to get used to being ill. And modern-day medicine facilitates this. 'You have a pain in your liver? Here are some tablets. No, your liver cells won't recover, they won't function any better, but you won't have to put up with the pain.' And so, instead of fighting their illnesses people simply swallow tablets. Such passivity and resignation to illness is all too easy. Many medicines don't cure; all they do is help the human organism adapt to the disease that has taken a hold over it.

New problems have recently been encountered at the doctor's sessions, in children who have been saved from serious disease. If a child has suffered from a chronic illness for some time then, naturally enough, the parents have not treated the child as they would a healthy one. They've gone out of their way to let them have everything they want, without limits, in the hope that this will make the child feel better, give them something to be happy about. At long last the child is better, thanks to Dr Konovalov. But then the problems start again. The parents haven't yet got over the nightmare of what they've been through and so they carry on treating the child as they did before, as though it were still sick. And the child, even though a lot better, comes to expect it. A short while later and the parents are complaining to Dr Konovalov: 'He's throwing tantrums, he's become selfish and won't listen.' The fact is, the child has got used to being ill. So it isn't enough to re-establish the normal inner workings of the body; you have to restore the equilibrium of the family too.

## Gaining Inner Strength – Something We All Have to Work For

It isn't possible, at one stroke, to destroy all the negative things that have been accumulated inside a person over decades. Besides, if you were to do this and suddenly wipe out the whole of a person's inner world, their spirit would be empty, a vacuum. So what kind of health are we talking about here?

With the help of the energy of creation – not at its expense, but with its help – a person's inner strength can be sufficiently reinforced that they are able themselves to sweep away old habits and attitudes and allow new ones to develop. You mustn't rely just on the energy of creation and do nothing yourself.

But when it comes down to getting rid of old habits, many people simply want to throw in the towel. There's a Russian saying 'Habit is second nature' and we often keep jealous guard over our habits, more so than we do our health. We're deluding ourselves, of course, by hanging on to the past and trying to find whatever justification we can for not changing things (in other words, for not getting better).

## Developing a New Outlook on Life Takes Time

There are two ways in which patients react to the energy of creation. The first is like a moment of insight: a sudden flash of light, when the scales fall from their eyes and they see their life as it is and realize why they are ill. Such an instantaneous revelation and with it a transformation in the person themselves means that their diseases quickly go away. This is wonderful, of course, but without having a new outlook on life to fall back on, the recovering patient can very quickly relapse back into illness. This is why, despite the fact that many (or even all) of their clinical diagnoses disappear, the patient must first of all have a healthy world outlook. It's the same outlook that Sergey Sergeevich describes in his books; it forms a whole philosophy on the healthy way of living. And if you don't follow it you will not be able to maintain your health for long.

The second way in which patients recover is more protracted. Why? This question can only be answered by working with every patient on an individual basis. But patients are, nevertheless, able to help themselves. Everything does not disappear at once, but by degrees, and often it seems as though progress is terribly slow. So, if you really want to help yourself, your priority should be to get to grips with Dr Konovalov's philosophy of health. If you do this, without leaving out the things that seem trivial to you, if you follow the same path to health as that laid out in the doctor's books, and which he elaborates on in every healing session, then you are sure to get well. This is as relevant to the patients who join in link-up sessions as to readers, because there's only one path to health and that's to do away with your old habits that have been ingrained by illness and exchange them for new ones which will help strengthen your sensitive-body system and your energy-information structures.

# CHAPTER 31

# HOW TO BRING UP HEALTHY CHILDREN

This chapter describes how a child comes into the world, and discusses how its upbringing should be in an ideal situation so that the child grows up a healthy and well-rounded person. All these suggestions will, of course, be of much greater help to those who have just started having a family or who are thinking about it. But don't assume that if your children are grown up, if they are already 10, 15 or even 30, that it's now too late and you can do nothing to help them. It isn't so. It's never too late to make a start.

## Healthy Parents Make For Healthy Children

As has already been said, the health of the child depends to a large extent on the health of its parents, and also on relations within the family into which it is born. A great many factors exert an influence over the child's destiny before he or she is even born. In order to make sense of them one must read all of Dr Konovalov's books, enlightening oneself on the reasons for illness and preparing in all seriousness for things that may happen. I shall only touch briefly here on the main factors which have an influence on the health and fate of the unborn child. It goes without saying that before their child is born parents should give up all their harmful habits and adopt a healthy lifestyle. Sergey Sergeevich thinks that this should be done for at least a year before a child is conceived.

## How Parents Should Behave Towards Each Other

The love and respect parents have for each other is in itself a guarantee of good health. If nature has given two people the ability to love each other then they must also learn respect.

The cornerstone of the respect that partners have for each other is first of all equality. Without equality there can be no well-rounded family. If one partner tries to control the other, whether physically, emotionally or intellectually then the inevitable collapse of the family can be predicted: love will die, sickness will take the upper hand and in the end life will become utterly intolerable.

In terms of the theory of information-energy how then does this happen? Let's say that the woman finds herself dependent on her husband; he beats her, humiliates her, or perhaps simply keeps trying to assert his superiority over her. For various reasons, she can't get a divorce. You'd agree that any woman, finding herself in this situation, would summon up a hundred and one reasons to keep herself chained to this despot of a husband rather than leave him: she can't support herself financially, she's nowhere else to live, 'And what about the children?', etc., etc. But even though, on the outside, the woman seems to be playing to the rules: subordinating herself to her husband, doing what he demands of her, giving in to him, nevertheless, inside, and sometimes without even consciously being aware of it, she's resisting him. She allows her sense of hurt to grow inside her, and it turns to hatred. We aren't always consciously aware of hatred. It can manifest itself in uncontrollable fits of anger, in hostile outbursts, teasing, or making rude gestures. In this way, the 'downtrodden' wife gets her own back on her husband – and this is where the energy is at work. So the husband, who thinks he's in control, is already feeling his wife's anger in his heart and his liver, and his blood pressure has gone up too. And this is all because the desire to control somebody else against their will cannot be fulfilled without paying a price. You pay the price for it with a drop in your own energy levels, and that, of course, means it affects your health too.

A sense of justice, of equality between partners, must be nurtured by them in each other. And it must be done from the very first days of their life together. So, for example, a girl meets a young man. From time to time, when they go on a date, it's clear he's had a drink or two, but she pretends not to notice. And then, during the first years of their marriage, the same girl starts getting upset when her husband comes homes drunk. 'Why is this happening? she'll ask herself indignantly. Well, it's a consequence of those first dates when she turned a blind eye to his drinking habits.

The first time her boyfriend had turned up drunk, she should have told him in no uncertain terms that she didn't like it and to go home. But she didn't. She thought he must know what he's doing and didn't need her to tell him. Or maybe she was frightened: he might leave and never come back. As a result, she said nothing for a long time and left things as they were, which led the young man to believe that what he was doing was alright.

If you don't tell your husband when you're first married that you can't stand cigarette smoke, and you don't insist he goes outside to smoke, he will get into the habit of smoking at home. If, the first time he stays behind after work to be with his friends, you don't tell him you're unhappy about this, then he'll spend more and more of his time without you. The thought of taking you with him won't enter his head, and after a few years you'll be so fed up with this that it might even lead to divorce.

All these things seem so trivial at first; the trouble is that, after ten years or so, people will start quarrelling over such trivialities and love turns into hatred. I'm not saying here that equality and respect necessarily mean an equal responsibility for domestic, everyday affairs. The husband having a rest on the settee in front of the TV whilst the wife dashes from the cooker to the washing machine, although something of a cliché, is all too commonplace. But it shouldn't be like that in a well-balanced family.

## Your Own Interests Come First

Despite all the love she has for her husband, her parents and her children, a woman must always remember that her own life is the important thing. Her interests should come first. I'm not talking about the selfish woman who satisfies her own desires at the expense of her family. I'm talking about women who all too readily sacrifice their own sleep and rest, their own education or career, their health and their peace of mind, for the sake of their husband and children. (Have you noticed how men are considerably less inclined to make similar sacrifices?) And what does this lead to? It means that in several years (maybe even a couple of decades) a woman who behaves so selflessly will end up alone and full of bitter regrets. 'I've given them everything, and what have they done? ... They're so ungrateful!' On top of that, by now she's already suffering from some chronic complaint or other, her face is furrowed with wrinkles and she has the downtrodden look of someone who has no interests of her own in life. By this time, her husband has already taken up with someone younger, healthier and better looking. The children have long since left home and don't want to visit her unless they have to because they can't bear the reproachful looks she gives them. The children have also got used to taking, because nobody ever taught them how to give.

In the end, life is a gift from God, and it's given to you and you alone. Remember this when you find yourself wasting this precious gift needlessly.

The foregoing remarks should not be taken as some kind of attack on women who choose to stay at home and don't go to work. It's great if a woman has a job she likes doing. And if the work she likes doing is confined to the home then that's great too. The important thing is to be doing something you enjoy and not to go overboard in slavishly serving the interests of somebody or something else.

Every time we come to the subject of housewives I remember my own grandmother. She's 93 now; her children are all over 60 and her oldest great-grandson is 14. But not a single family matter is decided without her being consulted. Here's a particular instance. At the end of the 1940s grandmother fell ill. She was diagnosed as having a stomach ulcer. She left her children with grandfather and went to her mother's in the country for two months, where she was treated with some special, herbal remedies. It was difficult for grandfather looking after the children; he had to work hard and, although some good neighbours helped him, the children were pretty much left to their own devices.

Grandmother had obviously found it hard to make this decision, but to take time out for herself and abandon her usual domestic routine was a wise one, nevertheless. As always, she was right: it was better for her children to be without her for a few months and for her to recover her health than for them to be made orphans in a few years' time.

## Working with the Body of Thought: the Primary Task of Parents-to-be

One of the basic tasks of all parents-to-be is to work with what Dr Konovalov calls the 'body of thought'. Our thoughts are miniature copies of the body of thought of the divine universe. That is, whenever our thoughts are in motion we are simultaneously creating the programme of things to be fulfilled.

So the first thing we need to do is to cleanse ourselves of all bad and stress-inducing thoughts. One of these, which seriously hampers the child's entry into the world or makes it more prone to disease, is the thought that a child is unwanted. Everybody in the family must be happy about the arrival of a new baby. If, during her pregnancy, the mother can only think of the responsibilities, the difficulties and the unwanted restrictions to her own life that the child will bring, if her thoughts about her unborn child are negative ones, then it's unlikely that the baby will be born healthy, strong or happy.

Where, in your opinion, do lacklustre, dull people, who have no joy in life, come from? Look at children and see how different they are. There's one whose eyes burn with curiosity; everything interests him. He takes a tumble, gets up and carries on laughing, taking everything in his stride. And then there's the other kind: he's sullen and nothing interests him. And no matter how hard you try to entertain him with toys or books he does nothing but whine and sulk. Are such striking differences the result of nature's programming or does it all depend on the parents' programming? If the child was conceived by loving parents, who had surrendered to their passion with joy and had awaited the child's birth with impatience and anticipation, then their child would, from the start, have been endowed with enormous resources from which to draw strength and love in its own life. But if the child was conceived not out of love and passion but out of dull, sexual routine, and without emotional commitment, the child's potential (for love, strength in life and health) will turn out to be low.

Our thoughts programme not just our own lives but those of our children too. For this reason, Sergey Sergeevich regularly warns his patients in no uncertain terms about the danger of paying attention to omens, superstitions and clairvoyant predictions, because all of these things programme our consciousness. Say a black cat runs across the road in front of you. This in itself cannot do you any harm. It's what you think about it that's harmful – whether this alarms you or you think something nasty is sure to happen to you as a result. It's not the cat that makes bad things happen to you but your own thoughts; and it is these thoughts of the awful things that might happen which lay down a programme for misfortune which ensures that they actually do.

This is why I'd like to tell you a story about how I came to make black cats my allies. In order to get into university I had to compete against 20 other people for a place. Just thinking about this terrified me. And in the maths exam the questions were much harder than those I'd sat at the Mathematics and Mechanic Faculty. (The logic behind this was simple: everybody wants to do psychology but far fewer want to do maths, so they'd made it deliberately harder for us by setting a tough maths paper). At Peterhof, whilst walking though the woods on my way to the maths exam, my knees were knocking and I was feeling agitated. Then suddenly a black cat leapt out of the bushes and ran across my path. 'Well that's it', I thought, 'I might as well go home'. So I carried on walking like a condemned person. Suddenly another black cat appeared, and it too crossed the path in front of me. I stopped and thought for a moment. What did the second one signify? The worst they could do would be to give me a low mark for the exam. Could anything worse happen? I carried on walking …. And then black cats started coming at me from every direction; it was literally raining cats. A third, a fourth, a fifth … after the seventh one I gave up counting and laughed: 'It's absolutely impossible things could get any worse!' I went into the exam feeling light-hearted and got a high mark. And because only 15 lucky people out of 600 got through the exam that day, I've been very fond of black cats ever since. Whenever I meet them I say to myself: 'Be lucky!' and I imagine to myself that it will happen. Because it isn't to do with cats, it's to do with what we think about cats and what we expect to happen if they cross our path.

As regards astrological predictions, Sergey Sergeevich gives a categorical warning: 'People don't need to know what the future holds for them.' And this is because a person's future has not been set in stone. Many changes in our lives are within our own power; a lot depends on how we live, the things we strive for, what we do. But to predict a person's future means to lay down a clearly defined programme which, penetrating our thoughts, will then ensure that the predicted events happen. And on top of this, the majority of today's psychics and clairvoyants are nothing but charlatans. It's no secret what they depend on for their reputations. A person comes for a consultation and is told the programme of their future life. They're not going to turn a deaf ear to it and will start thinking of the bad things that might happen. And sure enough, bad things follow on from this. And so they go around telling their friends: 'That's exactly what they predicted would happen.' And before you know it they're queuing up outside the clairvoyant's door.

Because Sergey Sergeevich is in constant contact with the energy of creation, he can, of course, extract from it information specific to the future and well-being of a particular person. He's well aware that this is no simple thing to do and only makes use of this ability on rare occasions, when it is essential for him to help relieve someone of a very real burden.

On one occasion, a friend of the doctor's was about to travel to another town. For some reason he felt uneasy about this and told Dr Konovalov. Sergey Sergeevich didn't say anything straight away, but a while later phoned him and warned him: 'Go if you must, but don't set foot outside the town!' His friend wasn't intending to go anywhere else so he didn't pay any attention to what the doctor said. But he soon had reason to remember the doctor's words.

The town he had gone to is situated not far from Makhachkala on the Caspian Sea. Several of his travelling companions were intending to go into Makhachkala to watch a wrestling competition. And that's when he remembered what Dr Konovalov had said. He hesitated for a while, because he very rarely had the chance to go and watch a competition of that class. But, in the end, he decided not to risk it. This very same competition was soon in all the newspapers – because during it the ceiling had collapsed and many people had been killed. You can just imagine how Dr Konovalov's friend felt to have escaped the fate of his companions.

## Things to Remember in Bringing Up Your Child

Bringing up your child is an everyday duty. A missed day can mean lost years. And you must set about your child's upbringing from the first days of its life.

This newly created soul, this little ray of God's light, has been born into this world small and helpless. 'When contemplating the mystery of birth,' Sergey Sergeevich says, 'you must not think that you are stronger and cleverer, that you know more and that you will teach the child to walk, speak and live. You too will learn from him! For the child's soul has not yet lost the divine spark which it carries within it.'

Being made flesh is a new and unfamiliar mode of existence for the soul. So don't go swamping your child all at once with all the pleasures of the physical world, and especially of our civilization. Take, for example, the television. Babies don't need a TV in their room. Don't shake bright toys in front of their faces; this will only frighten them. If they are fractious at night, under no circumstances switch on bright overhead lights. This will alarm them and also burn the retina of their eyes. Don't think that if you put a baby in a wide, open-sided bed that they will feel cosier. They're better off in their own little nest of blankets.

You'll find it hard to understand what your child wants until he learns to speak. But you mustn't think that as soon as he is able to say something to you that everything will be all right. Mutual understanding is the most important thing you must learn together in your lives.

Personal example is an important tool in the process of bringing up a child. If you yourself do not behave as you teach your child to behave, then you'll never manage to teach him anything. So just remember the magic formula: 'Begin with yourself!'

Today's world provides us with a model for bringing up children in which violence and fear prevail. Violence begins when you make an issue of insisting that a child eats something and it ends in physical reprimands (and this happens even in normal families). Such things should not happen, says Dr Konovalov. Our world is full of people who are being coerced. The majority of children grow up afraid of their parents. Even when they become adults they still can't avoid being constrained and subordinated.

Many mothers, particularly anxious ones, often say to their children when trying to make them do something: 'You'll thank me when you're bigger.' Well don't bank on it! You're fooling yourself. Your child will quietly hate you when you say it. He won't say anything – he's not allowed to contradict you – but no one can stop him from storing up hatred in his heart. Bringing children up by means of force suppresses the development of their personalities. This way, all you'll do is create illnesses.

Earlier in this book, Dr Konovalov spoke about energy exchange and the way in which one person can feed off the energy of another. I'd like briefly to remind you about this process here. One person, who is utterly composed, provokes another with unkind words, actions or deeds, producing in them a strong reaction which takes the form of indignation, annoyance or resentment. When in an angry state (as well as experiencing other strong emotions) a person sends their own energy out in all directions, the person who has upset them feeds off it. As a result, the person who loses their temper also loses energy from their sensitive body, which can lead to all sorts of illnesses. Meanwhile, the energy vampire takes in this energy, which has a therapeutic effect on them at first but nevertheless, with time, will also cause damage to their information fields.

An upbringing founded on being lectured to and shouted at is a bad energy exchange, as a result of which everyone will suffer: the parents and the child. Dissipating their energy by getting irritable and anxious, parents do nothing but weaken their own sensitive-body systems. And the child meanwhile learns to take in that energy whilst letting their parents' angry demands wash over them.

In so far as the processes I've just described take place at an unconscious level and we aren't always able to control them, Dr Konovalov advises people to remember one important thing: if you're out with a small child, don't focus your attention on whether they do things right or not. Your son's walked straight into a puddle? Calmly take him to one side and explain that he mustn't do this. He does it again. Are you on the point of losing your temper? Are you getting irritated? Then just remember that this is the beginning. If you start giving vent to your anger – that is, if you start dissipating energy – the child is sure to look for other ways to make you give him more of your energy again, and will keep doing everything he can to annoy you.

The best solution is to explain things calmly, without getting angry (which sends out energy). If you don't like what your child is doing, it is better sometimes to pay no attention to it, rather than reward the child with even the smallest amount of your own energy.

I'm not referring here, of course, to serious misdemeanours, such as fighting or stealing. Things like that should never be allowed to pass. You mustn't stay silent on the matter. All the members of the family should be informed, or those at the child's nursery school if it happens there.

What's important is never to give up or lose heart; don't think that everything you do is to no effect. The process of bringing up children, if done properly, always bears fruit. But let them ripen in their own time and not when you want them to. That way, it happens naturally. Only advertisements promise us quick results. Such naivety, as the Russian saying goes, only leads to trouble.

# PART V

# THE LAWS OF THE ENERGY OF CREATION

# CHAPTER 32

# THE VOICE OF THE LIVING UNIVERSE

## Practice – the Basis of All Dr Konovalov's Theories

Dr Sergey Sergeevich Konovalov's energy-information theory is inextricably linked with every aspect of his treatment methods. I can say that now, with absolute conviction, on the basis of a miraculous turnaround in my own life. And I have every right to say so. During the short time I've known the doctor (since October 1998), I have been witness to innumerable victories over the most acute forms of disease. Among those who have, to their own amazement, had some complaint or other diagnosed at the doctor's sessions are my own children, my closest friends and acquaintances. There's one particular miracle I still find hard to take in: I have in front of me two X-rays, taken several months apart, bearing witness to the disappearance of a serious disease, and not just in anybody, but in somebody close to me. This has brought so much happiness in such a short space of time!

The theory of illness and health is linked to our everyday lives in the most intricate of ways. The final part of this book comprises Dr Konovalov's answers to some of the questions most frequently asked by patients about his overall philosophy, his medical theories and his practice as both doctor and healer.

## Understanding the Language of the Living Universe

The universe looks upon us as its younger siblings and we have only just begun to understand its intricate workings. Even those few among us, such as Dr Konovalov, who have been initiated into some of its innermost secrets, are not yet ready to understand things in their entirety. For the human race, which has for centuries boldly been exploring the vast expanses of the cosmos, is like a moth which, having dared to fly up from the topmost branch of a birch sapling, stiffens in astonishment at the boundlessness of space opening out on all sides before it. The material universe is ageless and infinite; but, in comparison, our own material possibilities, as transient beings, are very highly circumscribed.

The world of modern-day people is hemmed in by their scanty knowledge of the world that they inhabit. They do not feel themselves to be children of the universe. Modern-day people are the step-children of civilization; they are no longer sensitive to their relationship with the cosmos. Once, long ago, people looked up at the stars in fear and worshipped the heavenly bodies. It was not, as such, a fear born of superstition. In those days people were aware of their bond with nature and sensed they were an integral part of it.

But science has never been able to fathom the language of the living universe and grasp its subtle intonations. Perhaps this is because today's scientists are more predisposed to studying substance. Children who study basic astronomy at school only know that the universe is an accumulation of gases, planets, nebulae and stars. It looks down on us from its cold, lifeless, black emptiness. And if this is how things are, then why should anyone care whether new stars are beginning to shine and why others are dying?

However, now that you know that the universe is not just an accumulation of either cold or red-hot material, that it is not simply a cosmic void nor a conglomeration of planets unable to sustain human life, and when you finally realize too that the human organism is an energy system, indissolubly connected to the cosmos, it is then that you will understand that the voice of the cosmos cannot remain indifferent to us. It has good reason to call to us through those who have been initiated. And this is not some trivial prompting to listen; it is rather, a law, a command. It is part of the very same law that Moses passed to his people, and which was then passed down to us by Christ. There's no way of knowing to what extent these ancient laws have been altered over time. But by not observing them, mankind has been led down the path of self-destruction. The voice of the universe is the voice of an attentive mother who warns her child not to go up to the edge of a cliff or they will fall.

## The Universe Has Its Own Language

The universe communicates with us as we do with children. We are its young. And what, may I ask, can a baby grasp when it has not yet learnt to talk or understand what is being said to it by those whose duty it is take care of it, who love it and wish only the best for it? The universe is trying to attract our attention, but, like small children, we don't hear it and don't understand. We don't even realize that we should be listening out for its call.

However, the universe does have its chosen ones, those who can hear its voice. They hear, understand and pass on what it says to others. If only we could learn to listen to its intonations. For example, take the bird that sings all year round outside your window – what is human speech to it? Its world extends from its nest to the nearest field and back. Its interests are geared to feeding and bringing up its young and making sure they don't die or freeze to death. Are you going to tell it about your thoughts and feelings? And would it be able to understand you? But if you make a bird table for it and put out food at the same time every day, the bird will quickly learn your language, because this is a vital necessity for it.

But would the bird really be interested, even if it could understand your complaints about how life treats you? Why should it care? What significance do your plans and hopes have for this creature?

Do people really need to know precisely why stars come into existence, how the universe is developing or what will happen to the human race in the next two million years? No, they don't. It's for the scientists to take an interest in such things, even though their work in this regard will have no practical application. However, the human race will always need to find out from the universe about things that affect its daily life and how it obtains its daily bread. When it comes down to matters of life and death, or the health of our children and grandchildren, then we'd make any sacrifices in order to do the right thing. 'Just give us back our health!' you say. ' Just make this pain go away. Just let our children grow up healthy!'

## How Dr Kònovalov Teaches Us to Listen

But disease is crafty, and even today's medicine does not have all the resources to help us get to grips with it. And when tablets and medicines can't help, when your patience is exhausted, and when your suffering body is endlessly wracked with pain, then you've only one chance left: attending Dr Konovalov's healing sessions, or making full use of the biomaterials, doing the energizing exercises and taking part in link-up sessions. People don't come to the centre the first time to find out about the laws of the universe, they are driven there by a desperate need; it's their last hope of holding on to the strength that is draining away from them and being able to go on living.

And once they start attending the centre the pain really does go quickly. As soon as it goes and the patient once more learns how to listen, he or she will begin to hear the voice of the living universe. Dr Konovalov not only knows its language, he communicates with people on its behalf, and draws on its help in healing them. What does he have to say on the matter? We don't need to turn the world upside down in order to regain our health; it is enough that we make radical changes in our own, everyday lives, and our inner feelings and attitudes.

'It's so simple!' you say, thinking that radical change can come overnight, as if by magic. 'It's so difficult,' the doctor in turn replies. 'It's so difficult to change oneself.'

What matters the most to ordinary people? Good health and happiness. The cards sent in by patients are full of such wishes, full of a yearning to regain their health and stay well. We all say similar things on birthdays and anniversaries, no matter how old a person is – 10 or 110. And it's true, because health and happiness cannot exist without each other. But what exactly is human happiness, and what do we have to do to achieve it? Many people will assert that you can be happy without a penny to your name, but nobody can be happy without love, or without dreams.

# CHAPTER 33

# THE THINGS WE LONG FOR

## It's Only Natural to Want Things

Every one of us has their own particular desires or, to be precise, our heads are always full of a whole range of desires and aspirations. We have already discussed some of this in Chapter 26. Many of these are trivial, insignificant desires which we hope to achieve in the short term – for example, to go to the theatre next week, do some decorating next month, or visit friends in the not too distant future. But there are also other things we desire, objectives which we strive towards over the course of several years – for example: getting an education, bringing up our children, reaching certain levels of creative achievement, making a career for ourselves. These are all-embracing desires, which will require a lifetime's hard work to achieve.

The ability to dream in this way is something common to each and every one of us: from the miserable, hung-over drunk who wakes with a terrible desire for the hair of the dog, to the Napoleon Buonapartes who drift off to sleep dreaming of world domination. People cannot live through a single day without having dreams and desires. Otherwise, their lives would become meaningless.

So why then are people always wishing for something, dreaming of things, wanting things so desperately? It's because this is how we are made, because nature has created us to want things. And this 'body of desire' in each of us is, in the doctor's opinion, one of the major components of the divine plan.

## The Body of Desire as Part of the Divine Universe

Dr Konovalov's information-energy theory describes how the body of desire is not only laid down in a person's nature but is in turn part of the overall structure of the divine universe. In other words, the absolute (God) realizes his grand design with the help of the divine universe. The energy of creation's role is to bring this into being, by penetrating the lower echelons of the hierarchy of the divine universe – what Dr Konovalov calls 'the world of the life force' – which borders on the real, physical world. It is in this way that the programme of creation and the evolution of life are realized in the universe. As it is realized, God's grand design passes across the world of thought and into the world of desire of the divine universe. The grand design enters the information field and concentrates itself there as the will of God.

A person's desires – the ones they set their minds on – are not trivial, passing desires, but can only be fulfilled with difficulty. When people desire something they draw their own information field towards what it is they are striving for and concentrate their energies on it; that is, they pass through exactly the same process as that accomplished by the higher plan, only in miniature. It was thus no accident that man was created in God's image.

## How to Protect and Fulfill Your Primary Desire

During Dr Konovalov's sessions, where there is a high concentration of the energy of creation, patients go through a procedure for 'protecting the primary desire', and for this reason it has a great significance. A person's body of desire is one of their highest bodies, as it is contiguous to the planet's information fields. In this way, when it comes into contact with the information field of the energy of creation, a person's desire enters the fourth dimension of space, which is called time. The vibrations of human desires enter the information field of the energy of creation. It doesn't happen straightaway, nor in an hour or so. The desire has to work its way through. How does it do this? Precisely as Sergey Sergeevich says it does: 'You only need to have one desire. Or at least one desire during the course of a single treatment programme.'

If a person has a concrete goal (one desire), and if they don't change it, then with time that desire will penetrate the information field of the world of the life spirit and begin to be fulfilled.

As regards the ways in which desires are realized by the information field, it must be pointed out that their fulfilment does not always bring a person complete satisfaction. There are two reasons for this.

First of all, the existing mechanism in which the information field works does not necessarily indicate that the universe directs its powers solely towards indulging people's every whim. The bringing into being of God's grand design in the lower echelons leaves its own mark on the realization of human desires.

So, for example:

- A desire that goes against God's plan cannot be realized (for example, the desire to do harm to someone);
- The fulfilment of a desire is sometimes linked to the gradual 'summoning' into someone's life of certain opportunities, of which they must make use. If they don't recognize them and make full use of the chance with which they're presented, then this desire also may not be fulfilled.

Take, for example, a person who particularly wants their career to take off. Yet they don't seize the opportunity when the chance of changing jobs presents itself, and they fail to do so on more than one occasion. They dream of being promoted within the company that they've already been working for for five years and don't try any other options. The problem is that they don't want to accept the fulfilment of their desire in a different, unfamiliar form. And for this reason, likely as not, they will end up with nothing.

An ordinary person, with ordinary material desires, is incapable of comprehending that the universe is wiser, that the divine plan, the desire of God, is for them a greater blessing than his their personal aspirations.

Secondly, a person doesn't obtain satisfaction from the fulfilment of their desires if they don't clearly understand what it is they want, and what, for them, is a blessing and what is not.

At one of his healing sessions, Dr Konovalov told a story about one of his patients. The woman had an unhappy marriage and her relationship with her husband was so difficult that she often hoped he'd end up leaving her. She was coming to healing sessions at the time, and thus found herself in close contact with the energy of creation, which meant her desire was soon fulfilled. Her husband left her for another woman. After he first left she was enormously relieved and happy. But as time went on, her happiness turned into longing; she missed her husband and began weeping at night. She asked him to come back, but he wouldn't. On the one hand, the woman's desire had been fulfilled but, on the other, it turned out that she hadn't really wanted it in the first place.

And this is why the doctor talks about how important it is to settle on a particular goal in life and be aware of our true desires. Otherwise, the same thing will happen to others as happened to this woman: the fulfilment of a desire that may bring not pleasure, but suffering.

# CHAPTER 34

# HOW TO DEAL WITH EVERYDAY EVENTS IN OUR LIVES

## If You're Afraid of Something Then It's Sure to Happen

The mechanism of interaction between a person's information fields and the universe lies at the root of many things that happen to people during the course of their lives. You'll agree that most of the fears and apprehensions people have usually turn out to be groundless. It's like people say: 'If you're afraid of something, then it's sure to happen.' Fear is primarily the thought that something unpleasant or harmful might happen. It is a troubling emotion that, when it occurs, can have an effect on the interaction of the information fields in the aforementioned mechanism. Day after day the person will be sending their apprehensions, in the form of information vibrations, out into the information field of the energy of creation.

'I always worry when my daughter goes out with my son-in-law in the car and they don't come back for a long time. I imagine there's been a car crash and they have all been killed ...'

'There's no way I'd be able to cope if I were in that situation ...'

'I'm a terrible worrier as a mother. I'm always scared that something will happen to my children ...'

Worries like this very often lead to the most unpleasant consequences. For, when it comes down to it, the information field will make the 'wishes' of those who love and care for us come true.

## Social Stereotypes and How Our Destiny is Shaped

Certain fixed stereotypes of human behaviour have already been laid down in society. If, for example, a woman isn't constantly preoccupied with her children and worrying about them then, likely as not, she'll be criticized for being a bad mother. If a person isn't forever conjuring up ideas of the worst things that can happen to them, then they are often thought insensitive or complacent. The stereotypes of anxiety and fear are often imposed on us by external sources: for example, television and other mass media.

We worry not just about our loved ones, but also about our health. For many, pain and physical illness conjure up feelings of fear. Is their illness serious? Fear in turn engenders obsessive and disturbed thoughts. What starts as a slight indisposition is followed by unusual symptoms, by which time the person is already painting a picture for themselves of some dreadful disease creeping up on them. And if the condition persists for a long time, it will work on the transmission of information and a serious illness really will develop.

## When Programming Becomes Dangerous

Every minute of the day, we are all programming our own lives. Only, more often than not, this process happens subconsciously. The most dangerous thing in such programming is unconscious anger. 'Damn you!', 'Get lost!', 'Go to hell!' – these are some of the things we say in anger to those close to us, and they sound like a real threat. Such words are particularly dangerous when a mother says them to her children, because the mother and child's information fields are very closely connected. In life, it often happens that unrestrained anger is expressed in the form of driving someone away. And this is often exactly what happens. To be honest, it doesn't happen straight away, or even the next day. It may take six months or even a year before something happens. And when something unpleasant finally does happen, people are often baffled: 'Why did this happen? What for?', forgetting it was they who had brought these events upon themselves in the first place.

## How Negative Energy Affects Us

The energy of creation cannot, in principle, be used to do someone harm, mainly because it is not subject to human control.

In situations where an angry mother curses her naughty child behind its back, the energy will not react in a negative way as a result of this. It will absorb this outburst as a well-intentioned wish. This is because a *mother cannot wish her own child harm – that's one of the fundamental laws of the universe!* The information field, however, is not in a position to distinguish between the desire sent out unconsciously by the mother, in the heat of the moment, and what she really wants. And people aren't well enough acquainted with the way the world in which they live works in order to attach the correct meaning to the words they say on the spur of the moment, without thinking.

*'Dear mothers. Think carefully about the words you use. Control your emotions, whatever the situation. If you still manage to let some swear words slip, you can only take them back by repenting. But your repentance must be genuine and not momentary. If you find this difficult to do on your own, then come to the centre and confess what you have done. If you live abroad and can't do this, write a letter of confession to me, the doctor. And, of course, if you are a religious believer, then go to your church, synagogue or mosque. The important thing is that you sincerely repent what you have done.'*

## People Wishing Harm to Others Only Destroy Themselves

Yes, ordinary people cannot control the energy of creation, but the doctor's patients, especially those who have been attending his centre for a considerable length of time, can draw on some of this energy in their own treatment. (And self-treatment in the home or via link-up sessions is, by the way, based on this phenomenon). Many patients are able to experience the transmission of energy like this, at a distance. There are many good examples of how relatives can come to the clinic in order to alleviate the condition of a seriously ill loved one who is in no condition themselves to come in for treatment.

This raises the question: couldn't somebody in exactly the same way – with the help of the transmission of energy – have a negative effect over another person? Dr Konovalov has a categorical response to this question:

*'A person deliberately setting out to cause harm to another person will only destroy themselves.'*

As I have already stated, the sensitive-body system has a reflecting layer, the purpose of which is to hold back the annihilating energy produced by the cells.

If, during a session, the patient is calm and composed, the energy penetrates their organs, tissues and cells, restoring the sensitive-body system. But if a person forces evil through the body of thought, then the vibration from such a transfer will not correspond with the vibration in the reflecting field. This is something else altogether and, as a result, the person with evil intentions will only soak up the 'evil' vibrations themselves, and this in turn will destroy their sensitive-body system.

A person coming to the centre for the first time, without yet understanding all the intricacies of the process taking place there, is more than capable of carrying evil plans or intentions with them. It's also possible that they have an unconscious desire to cause someone harm. In such cases, contact with the energy of creation will only make their own condition worse. 'Tell me, doctor, why am I not getting better? Why are things so bad for me all the time?' Questions like this are most often asked by such patients. 'Ask yourself why', is the doctor's reply.

Indeed, it's not just the desire to cause someone harm that destroys the human organism. People can, at times, be very impatient. 'There you are, doctor! The woman who's sitting next to me has already got better. Why her and not me? Perhaps you're not paying me as much attention?' Impatience, the habit of always being in a rush for things, does nothing but generate more irritation. And people have grown used to inflicting their irritation on somebody else. How could it be otherwise? They just don't know any different. But the energy of creation doesn't absorb their irritation and transmit it to the information field. Instead, the reflecting layer 'bottles up' the irritation in their sensitive-body system. The result is that they mark time in their treatment, and there's no forward movement.

## 'Start with yourself ...' says the doctor.

But people often don't hear the doctor; they don't understand the meaning of this instruction. All the sick person is aware of is that they are carrying a disease in their body, because the doctors have diagnosed it and because it constantly reminds them of its existence with pain and discomfort. But they don't stop to think about the things they carry in their own psyche – irritation, intransigence, stubbornness, discontent, arrogance, hypocrisy. They don't consider the fact that all of this eats away at them from the inside, eats away not just at their soul but also at their physical health. It's as though the vast powers of the energy of creation, which the doctor is channelling in order to improve the patient's condition and treat their ailments, weren't there at all. It isn't possible to heal the soul in the same way as one would the body, if the person themselves does not really wish for it, if they cannot see, cannot feel. ...

'We shall carry on with our struggle against disease ...' says the doctor. '*Our* struggle'. And that means that passivity in the patient cannot be tolerated. It means that a person needs to fight their illness with as much passion as the doctor does in turning to the universe for help in bringing about their recovery.

We have today learned how to conquer almost every disease known to man. And you too will overcome your own disease if you really want to. But doesn't it sound odd and unfamiliar to hear a doctor telling a patient that it's all down to a matter of how much they want to get better?

*'To love yourself means that you must be ruthless about your own shortcomings and your own laziness.'*

Disease often lies in wait for us in the sharp twists and turns of fate. Something awful has happened; a person goes through a profound upheaval in their life, someone close to them suddenly dies – and the grief can literally tear that person apart. That is, the cells of their body respond negatively to this upheaval. Grief becomes the cause of the person falling ill, and soon that illness will make itself felt.

What should we do in such difficult situations? People can't, after all, insure themselves against every possible thing – all the traumas and misfortunes – that life will throw at them. We're none of us immortal, and sooner or later we're going to lose our loved ones. We need to learn how to get through the grief, so that it doesn't become the cause of illness.

The first thing is to allow yourself to grieve – weeping, either in the company of loved ones or alone. You shouldn't let yourself get in such a state that you're choking on your tears. Do you know how this happens? A person tries to be strong and overestimates their own strength. They suppress their tears; they go to work, get on with things, but all the time they can feel the tears welling up inside and choking them. Tears like this can literally choke you. You mustn't keep them bottled up. You've heard the saying 'It never rains, but it pours'? Many people misinterpret this: they say that if one bad thing happens then others are sure to follow. Nothing of the sort! Open the floodgates and let your tears flow; don't bottle up your grief. Open the gates to your soul as wide as you can, so that all your misfortunes can flow out of you as quickly as possibly.

# CHAPTER 35

# THE BOOKS THAT WILL CHANGE OUR LIVES

## The Constant and the Inconstant

They say that as time moves on everything changes. It's now more than six years since the book *The Energy of Creation* was published, telling readers about the wonderful work being carried out in St Petersburg by Dr Sergey Sergeevich Konovalov. This doesn't seem a very long time; the reader who today opens the first book in the series known as the 'Books That Heal' might get the impression that it's all still happening now, precisely as it did then, and that nothing has changed.

But in fact the only thing that hasn't changed is that Dr Konovalov still comes out on stage, in front of his patients, as he always has; he sits down at the piano, as he has always done, and fills the auditorium with the sound of his captivating music. Just as before, the centre keeps up the fight against disease; and disease, as before, retreats in the face of an onslaught from the energy of creation. But that is all. Having now missed a few treatment programmes (adding up to a year in all), I feel like a student who has fallen behind with their studies (and this despite the fact that during this time I've read all of Sergey Sergeevich's new books). There's a feeling that here, in the hall, everybody has already forged so far ahead that they are somewhere in the future, a future which readers are yet to experience. But don't worry: work is in progress now to have these books translated for the many patients outside Russia who are keen to know more about the doctor's work and practice.

## The Doctor's Books Are the Centre's Textbooks

The possibility of being able to transfer his knowledge to his books has untied the doctor's hands. He now no longer needs to begin every new treatment programme by going through the basics with his patients. Why should he? Every new patient already has a minimum amount of knowledge under their belt, which they've picked up from the first seven books. These have prepared them for the treatment programme and he doesn't need to start from scratch; he's already striving to move along a new path in rhythm with everyone else.

Sergey Sergeevich has become even more skilful in channelling that tremendous power, long since revealed to him, in the way he treats people. Going on some of the things he has not said before (and he has of course already forged further ahead in his acquisition of knowledge – considerably further than even the most industrious of his students) one can see that the doctor's contact with the energy of creation has become even more profound, and that he has now perfected his control of the energy and information fields. He now shares more fully with his patients attending the centre at St Petersburg the revelations made to him during sessions when he is in contact with the energy of creation. And the patients themselves are ready to accept these revelations. There's a feeling that patients have, in a year, graduated from the preparatory stages to being senior students.

The doctor's commitment grows with every day. Letters and questionnaires continue to pour in from all over Russia, and they always contain 'unbelievable' stories of rapid recovery from serious disease. Here are just a few of them.

*From case history A-017981 (born 1962)*
'My dreams have finally come true. My daughter and I have been coming to your wonderful healing sessions. My acquaintance with you dates back to March 2001. The mother of a friend of mine, who comes to sessions, gave me the leaflet. My daughter and I had only just been discharged from hospital. Our whole family has been affected by this particular disease. I bought and avidly read all your books and started doing all the things they recommended. I charged my water and drank only water charged by the leaflet; I put the leaflet against where it hurt; I slept on the leaflet, took part

in link-up sessions; the morning and evening prayers became essential for me. At home there was a leaflet in every room. The whole family sleeps on the leaflet. I'll describe a little of how things have changed since *The Book That Heals* came into my life.

At that time, I was sick with bronchitis and, having read the book, I laid the leaflet on my chest and fell asleep. I was woken by an incredibly strong vibration inside – it was as though something large and powerful was leaping around inside me, that it was shaking and rattling all my insides. I grabbed the leaflet and gradually everything subsided. This happened three nights in a row. It didn't frighten me; on the contrary, I was fascinated by it. I wanted to go on experiencing the feeling, but it didn't happen again. And then something new started happening – I started receiving a charge of energy in my spine. I got into bed at night and my legs would stretch out, one after the other, for five nights in a row. I felt a crunch in the small of my back; my spine was gradually getting back into place and the small of my back stopped hurting. I had a surge of vitality and energy, my legs didn't get tired as easily, the little toe on my left foot straightened out completely, and I began to sleep soundly. Previously, I'd have bad dreams all night, would get up feeling irritable, exhausted, and with a thick head. I was very on edge, short-tempered, always shouting and aggressive, and waves of spitefulness would take hold of me for no good reason. I couldn't do a thing with myself, even though I knew that something awful was happening to me and that I had to stop behaving like this. My husband's a good, kind father, a family man, but my aggressive, domineering behaviour and my bad temper were very hard for him to take. He doesn't like being shouted at, and I'd begun shouting at him for no reason at all. Now I'm so much calmer, confident, easy-going, because I've thought many things over, thanks to your books. I'm convinced there's no turning back.

As for my physical problems, I'm getting good results. Thank you.'

*July 2001, Pskov*

### From case history M-017984 (born 1938)

I first heard and read about you at the beginning of the 1990s, when my husband, who is a real bookworm, brought home a book which talked about you. I read the whole thing and thought: 'it's the usual psychic nonsense' and put it to one side. Now I understand of course that it was a sign from above, only I didn't listen. How many years I lost as a result! However, despite this, higher powers finally brought me to you. In December 2000 my husband got hold of another of your books. It was the first one, *The Book That Heals. The Energy of Creation. A Doctor's Story*. I started reading it and couldn't put it down. I knew it was for me. I accepted everything it said immediately, without question. My husband and I now eagerly look forward to each of your new books.

We've read and re-read them several times and every time we do so we discover something new. There's such a wealth of information in your books. And now our 22-year-old daughter has joined us as well.

I want to let you know the results of our external treatment sessions. I began taking part in them on 20 December 2000. I followed all your instructions to the letter. Morning and evening I did my energizing exercises *without fail* (I've only missed two in all this time), and on Sundays my husband and I took part in the basic link-up sessions. Since reading your book *Overcoming the Ageing Process,* in which you write that people can take part in the link-up healing sessions not just on Sundays but every day, my husband and I have changed our routine: one day we do the energizing exercises, and on the following one we do the exercises in the morning and in the evening we take part in the link-up session. I keep your leaflet around my waist all the time; I sleep on the leaflets, which I put under the mattress, and, of course, I drink the charged water regularly.

Right from the beginning of the link-up session, as I'm starting to get into the mood, I put on some music. I start getting a pleasant feeling of warmth in my feet which spreads up my legs (I'm getting the same sensation now, as I write this). I have a particularly strong sense of the energy between the palms of my hands, and also when I am channelling it.

*Results of my external treatment:*

- The pains in my right hip joint have completely gone. I can sleep on my right side without experiencing any pain. Before, I could only sleep on my back, and my spine and joints would ache when I did.
- All the pain I had in both shoulders has gone.
- The pain in my left hip joint (where I had the worst problem) has lessened by 50 per cent and the pains in the lumbar-sacral area of the spinal column have also lessened.

All of this happened in the space of seven months. I arrived in St Petersburg with these results and on 23 July I came to your sessions at the hall for the first time. I had dreamed of this for such a long time, having listened to my husband and daughter talking about it after they'd attended a treatment programme in May–June 2001. So everything in the hall seemed comforting and familiar. During the very first healing session, the pain in my left hip joint went away, and in the morning my hip didn't 'pop' (it usually made a popping noise whenever I walked).

Dear doctor, I can now sleep on my left side, but before I was always waking up with the pain. I can keep up with my daughter now, when we walk round St Petersburg. But only two weeks previously I wouldn't have been able to entertain such an idea. Thank you, dear doctor.

And now a word about your beautiful music. I love music very much, especially classical. My generation was, of course, brought up on the classics. And now, once more, as I did when I was young, I'm listening to these beautiful sounds, and the tears pour from my eyes and my soul is reborn. Take me to you and bless me.'

*4 August, 2001, Moscow*

### From case history M-018003 (born 1985)

I'm writing to you with all my heart and soul. I am fifteen and will soon be sixteen. I want to thank you for your wonderful work, that is, for your books which open up a new and beautiful world for people. After reading these books you want to somehow start living your life differently.

As soon as I opened your book and started reading the first lines, I felt extraordinarily uplifted. I felt I was a self-sufficient person who could take on anything. My hang-ups disappeared and I had this feeling, as though you were shining a light from inside of me and my life seemed entirely transformed and the people around me were different. I've very rarely experienced such a feeling in my life – this feeling of being content with everything. And now I don't even want to talk about the bad things that have happened in my life. I've been through a lot, but I now no longer have the feelings of depression and loss that I had before, and I've even forgotten about all the bad things. I want to thank you for bringing my grandmother back to life. She was literally dying, but now she runs to your healing session, whereas before my mum literally had to carry her.

When I began to take part externally, I immediately noticed improvements, particularly in my emotional state. There were some big improvements at school – they changed my teacher. The problems I'd had with my digestive tract went away; the heartburn went, and so on. I'm very grateful to you for taking the time to listen.'

*July 2001, Moscow*

### From case history A-018005 (born 1938)
'I want to tell you how I became acquainted with your books. Some friends in our literary society who were trying to reach an understanding of the world and the cosmos gave me your first book A Doctor's Story to read. We have accepted it unconditionally. Believing you and your every word, we have, as you have advised, absorbed every single word. If only you knew the joy we have had from reading this book. It's as though our souls have been bathed in healing balm. We have many books, and my son-in-law's always buying something new and interesting, but this knowledge offers a new approach to healing and an understanding of the human organism as a single entity, and it's the first time that we've become aware of the consequences that follow on from it. What is there today that can be compared with the power of the living, divine energy of creation? And, of course, all of this knowledge is so new and stunning and awe-inspiring. One never ceases to be amazed and inspired by your unique gift. I never cease to thank God for sending you to us sinners as his envoy, his chosen one, a person who loves us so much that you have taken our pain upon yourself. I see you as being like Atlantis, who carries all the pain of humanity on his shoulders, and not just that, but as someone who also heals humanity of its pain and suffering, making us into new people.

At that time we still couldn't buy your books in Ulyanovsk. But very soon (because we prayed about it) my son-in-law had the chance of going to Petersburg and bought all your books there. So now we have all of them. And so we started studying them and doing the exercises, morning and evening. I found I had so much energy, more even than when I was young. It was as though my strength had increased tenfold, despite the frailness of my body.

Doing your exercises I gained a love of life, joy, and the desire to help other people experience the same joy as mine. My bowels became regular and other illnesses began to bother me less.

At home we organized a club and called it "The Path to Health". We help people find themselves, find their faith, and we study your books with them. My daughter wrote a wonderful article in the magazine *Health* about your unique gift, about the energy of creation, so that more people in our town should know about you and try to follow this path. ...

What you do is to heal people who are utterly without hope of recovery from their incurable diseases. But you do more than that; you cleanse their souls, and return them to life as entirely different people, with different inner qualities and with an understanding of the laws of being, God's laws. Such a triumph has no equal. With love and respect ...'

*July 2001, Ulyanovsk*

## 'Living Books' Which Are Hard to Live Without

*From case history A-018007 (born 1947)*
'My daughter brought me the living books and I straight away took them to heart. I have come to trust you, dear doctor, and believe in the power which you are able to direct and use to help sick people not only regain their health but also heal their souls. Having started to read your books, I cannot live without them. I've read and re-read them, not understanding much the first time I did so. Having only just discovered them, when I was first reading them it was as though some unknown force was taking hold of me: I was in such a state of bliss. But at the same time, the sick organs in my body were hurting. Your books, Sergey Sergeevich, have become the books of my life. They are like the air, without which there'd be no life on this blue planet. And I've now begun to do the energizing exercises in the mornings and evenings and to charge water with the leaflet, never forgetting to dab water on the places that hurt. Soon the process was being continued with God's help, yours, dear doctor, and the energy of creation. I had more life in me, became more energetic, better able to work, calmer, my body felt easier. I can walk normally, just like everyone else. I don't have any pains round my heart. They did a cardiogram and the doctor said that I don't have coronary

315

heart disease any more. And I can sense this myself – I don't take the tablets, and I couldn't get through a day without them before. The pains in the sacrum area of my spine have gone. And yet, going up the slightest incline, or doing my housework, the pain had been intolerable, especially on the right side. I seem to have acquired flexibility in my spine.

After my operation, the stitches began to hurt. They were pulling. But now I hardly notice them. The middle toe on my right foot has straightened.

My feet have become nice and smooth, but, as I remember, they used to be rough even though I was always rubbing cream on them. My heels were so cracked they bled. The things I didn't do to make them better! Now they're pink, soft and no longer dry. The wart on my right hand has shrivelled and fallen off. So there's the run-down on my 32 Sunday link-up healing sessions. How can anyone not believe you, doctor?

There are no words to express how grateful I am to you. I thank the Good Lord for sending you to save our souls. With respect and love …'

*7 August 2001, Odessa, Ukraine*

### From case history 1018011 (born 1934)
'I've been suffering from radiculitis for twenty years. I fell ill in October 2000 and was in hospital for three months. I was in such pain for a whole month that I cried. I couldn't walk, or lie or even sit – the pain was so dreadful. All I could do was crawl along on my knees. The doctors made house calls, and nurses who did pain management gave me injections, but the pain wouldn't go. One day my neighbour looked in and brought your leaflet, and I put it against my back. I kept it there for two days and then my husband bought another three. To my amazement, on the third day the pain vanished.

Thank you very much; even your books can heal. With respect.'

*July 2001, St Petersburg*

### From case history A-018012 (born 1941)
'It's now already a year since I first discovered your books and, not long after that, your leaflet. For six years I'd been in pain with a dislocation of the left knee. Sudden movements would make the pain worse and the leg would

swell. I began tying the leaflets to my leg and bathing it in your water and the leg got better. On top of that, my duodenal ulcer hasn't troubled me for a year, my liver too. The heartburn's gone, and the burning under my right ribcage. My fingers have straightened out.

There's a lot of other things that have got better too. I'm very grateful to you and to the Good Lord.'

*August 2001, Lebyazhe, in the Lomonosov region of Leningrad province.*

### From case history 1018014 (born 1930)
'I have a pet parrot which is seven years old. He talks. Something miraculous happened to him. The vet had said he had cancer and wouldn't last more than another month. This was in December last year. My friends bought some leaflets and books for me at one of the healing sessions, and I started treating my parrot with them. I gave him water to drink that had been charged with the leaflet, and put another leaflet in his cage. And what do you think? In two weeks my Kira began showing signs of life and on the following day he was talking away and flying around cheerfully, just as he did the first year of his life.

Take care of yourself, Sergey Sergeevich, we need you.'

*July 2001, St Petersburg*

### From case history A-018015 (born 1938)
'My sister sent me your leaflet and book.

I read your book over a six month period and charged my water and did the exercises. Dear Sergey Sergeevich, I noticed I became calmer after reading your book and doing the exercises; my irritability disappeared. I had a weak throat, and couldn't eat or drink anything cold or my angina would straight away come back, and I'd regularly get colds. Then suddenly I realized that when I ate something straight from the fridge my throat didn't hurt. I've forgotten all about colds and I'm hardly bothered by indigestion.

A huge thank you to you, Sergey Sergeevich, for your gift and your kind heart.'

*July 2001, Murmansk*

*From case history 1018016 (born 1940)*

'I found out about you a while back – four years ago – but I didn't have any particular problems then. It was one particular misfortune that made me place my unconditional trust in you. In December 2000 my grandson fell ill (he was about five then). He was rushed to hospital by ambulance with "severe appendicitis". The doctors at the hospital weren't able to confirm this diagnosis and they couldn't take the pain away. We didn't sleep for ten nights: my grandson was crying with pain, and the doctors were helpless and could only inject him with pain-relieving drugs. On the tenth day someone brought your *Book That Heals the Digestive Organs* to me at the clinic. In the evening, I placed the book near my grandson and, for the first time, we both slept through most of the night. After this he wouldn't be separated from the booklet and drank your water. Three days later they finally gave us a diagnosis: "pseudotuberculosis".

But the pain had stopped and a week later we were discharged. Now, thanks to you and to God, he is healthy. After this happened, I started buying and reading all your books. Thank you very much for them, and for your hard work!

I came to my first lesson with you on 24 July. Thank you! The lesson flew by, and seemed to last only 15–20 minutes.

My overriding sensation has been one of calm, goodness and of a radiating power. With respect.'

*July 2001, St Petersburg*

*From case history 1018017 (born 1955)*

'A year and a half ago I fell down the stairs on my back. Exactly a year later the pain had become so bad that that I was climbing the wall with it. A growth began developing, in the shape of two lumps which kept getting bigger. This was accompanied by terrible pain in my legs. I didn't yet know that these were bony spurs. In the morning I would literally crawl out of bed and my torment would last from six in the morning till ten at night. And then came that long-awaited day when God helped put an end to my suffering.

I was on my way home from work; my legs took me into a bookshop, where my arm reached out and picked up your book.

This was your sixth one, about the spine. I'd never heard of you before and didn't pay any attention to the fact that it was not the first book. I bought it and started treating myself. I bought the other booklets and all the books, but I didn't read them all in one go, like some people do, but spent from February till June. They healed me at a stroke. I'd often fall asleep with the book in my hand. I tied the leaflet above my waist, where the damage had been done, and slept on three more of them. I charged the water on the leaflet and drank it. By June the growths on my spine had begun to go away. And the pain in my spine died down, so I almost forgot about it. When I first discovered your book, I hadn't had a period for three months. I started reading it, and two weeks later my periods started again and now they're regular. Thank you for your books.'

*July 2001, St Petersburg*

There are thousands of letters like this, a flood of them that is growing all the time. Sergey Sergeevich is already prepared for the fact that the number of his patients (both at live sessions and the link-up ones) will keep on increasing, day by day. He is ready, without hesitation, to take the whole world in his embrace. He doesn't worry about how difficult this will be for him personally, as a man, or how it will be for his loved ones, but is fully aware of all the burdens he will have to bear on the path to ordination, a path along which every step is an act of creation, of goodness and light.

# CHAPTER 36

# PATIENTS FROM ALL OVER THE WORLD

## The Energy Knows and Understands Each of Us

It goes without saying that Dr Konovalov's Human Rehabilitation Centre in St Petersburg is not able to take everybody who wants to attend sessions there, even though their numbers are growing with every year and will continue to do so. But those who cannot attend should not be discouraged, for every one of us can come into contact with and benefit from the energy of creation – through the doctor's books and by means of their healing energy. This why it is up to each of us to establish a solid, long-lasting contact with the energy of creation and to do it in such a way that there is no power on earth that can break that bonds that binds us to it.

*From case history 1018021 (born 1957)*
'This is the first time I've written to you. I couldn't bring myself to do it before. Yesterday I completed my first treatment programme. Unfortunately I don't have enough tickets for the next programme, but I'm not that upset because I shall definitely try to get to the hall again some time.

I use the word "hall" because I feel as though the doors to the temple of the creator have been opened, just a little, to me. I have always had a vague feeling that some great force of love, righteousness and purity was leading me through life, protecting me and giving me strength. Thank you for opening up the energy of creation to mankind. I want to learn, together with you and your students (not patients), how to consciously become part on the divine universe and how to make conscientious and careful use of this gift we call life.

Please accept me as one of your followers and bless me on the Path to Understanding and Insight! For I now realize that you are leading us to the true faith.

I'm not going to write about my illnesses today. Too little time has passed since that moment in May this year when, quite out of the blue, I suddenly bought your book. I opened it and straight away wanted to come to you, especially as I'd been hearing, since 1994, about the wonders that you work. People had been advising me to turn to you, as I live only ten-minutes' walk from your treatment halls. I can't say I was sceptical about any of it; no I wasn't. I don't know how to explain it but I thought my turn had come and I saw the light. A power I didn't understand led me – me, a woman who by nature is complacent and self-sufficient – and it made me stand in line to buy tickets. And I wasn't even surprised when I managed to buy a subscription, because I could already feel the faith inside me, could sense the presence of the energy of creation.

I believe that I'm becoming healthy and full of strength despite my age. I believe I'm becoming a happier mother and will bring up good, healthy, capable children. I believe that my husband and our mothers will help our children rear their children and grandchildren. I believe that, with your help, the human race will become both spiritually and physically healthy. Let it be! With respect and love ...'

*23 August 2001, St Petersburg*

## Contact with the Energy of Creation Comes to You Through This Book

The energy of creation cannot be resorted to like medication or some fashionable type of treatment; that is, you can't make use of it as a one-off, for some specific personal need or other (to recover from illness, or make your life better, etc.) and then simply forget all about it and carry on living as though you'd never encountered it. No. A single encounter with the energy such as this will not make further development or recovery from illness possible. And if by chance some of your ailments go away then the future preservation of your health will become problematic. All you can do, once having come into contact with the energy, is to obey its laws and not stray from the chosen path, making sure of your every step by means of the truth revealed to you.

Having already spent one year as an external patient, I can say with all certainty that this form of treatment, and contact with the energy and, of course, with the doctor too, can bring almost the same results as coming to the centre in person. The only precondition is that you must make Dr Konovalov's information-energy theory the basis of your own world outlook, and the practice of interaction with the energy (by means of the leaflet, the charged water, the energizing exercises and mental appeals to the doctor) a fundamental part of your everyday life.

Mastering and accepting this practice couldn't be simpler. All the more so as the majority of external patients have found their way to the centre (including some of those who now write about it in books) not believing in miracles, but drawn there by personal contact with the energy of creation. A reader's contact with it comes when they first take up the book, for it plunges them immediately into the information field with which they have not been familiar till then. From these very first moments the energy reveals its healing powers. Here are some letters from external patients who experienced contact with the energy of creation whilst they were reading the book:

'As I was reading the book, I felt as though something was being poured all over me,' writes an external patient from Sochi, on the Black Sea. 'I had this sort of jittery feeling, which I hadn't experienced for a long time. And almost immediately afterwards ... tests showed the total absence of any gynaecological complaints.'

'I started reading and fell asleep, because, for the first time, the pain which had been tormenting me for years, went away' (there are hundreds of letters like this).

'I put some water to be charged before I'd even finished reading the book. Three days later I felt an incredible sense of relief' (a seventy-year-old man who had suffered a stroke).

Another group of external patients includes people who have linked up with the information fields of the energy 'from a distance', as it were:

'I don't know why I went into the bookshop. I never usually read or buy books like that. But I saw your book and straight away knew why I had come in'.

'I've always been interested in books about alternative medicine. And that day, as usual, I bought five or six of them. I took one of them and went up to the second floor to have a read of it. But then I felt as though something was telling me to go back downstairs. I went down, and immediately pulled out your book *A Doctor's Story* from the pile.'

A third category of external patients can be described with the same kind of words repeated in thousands of letters:

'I finally found what I had been searching for all my life.'

'I have taken up Sergey Sergeevich's teachings with all my heart. I have literally been waiting all my life for this.'

'At long last we have found our true doctor.'

For all these people, the appearance of this unique doctor was more a matter of joy than any great surprise. For they had been searching for him; they had had an intuition that there might be such a person. They hoped for it, or perhaps only dreamed about it, and now enjoyed a huge sense of satisfaction that their hopes and dreams had come true. To tell the truth, I myself belong to this category of patients. I too had always felt that a man such as Sergey Sergeevich simply had to exist. But the most unexpected and unbelievable thing, and one that brought me great joy, was that such a person really is among us today. For we could so easily have passed each other by.

The overriding wish of many of the doctor's patients is that his teachings will become more widely known.

### From case history 1018022 (born 1941)

'If you would like some interesting observations from one of your patients, then I'd like to have that honour. ...

Today I went to one of the doctor's ordinary sessions (this is my first treatment programme). The session began ... As I see it, this is absolutely the ideal approach, both in meaning (content) as well as in the way it's conducted and the rationale behind it. On top of that, there's an excellent way with words and language. As I was listening, I became more and more caught up in it. I do wish that public appearances such as these could be held in a larger auditorium and on the radio and television.

I know not many young people will pay attention to such discourses, although more mature ones might, and I know a few who would. The vast majority of young people base the way they look at the world on stupid films and moronic songs which only fill their heads with every kind of rubbish and totally false ideas. I realize that they sometimes have a real, physical need for the rhythm of music, but there's no one capable of writing intelligent lyrics.

Why not try and exert some influence over youngsters (or maybe not just the young ones) by means of the things they're interested in – songs – and fill their heads not with rubbish but with a proper way of looking at the world.

If the doctor were to set out his basic tenets in verse form, they could be set to music, and who knows what might happen.

With deep respect. I consider myself to be healthy and happy and I'd like to see more people being happy.'

*22 August 2001, St Petersburg*

# How People in St Petersburg Find Out About Dr Konovalov via America

There are, of course, very few books about the doctor in comparison with the millions of people in Russia. There needs to be more of them and there certainly will be. But meanwhile, we can only be gratified by how news about Dr Konovalov's work is spreading. 'A friend of mine wrote to me from America,' writes a lady from Moscow, 'telling me how we in Russia now had some wonderful books about a doctor S. S. Konovalov. She'd heard about this on the television.' It's good to hear, even from an American, about our own, native-born doctor.

Sergey Sergeevich is now beginning to be known all over the world. And not just as a scientist – thanks to his appearances at international symposiums – or by his scientific work and lectures. He is known primarily as a doctor.

*Telex 2000, 30 June 2001*
'I want to share my great joy with you and say a huge thank you to you.

On 15 April, on holy Easter Monday, a little hero (4 kilos 270 grammes [9lbs 7 oz.]) was born here in Iceland. He was born thanks to you and your knowledge, your goodness and love for people. I don't know the right words to express my gratitude, good fortune and joy.

I am 38 years old. For the past three years I've heard nothing but people telling me you have to have children at an earlier age; that at my age I'd need an operation. And then in July this year I happened to come to one of your healing sessions and wrote down my major desire – a child. I knew and understood nothing at the time. It was just a hope. This is why I only wrote about my own, female, problems, not having the slightest idea that there are many illnesses but only one cause.

Having now read your books, I know that all my problems began with an injury to the lumbar region of my spine four years ago. It was right after this that the problems started building up: ovarian cysts, endometriosis, myoma, asthmatic bronchitis. And that's without mentioning the mastopathy, or the pain in my pancreas, the osteochondrosis in the vertebrae of my neck and chest, or the aching joints, the chronic inflammation of the ears, and fungal infections of my feet.

The most interesting and amazing thing, Sergey Sergeevich, is that all my aches and pains disappeared during the fourth month of my pregnancy, although I hadn't been making a note of it and wasn't worrying. I only had pain low down, below my stomach and it continued all through my pregnancy. I don't think I'd have been able to carry my child to term if I hadn't had your leaflets, books and exercises. All the same, we were lucky ... My little Sergey is already nearly two months old. He is a happy, smiling baby and gurgles away – you can make him smile whenever he's not busy eating or sleeping. Everything's fine for us, really wonderful. I'm going to continue my external treatment with you, together with my husband and older daughter.

I'd like to tell you about another interesting phenomenon. When I was pregnant, I often used the leaflet at night; either my stomach was hurting or I was plagued with heartburn, or something else. Whenever I picked up the leaflet, it would glow in the dark, where it came into contact with my fingers. I don't know if this still happens now, because the sun is still out during the night – it's the polar day here. There's nothing about this in any of the books and I'd be interested to know what it is exactly. Maybe I'll find the answer in the books to come.

Sergey Sergeevich, thank you so much for my children; thank you for your love and kindness and the way you help people, thank you for sharing with us the knowledge given to you from on high. With deep respect and humility.'
*Iceland*

# How External Patients Respond to Treatment

It's easy to tell, just from looking at their letters, who among the external patients have really understood and wholeheartedly accepted Dr Konovalov's teachings. They are those who've already started their own external treatment and take part in the link-up sessions, using the leaflet and working with the energy of creation. As a rule, they soon get positive results and write to the doctor telling him about them. Take one woman from deep in the heart of Russia who writes that she's never parted from her leaflet. She tells how once, when she was staying at her country cottage, she burnt her hand; because she didn't have the leaflet with her, she simply imagined that the water she used was specially charged and dabbed it on the burn. The pain went and it didn't blister. Nobody taught her to do this; she simply had an instinct about how to help herself.

Many people write and say that they haven't decided to take part in treatment and offer various reasons why: 'I didn't want to spoil the book by cutting the leaflet out of it', 'I'd like to send away for the actual leaflets patients use during healing sessions', and so on. Others complain that they've 'already taken part in two whole treatment programmes' and haven't noticed any results. And there are even those who, having had a superficial skim through one book, bombard Dr Konovalov with letters and questions, instead of taking a closer look at the text, taking things in properly and reading the other books, which between them give the answers to these questions. These people aren't the doctor's true patients, nor are they good readers either. But even they still have a chance.

*From case history 1017415 (born 1994)*
I've written to you about how my grandson had an operation for an astrocytoma on the spinal cord. In December 2000, I described the methods we were using to help him recover, based on your teachings about the information-energy. His MRI scan on 23 January 2001 showed an improvement; in fact, the tumour had stopped growing and the sacs of fluid above and below it had gone down.

The MRI on 23 April 2001 shows there is no deterioration. My daughter can now do the exercises herself and works with the leaflets.

May you stay healthy and full of strength! May hope and goodness shine forth from you. Thank you.'

*29 May 2001, St Petersburg*

**From case history A-017987 (born 1946)**
'I cannot describe the moment of happiness and delight when, for the first time, I was given your first book to read. This encounter happened on 27 October 2000. Knowing the very serious state of my health, the mother of one of my students (I'm a paediatrician) recommended I read it, with the words: "Maybe this is what you've been searching for. I think it will help you." And a miracle happened! At ten o'clock in the evening I was going home on the train and I read it, or rather, tried to read it all and understand, really get to the heart, of what was written in it. (At that time I read little, couldn't concentrate on things, I was in a terrible state. In 1997 my son had died of myocarditis and I've had no life since then. I'd been examined by Dr Weisman, who had diagnosed 16 conditions.)

I started sleeping on the leaflets at night, drinking the charged water and putting the leaflets against my body, and this was my salvation and joy. I felt, with all my heart and soul, that this was mine, the thing I've been waiting for, searching for, for so long, and the next morning – you won't believe it, dear Sergey Sergeevich – I went to the toilet, to answer the call of nature, *all by myself.* I couldn't explain it to myself, or understand why at long last this had happened. My joy knew no bounds, and this was after three years of intestinal inactivity (massage of the stomach and muscles, baths, special diets, and all without results). I was able to establish a daily routine between 10 and 11.30 a.m. What joy! Then I came to you and I'm now on my fifth treatment programme and want this to make you happy too. For the first time in 25 years my urine samples are normal. The doctor couldn't believe it and looked at me and then the results twice! My blood is fine, the stone in my left kidney has gone down by a third. This is wonderful! The cramps in my legs have practically stopped. I can now see better, my head's clearer. I'm recovering my ability to concentrate and with it the desire to grasp and comprehend things.

I'm thankful to destiny and to the Lord for giving me the chance to meet you, for the energy of creation, which has given me the strength and ability to live, work, teach and communicate with my beloved students. It's given me the strength and the desire to recover my health, my youthfulness of spirit and to become better, purer and more spiritual.

With sincere respect.'

*4 August 2001, St Petersburg*

*From case history M-018001 (born 1961)*
'About a year ago, when I was going through a bad patch in my life, your *Book That Heals Women's Ailments* caught my eye in a bookshop. I started looking through it and realized that this was a book that could give me the answers to my questions, a book I had long been waiting for. When I'd read it, I went to look for all your other books and bought them. I began doing the energizing exercises and took part in the link-up sessions on Sundays. Your books helped me recover my spiritual equilibrium and reading them became a necessity. They are written with love and convey such spiritual peace, filling one's heart with goodness. And, gradually, my physical problems began to recede under this influence. I've had problems with my ears, especially at night-time when I couldn't sleep from the pain. I'd been to the doctor's; he said he couldn't see what was making them hurt. Whatever I took for it, it didn't last long. And then, after a month of external treatment, my digestive tract began working better. My heart was beating more calmly. I had a lot of cysts in my breast when I started the external treatment. Before going to a live healing session, I had an ultrasound and the doctor said the cysts had gone. I'd had two myomas, but only one was left.

Your music is so wonderful, Sergey Sergeevich; it fills my soul with the light of love and tenderness.'

*31 July 2001, Moscow*

## Liberating Ourselves from Disease with the Help of Dr Konovalov's Books

As I write this it's not long since the summer treatment programme ended. It was different from the others, in that it was attended by many external patients from all over the country, as well as abroad. At one of the sessions, Sergey Sergeevich invited all those who had first treated themselves with the books and who, by the time they'd come to him, were already enjoying a good level of recovery, to come up onto the stage. It's a day that will be hard to forget for everyone who was there in the hall. We were all profoundly moved by what we heard and witnessed. A young woman, the mother of four, had been hostage to a terrible, incurable disease for nine years. She had flown in from Canada in the hope of a miracle, because conventional medicine had been powerless to help her condition. And a miracle had happened. She was released from the clutches of the disease. The books, as well as some healing sessions (that is, a few hours-worth) with the doctor had produced stunning results.

Another patient, from the Moscow suburbs, told how she had turned to the books as a last resort. She had cancer. The doctors had told her she'd be lucky to survive another two weeks. It was then that she began reading Dr Konovalov's books and since then she's had considerably longer than two weeks – or even two months – and what is more she managed to come by herself to see the doctor. In June 2001 the disease was in remission. (In November 2001 the patient was in the recovery stage.)

A middle-aged woman living in Leningrad province told how, not long before, she had been having great difficulty in walking even to the nearest shop. She'd cried with the pain and with thinking about the future: she lived with her little granddaughter and there was no one to help them. Her neighbour had told her all about a 'Dr Konovalov who cures all diseases'. She also told her that the doctor held link-up sessions every week from 9 to 9.30 pm. on Sunday evenings. And, knowing nothing more about the doctor, or yet having read his book (she got hold of it and read it much later on) or having the least ideas about the treatment or how long it took, this woman firmly ordered her granddaughter to sit quietly on Sunday, and at 9 p.m. she'd lie down on her bed and watch the minutes tick by. She didn't know about any of the energizing exercises and did everything wrong (Dr Konovalov recommends that you relax and don't place too much emphasis on the time), but there was a prayer she carried deep inside her: 'Please help me, doctor!' And suddenly, 'there was this light that started shining in front of my eyes,' the woman tells us, 'but I don't know what happened after that.' The second session went pretty much the same, and then the 'visions' disappeared. All she had was a sensation of lightness. Not very long after, she was already managing to get to the shop quite easily. What more is there to say? Now she can get into town and attend the healing sessions on her own. She looks after the other elderly people who can hardly walk and feels half her age; she's full of strength, having forgotten that she herself also once walked like that.

## Greeting the Future with Love

*Healing the Soul* is the name of Dr Konovalov's latest book. And the same title was used for the summer 2001 treatment programme that coincided with its publication in Russia, Germany and Latvia. Even the most masculine of men could not hold back the tears – the tears that cleanse the soul and which poured forth like a river during this programme – as people listened to patients tell their stories, their hearts beating in one rhythm. Even Sergey Sergeevich remarked, at the end of the programme, that he couldn't remember one when the tears had so often come to his own eyes. When a person's heart opens itself wide, in a welcoming fashion, to the heart of another, when there is absolute sincerity, and when the purity of intentions reach out across the world, then the soul is healed, which means that that person will without question be released from the bondage of all their illnesses.

In conclusion, I'd like to quote some lines from a letter written by a woman on a train travelling from Moscow right across Russia. The author's first name is Lyubov (meaning 'love' in Russian), and she writes about love. The letter closes thus:

'I feel it; I know in my heart that you are my teacher. I am grateful that there is someone like you here in the world. *I love you with all my heart and soul. I love you, doctor, and I want you to be aware of my feelings of unbounded love as well.* At this very moment I love all the passengers in my carriage too, for I work as an attendant. (To tell the truth, it's probably not quite love, but I'm learning.) I want them to be healed too, with the help of God's great love.'

Today, Dr Konovalov's teachings are not unlike this train as it hurtles along, from one end of Russia to the other, carrying to people everywhere *love, hope, health and faith.* Those whose hearts have been touched by the wave of heat emanating from the energy of creation already carry the reflection of this love within themselves and, with it, the hope of recovery for all their loved ones, friends – and even those they don't know – throughout the country and across the whole planet. And there are more and more of them with every day.

If, on the difficult path of your own struggle against disease, against evil and your own shortcomings, if at some point you find it hard to move ahead, then remember that you are not alone. Think of that train full of love speeding across the country, and remember how many there are of us already! And then boldly carry on, because this world – where the doctor loves his patients, the train conductor loves his passengers, the teacher his students, and so on – this world is real. It is within our powers to create it and live in it. And only this world – where love and the energy of creation reign supreme – is truly beautiful.

# CHAPTER 37

# THE MAN AT THE CENTRE OF A WHOLE NEW WORLD OUTLOOK

Let us try once more to fathom the phenomenon that is Dr Sergey Konovalov. He has held out the hand of hope and support to millions of people, has returned them to health and given meaning and joy to their lives. For 14 years now he has been following a difficult path, a path that has taken him away from conventional medicine and towards a healing power without equal and whose name will soon be known worldwide. It is now extremely difficult to get into his healing sessions without booking well in advance. But, thanks to the books and the specially charged leaflets which can be found in them, it has become possible for people to treat themselves at home, in whatever corner of the world they find themselves.

Today Dr Sergey Sergeevich Konovalov is offering us not just the chance of recovery but also of getting rid of our pain and misfortunes for good. This is a man who is opening up for us a whole new way of looking at the world, a world which encompasses all of life's most important aspects: science, medicine, philosophy, morality and even faith. But by faith, I don't mean a religion, but a whole new way of looking at the world, with the human being, the universe's highest creation, at its centre. For the human being is a body and information field linked, as one organism, with the universe and its information-energy fields.

## Showing Our Gratitude to the Energy of Creation

When a person is overcome with grief and pain they often automatically turn their gaze upwards and ask 'Why is this happening to me?' They forget that they were once a convinced atheist and that they didn't believe in God.

And yet, quite suddenly, here they are, being presented in the most amazing fashion with the chance of being freed from suffering and of being well again. And what happens next? Do they then ask 'Why am I being given this chance?' I doubt it. But it's still the most important question and it's one they should be asking. What was the purpose of us being given the chance to regain our health, to feel the might of the universe and the limitless reserves of our own organism? Is it really only in order that, having recovered our health, we immediately go back to our old way of life, the one that had brought us to the edge of the abyss? Is it only that we should once more fall back down into the chasm of moral insensibility? If so, why?

Everyone who has experienced the amazing power of the energy of creation at first hand is quick to thank Dr Konovalov for making them well. And, of course, if there were no Sergey Sergeevich then there'd be nothing to say on the matter. There's no doubt he makes a personal investment in the recovery of hundreds of thousands of people. And although not everybody does this, many people also thank themselves and their own body. Dr Konovalov advises people to do just this at healing sessions, for it plays a significant part in the recovery process.

One might also go so far as to thank the energy of creation – that power which turns out to be a direct participant in the healing process. Only how can you show your gratitude? You can't give it flowers, like you can the doctor; you can't show it the care and attention you show your own body. So how exactly does one show 'gratitude' to the energy of creation? One does so by following the higher laws of the universe, the laws of the energy-information theory, and respecting the need for harmony in the construction of our world. These laws put us to the test from the very beginning: how we encounter the energy of creation; how we relate to the doctor; whether we are able to heed the voice of the universe; whether we are responsive to a new world outlook that is different from the one so far imposed on our everyday lives. They test us by offering several different paths. It's possible for us to get treated quickly and then just carry on with our descent into the abyss of moral insensibility and sickness. But it's also possible for us to change the present order of things.

## Humanity at the Crossroads: We Must Decide Its Future

The time has come when we can see the future of humanity mapped out all too clearly before us: AIDS, international terrorism, organized crime, murder and the worldwide rule of violence; global warming and the destruction of the environment – all of these things could quickly bring about the destruction of our planet. This is why the universe is calling out to us and trying to bring mankind to its senses. And Dr Konovalov is its mouthpiece, a man possessed of the ability to make contact with its powers. He's a real-life person, who lives in St Petersburg, where he works real-life miracles. He is a man of penetrating vision, with the most wonderful, enigmatic, kind brown eyes, who is always surrounded by an atmosphere of calm. You can physically sense the power that emanates from him.

The doctor's energy-information theory has been repeatedly endorsed in practice. But if we don't stop and ask ourselves why he is here, among us, today, then tomorrow it may already be too late. Dr Konovalov is here among us not so that we can run to him for help as we would to our local doctor, preoccupied only with the way we feel today and in ignorance of the presence of the universe and what it can do for us. He is here so that we should at last hear the real voice of the universe, its warnings, the things it demands of us, and that we should also feel its love. Are we ready for this?

## Begin Your Next Day with the Energy of Creation

If we really are ready, then let's begin our next day with the energy of creation as we strive to attain the health of the body and the purity of the mind. For the book that you have been reading is not just a bearer of good news, of news about the power which can save us and our children, and which gives us a chance to change our lives for good. It is there first and foremost to lead us into action, to the path which we must take without delay, having first equipped ourselves with this new science, philosophy and faith.

I know that as you read this book you will become caught up in the wonderful world of the energy of creation. Maybe some among you are already celebrating having come into direct contact with the energy as you've been reading. But, equally, I also know that, having finished the book, many of you will return to your normal life, in which there is so much pain and so many tears, such solitude and lack of warmth. You'll go out on to the street, where bad behaviour prevails; you'll turn on your television and be swamped in a torrent of depressing news. And you'll say to yourself: 'What can I do? I'm only a speck in this vast world. Everywhere around me there is injustice and dishonesty, violence, bad behaviour, bureaucracy, drunkenness and depravity. This is how it was before I was born and how it will be after I'm dead. It's been the same from century to century. What difference can I make on my own?'

## You Are Not Alone!

The best thing you can do is remember at such moments what Dr Konovalov says:

*'Start with yourself! Start today, right now. Don't wait until the world falls apart and buries you in its debris.'*

If things turn out right for you, you'll remain a small island of hope in this world. And you're not alone – just remember that. There are many of us. The 'Books That Heal' have millions of readers. Even if not all of them, but only a small proportion of those strongest in spirit and ready to listen to the voice of the universe, were to listen to what the universe has so say, then there would be many more of us. Try to feel it! During your own regular evening self-treatment session, wherever you may find yourself – on another continent, in another country – listen carefully and you will hear the breathing of *hundreds of thousands of us* – those of us who have heard the call of the universe; you'll hear our hearts beating as we strive for health and happiness for ourselves and our children. It will give you courage and the confidence to carry on along the difficult path that you have now chosen. There are many of us and we are with you. And all of us want to make the world a better place to live in.

## You Can Only Know the Road by Travelling Along It

But, all the same, how does one find the strength? How do you work out which direction to go in. You can start by getting hold of the 'Books That Heal' as they become available in English. For details, contact the Creation Publishing website on www.creationpublishing.co.uk In them, you will find the answers to all your questions. Dr Konovalov is continuing to work on his books, and we can expect many more stunning revelations and insights from them. Together, the energizing exercises, the leaflet and the link-up sessions will become your trusty sword as you fight against disease. The new knowledge you gain in the realms of the energy-information teaching will also be your protection along the path to spiritual harmony – both personal and in the world as a whole. Dr Konovalov's books do not allow us to stop or to stumble. They support us in times of need, they prompt us to keep going and give us hope. They soothe away pain and fill our hearts with love. So set out bravely on your path and remember: 'You can only know the road by travelling along it.'

# CHAPTER 38

# LEARNING TO RESPOND TO THE ENERGY

## The Genius of Communicating with the Energy of Creation

'*Genius of any kind,*' explains Sergey Sergeevich, '*whether it be that of a poet, an artist, a musician or a scientist, is always linked to the penetration of the energy into the information field and the living universe. That which creates genius already exists in the universe, and by coming into contact with the energy the man or woman of genius is merely reproducing it.*'

This book contains many things: it brings news of how to find a priceless way of returning to full health; it tells the story of a unique doctor, who heals patients with the help of the energy of creation. But it is also a means of preparing the reader to be receptive to the information emanating from the living universe, which is channelled through the doctor. Readers need to have followed this path with the doctor, in order to become familiar with the results of his healing methods and in order to comprehend the global significance of what is being opened up to them. They need also to become fully acquainted with the doctor's theories on health and disease, learn how the sensitive body is constructed and take in a whole mass of information that has been opened up to Dr Konovalov by the living universe.

Sergey Sergeevich has been in contact with the energy of creation and with the living universe for many years now. And, as you'll realize, this contact has been developing and changing over the years and now takes place rather differently than it did at first. A mutual trust has grown up; the doctor's knowledge is increasing all the time as more and more new information comes to him.

## We Are All Touched by the Energy of Creation

Today, Dr Konovalov is convinced that every one of us on earth is in contact with the energy. It is a living substance of the universe; it makes itself known to each and every one of us and ascertains how receptive we are to it. Of course, in millions of cases it simply bounces back, finding no point of contact and can only start entering a person when they are open to receive it. It then passes on to them its knowledge; it makes them sensitive to the fact that something is happening to them. In real life, this corresponds with a person's search for and discovery of a path in life. And as soon as that person has found their path, when the contact with the energy is established, even if it is weak, the most important thing is for them to preserve their purity of thought and integrity as they make their way along it. Contact with the energy is a means of selecting someone to accomplish specific objectives. Why have you been chosen? What is it you must do? Giving yourself up completely to it and being entirely honest will bring about rapprochement and an intimate knowledge of the living substance of the universe, at which point you will enter into a dialogue with it.

Sergey Sergeevich has already followed the long path of initiation and can confirm that following this path brings us to an extremely significant moment, when the energy of creation will begin to communicate with our very own thoughts. This won't happen straight away, but in the course of several weeks or months. And it will only happen when the contact has become stable and we are able to listen and understand that these thoughts and knowledge are not our own, for we did not have them before: they have been placed there by the universe.

## The Doctor's Teaching Continues

Sergey Sergeevich can summon up the energy and direct it. This is the culmination of mutual trust, but he knows that even from this height there is another even higher and unknown one to be reached, a height that is as yet unattainable. Knowledge becomes more profound as experience grows. The doctor can now take patients' pain away at the very beginning of treatment. He didn't do this before because he didn't have the ability, didn't know how to do it. He now uses music to take pain away. When he appears on stage in the hall, his fingers barely touch the keyboard and already somebody's pain has gone; somebody else now finds it easier to breathe or carry on with their life. In the past he couldn't make organs go back into their correct position, but now, in the course of a single healing session – i.e. two hours – this happens to hundreds of patients.

Previously, when starting out on his journey, Sergey Sergeevich had a sense of the energy as an enormous weight, as almost a physical pressure on him. This was how it made itself known to him. The pressure was unbearable, uncontrollable and even unpleasant at times, for the energy had no idea of the force it was exerting on him. Now, the doctor has learnt how to tolerate this pressure when it comes to him. Its arrival always signals that the moment of contact has arrived, only nowadays that contact is at the level of his thought processes.

There was a time in Dr Konovalov's life when the energy came to him with a different objective. In 1995, he and his wife were travelling from St Petersburg to the Ukraine by car. It was the same quiet road they always travelled. But as they were approaching Vitebsk, they suddenly felt as though they were being accompanied by the energy. Antonina Konstantinovna was surprised and said to her husband: 'We're so far from home and travelling so fast and yet it has caught up and overtaken us.' Nothing like this had ever happened before.

The further on they travelled, the more aware they became of the energy's pressure, and the stronger it became. The Konovalovs sensed that something strange was happening but they couldn't understand why they were being accompanied in this unexpected way. The closer they got to the outskirts of the city the stronger the pressure from the energy became.

The road continued to fly past when at some point Sergey Sergeevich began to overtake a van with a trailer. Then suddenly when his car was alongside the van and the trailer, the van unexpectedly and without signalling started turning to the left, onto a country road (in Russia they drive on the right). Travelling at a speed of 80 miles an hour the fast-moving car was on the brink of crashing into the van. Sergey Sergeevich was no longer in control of the situation, the steering wheel was wrenched from his hands; there was absolutely nothing he could do. At that precise moment, death seemed inevitable, inescapable.

And then something amazing happened. The energy, which had so relentlessly been accompanying them for the last few miles, lifted the car off the road, increasing its speed in a flash to 110 miles an hour, and somehow 'yanked' the car forward, leaving the van far behind on the road. The momentum carried the car forward for another 300 yards and then it came to a stop at the side of the road. It took several minutes before the Konovalovs were able to grasp that something incredible, if not impossible, had happened: they were alive and unharmed. After they'd got over the initial shock, Antonina Konstantinovna, overcome by a great wave of emotion, could only manage to say to her husband: 'God really must want us to live.' They were both so overwhelmed by the unexpected intervention of the energy in their fate that they were frozen to their seats. They thanked it for saving them. Soon after, some people drove by who had seen what had happened and they were clutching at their heads in amazement, their eyes as wide as saucers. As for the driver of the lorry – he just stood there by his vehicle for a long time, as though transfixed.

## Everybody Has the Chance to Get Well

I once asked Sergey Sergeevich whether there was anything that could possibly force him away from the path he had chosen, to which he replied: 'Well, of course, if some catastrophe happened to the planet, if our entire civilization were wiped out ...' And this is why the doctor's path, the eternal path to knowledge, continues and why you and I have a chance to share in this unique knowledge given to him by the living universe. This book contains not only good news but also a programme that gives man not just the hope of recovery but also the possibility of doing so quickly. Take care of this book; read and re-read it from time to time, and always carry it with you. If after a while you notice that some of your physical problems have disappeared or something that the doctors have diagnosed has got better, then do please tell the doctor about it. You can do so by contacting Creation Publishing at info@creationpublishing.co.uk or writing to: PO Box 43291, London E14 3XP, UK.

In conclusion, I want to remind you about your encounter with this extraordinary doctor on the pages of this book. He not only gives us the gift of health, and heals our spiritual wounds, but he also compels us to take a closer look at ourselves, to search deep in our souls and listen for the voice of the living universe and learn how to heed its call. Dr Konovalov believes that all people are capable of going down this difficult path and that, if they make a strong enough commitment to following it, then they will reach its end.

'*If, my dear reader, you have accepted this book as bringing good news, then try to take part in our link-up healing sessions. This means that, at a designated hour by Moscow time, you can be one of millions of people on the planet who will be bathed in the creation energy directed by the person who has been initiated.*

*I have no doubt that the results will be unexpected for you; you will be amazed, for it will be as much a release from your illnesses as it will be an escape from many of life's problems.*

*Just remember that everything doesn't happen at once. For some people it takes a long time, perhaps even several years. But the main thing is to have faith, like so many of our precious patients have.*'

Let the final word come from this, most eloquent, of patient testimonials:

### From case history 1012029

'I'm attending my 7th treatment programme. ... Whilst filling in the questionnaire, I took a new look at the results of my treatment ... Out of 20 major complaints, 5 showed an improvement of 25 per cent, 7 of 50 per cent, 2 of 75 per cent, and 1 of 100 per cent. And this is not counting the overall improvement in my general state, my sleep, the working of my bowels, as well as fewer pains in my heart. The most important thing is that I've gained confidence in the trueness of the path and in my mental equilibrium, which is gradually getting back to normal. Sergey Sergeevich, during the time I've been coming to your sessions I've had to make my own way along the path towards spiritual renewal, towards an understanding of the meaning of existence for each of us, and especially myself. Before I met you I had thought and read and reflected a lot on things, horrified by this terrible spiritual desert which had, in reality, turned my life into a mechanical-biological existence based on the joyless fulfilment of everyday functions. ... My encounter with you made me consciously aware of the most important thing, and it once and for all gave definition to my relationship with the Orthodox faith. Here, in our temple, I feel the power of other people, all united by one spiritual goal. I feel that if the church is none other than a fellowship of people, of one spirit, and believing in Christ in all his limitless power and love for each of us, then it can do everything. No doubt it is precisely because of this that the church has played a part in the most tumultuous moments in history; it has stood firm despite the attempts of cult followers, themselves far from perfect, to defile and discredit it. In May I decided to be baptized. ... Amongst true believers there always have been and still are great people with universal, world-reaching ideas. And if I, and others like me, still can't completely understand them, then it's not because they aren't what they say they are, but because we are not yet up to their level. ...

The 10th treatment programme. ... I think I've begun to understand you, at least in part, in that the clinical symptoms of disease appear when the body's compensatory possibilities are exhausted. After that, the period of an illness when there are no visible symptoms and which can last for as long as it wants, finally comes to an end. For this reason, it's not unusual for the destruction of this chain of symptoms (the eradication of the illness's framework) to take very little time (perhaps only as long as it took to get established). The conclusion I draw from this is that one must have faith and wait.

... And now, despite the fact that my body is getting older (because I've lived so long), I am in actual fact feeling younger. ... I am surprised and delighted to see how you are changing your treatment methods, how you are constantly perfecting them and introducing new things, and I am under no illusions that these changes are easy. I well understand the significance of constantly having to move forward, without allowing oneself the chance to stop and rest. It's clear to me that there's a massive amount of effort behind all of this coming from you and possibly also your staff. I wonder where you get the strength for such a huge task over such a long period of time. By ordinary standards, this amount of exertion would wear anyone out. It strikes me that going through all this pain and suffering must drain us of our energy. And if that is so, then the position you are in, of not being able to take time out from this process because of your sense of moral duty, is both noble and terrible. Seeing you with such a workload evokes feelings of the deepest respect and love for you. I pray for your health and I am grateful to God for sending heroes like you into our world. ...

The 14th treatment programme. ... As I analyse the progress of my treatment over the past two years, I am coming to the conclusion that my path to recovery has been based on the combined influence of all the things I see, hear, do, think and feel. Much of this, of course, is down to the influence of the energy, but I'm sure that the healing of the soul plays an important part in this, as well as the turnaround in one's way of thinking, one's attitude to life and a change in one's behaviour. ...

It was no accident that I met you; it was meant to happen. I was given the chance to try and transform myself and make my own contribution to human evolution. Of course, this in itself will scarcely be noticed but, then again, I am not the only one setting out on this path.

Every one of us coming to your sessions does so, of course, in the hope of getting better. For many sick people you are the last chance. ... And it often turns out that for many people (and that includes me) healing the body is proving not to be enough. This is only a part, a small part, of course, but still just a part of what people need, and which they cannot find anywhere else but with you.

My thoughts are taking me back to the time of Christ. People listened, and they were amazed at his wisdom. His words had an effect on people's minds, but all the same very few were sincere in their belief. He worked miracles but, even though they gasped in awe, people later put them down to black magic. They demanded he be crucified and crucified he was, and it was only then that they realized that his life and death had been necessary, in order that people should gain insight, be spiritually renewed, and that people as destroyers should be transformed into people as creators (not for the sake of technology or the good of civilization, but as creators of harmony in all living things). It was probably already clear then that the human race was on the road to destruction. And this has become especially clear now.

I often think about life. Everything must have its end, just as we are born. And in this respect, even being treated by you is not an absolute – one person goes, another comes along, nothing is forever. But to receive the gift of a few more years of life, so that one might try to live one's life differently and even improve just a little the things that you thought you couldn't, to feel joy at the fullness of life – isn't that happiness? Why is it then that a healthy person is so often not satisfied with their life?

It's probably because the ability to understand happiness is closely linked to the well-being of the flesh, of the physical body (even if this relates to material things, one's home, and so on). But now we know that the flesh is only one of ten bodies, and though it is the most perfected part it's still only a tenth of our whole organism. I think that absolute happiness in principle only appears when all ten bodies have achieved a state of harmony that allows the task of evolutionary development and the perfection of the world to be fully accomplished.

It is for this reason that those of us who are poor in spirit subconsciously feel the need to break out of the circle of convention, of constraints and dogmas, and move to a new level of knowledge. And this is the reason why people who have recovered their health continue to come to our temple.'

*(In October 2001 condition stable. Continues on the path to knowledge.)*

# CHAPTER 39

# INSTEAD OF AN AFTERWORD:

## PATIENTS OWN TESTIMONIES

### How Lives Can Be Transformed

The remaining letters in this book provide powerful and moving accounts of the extent to which patients are prompted by Dr Konovalov's teachings to embark on their own personal voyage of self-discovery and spiritual renewal, a journey which often brings with it the acquisition of a whole new philosophy and a dramatic transformation in the way in which patients live their lives.

*From case history 1015869 (born 1951, a teacher in an institute of higher education)*
'I'm writing to you for the first time, even though I've been one of your followers for a long time. I've been searching for the right word. Who am I? – a "patient"? For some reason I don't want to put myself in the same category as people plagued by many physical problems. And anyway, for many of us, contact with you means considerably more than just getting rid of our ailments; using the word 'patient' means only a doctor's client. An "adherent"? – that's not enough! A "student"? – on the one hand, we are all students in this life, but on the other, do you really have students? A "comrade" or "companion-in-arms" sounds too militaristic though, of course, it's important that the word should contain the idea of the path and of movement. ... So let's say "member of the congregation".

My encounters with you are very much geared to my primary desire to join my wife in progressing along the path to health and happiness. Way back in 1995, I was looking for a way of getting her to see you. Then a short time later I heard you talk at the hall at the Lensovet [in St Petersburg].

My wife, who'd been following your recommendations, had never told me in detail what went on at healing sessions. However, in the end, I turned up at the Lensovet hall. Then we transferred to the Hall of Music and now, by my calculations, I'm on my 12th or 13th treatment programme.

When I'm at the sessions in the hall I nearly always feel good, contented, comfortable and interested in things. ... I use the word 'nearly' because it depends more than anything on the state of several ongoing psychological conditions on particular days. For the most part, these are now in the past, but I felt I ought to qualify things with 'nearly' in order to give an accurate picture.

When I first started coming to the hall, I considered myself to be healthy. And I still try to think that way. In any case, once, during the 10th treatment programme, you used the term 'healthy or almost healthy' about one group – and I've never doubted I was in this group.

Something drew me, attracted me (and continues to attract me) to the hall. ... About once a year or every 10 months, I get to the end of my 'energy potential' (let's call it that). The clinical picture is always the same: heaviness in the head and feelings of confusion; unpleasant sensations in the stomach and bowels; usually problems with my stools. My temperature generally goes up to 37°C and I need to get a good night's rest of 10–12 hours. In more extreme cases, my temperature goes up to 38–39°C and I have to stay in bed for 1–2 days. All I want to do is to sleep, sleep, sleep. I don't like the medicines (even though I sometimes have to take something against flu). I'm never sick for more than 2–3 days; the temperature goes down and everything gets back to normal. This was what it had always been like before I came to Doctor Konovalov.

Now about the healing sessions: as I say, I feel good, comfortable and at ease during them. I'm able to relax and concentrate on myself. I really value the chance to completely unwind. Sometimes I catnap or even go to sleep during the preliminary session. I really enjoy the active section and I'm often sorry when you change the routine and cut short the time for head rotation or stretching. As regards how I feel when carrying out the procedures and the diagnoses, I can't boast of feeling any heat or a great number of sensations. Granted, I've felt warmth around my kidneys during some programmes, when you've worked on raising or improving the internal organs. However, there have been some very interesting and discernable after-effects. The pain I had in my spine and spinal column (rheumatic pain and a sense of heaviness) "worked its way up" from the sacral region to the neck area during the 1997 programme: first it was low down, then it was up to my shoulder-blades, then on my shoulder-blades and, finally, in the area of my collar bone. Then the pain went away. This was an amazing result for me, especially since I've always tried to take care of the state of my spinal column. My shoulders stayed as flexible as usual. I've known for some time, when exercising, that one must try not to overload the spine. And then, suddenly, this happened!

It made me very happy and it was also interesting. Before that, I'd had what is called 'radiculitis', a condition which submariners suffer from, twice before in my life. I'd not been able to get out of bed and had rubbed it with 'Fenalgon' cream.

Now about something else. I know very well that you can't break life down and compartmentalize it into different subjects and categories. But, all the same, when it comes down to the most interesting thing – spiritual life – then I still try to pick out the characteristic features.

Having now gone through the so-called 'mid-life crisis', it strikes me that everything that's happened in my life was natural and had a reason, especially with regard to my family upbringing (and, later on, when I was a member of the collective) as well as the different stages of my life working for the state. All of these were part of the background, the external factors to my inner development.

It seems as though I've always had a tendency for self-awareness and self-analysis in my search to find answers to the questions: "Why do I think like this? Why am I doing this?" I've always been able to visualize things, in other words, play around in my head with different ways of behaving in order to get to the bottom of my own actual behaviour and the way I think (which is not always a pleasant thing for me).

I'm not even going to start talking about my early childhood. I think I was a normal, active and inquisitive child. I was always good-natured and never a tearaway or a bully; I didn't hurt anyone. Other children always got on with me and I loved romping around with them. I started showing leadership qualities and was always thinking up new games and taking charge of them. This leadership quality lasted throughout my school years. Our class, our group of students, was in fact rather an exceptional bunch. All the teachers said we were "an amazing class, wonderful kids". So there is such a thing as "the spirit of the collective".

Once I grew up and had taken a bite out of life, and adapted to different social groups, one of my colleagues said: "They didn't bring us up right; we didn't have this, we didn't have that…" We could all agree with this, but it wasn't something we'd seriously complain about. So, in the end, I grew up a normal enough chap, only I was a little strange too. As the medics say "I'm a variant of the norm". Only this particular variant doesn't come somewhere in the middle or on the outer limits of what's normal, but somewhere on the borderline.

You'll find it easy to understand, therefore, that I found it very hard to fit in at the military academy barracks. My comrades treated me in one of two ways: as a normal chap, but one who was a bit quirky – I didn't smoke, didn't drink (on principle. The only time I had any vodka was at my father's wake in 1976). I was a bit of a loner (again, not the right words! I was no more withdrawn than I was a loner – I was the Komsomol organizer and leader, and I had a nickname "the commissar").

It was during those years in particular that it became clear to me that, in certain situations, what I myself thought became far more important to me than what others thought about things (and me). My behaviour was determined by this and how I perceived myself. Later on I'd come to define it as "egocentricity". But although the dictionary defines egocentricity as a more extreme (and worse) form of egoism, I've given it my own, different definition. In my opinion, egoism means me, and only me – at the expense of others. Everything is always for me. The egoist sees everything in relation to himself. Egocentricity, as I see it, is the acknowledgement that I alone am responsible for my own world, the world in which I live and function.

So, for example, during that period of my life I held to an idealistic principle: the first girl I kiss will be my wife. I had a wonderful first love with my school sweetheart, with all its suffering, joy and anxiety. During my years at university, I really wanted, had a need, to go dancing and be among other girls. But, as things turned out, it was as though I had made a vow of loyalty to this principle of mine. It was there inside me and I couldn't live or act or conduct myself in any other way. With time it seemed that I'd need to "lower my standards". But I couldn't do it and, as a result, I earned for myself the one thing I hadn't dared to hope for: I found a wonderful girl, who became my beloved one, my friend and my wife. We celebrated our silver anniversary at the beginning of this month. ...

Throughout my life, the main thing, as far as I was concerned, was always the search for a foundation, the search for a system, the search for an idea, the search for a path. The "fresh wind of change" had great significance for me when I was abroad in the 1990s – things such as glasnost, in the sense of the greater availability of books, journals, and newspapers; the personality and spiritual journey of Andrey Sakharov [the Soviet physicist and Nobel Prize winner; ed.]; the great wealth of people and ideas ...

Now I know one thing for a fact: all the people and books that we so needed all came at exactly the right time. And my own life confirms this in so many ways. (Only how do I convince my daughter of this?) I'm not going to run off a great list of names. But it's obvious that one of the important events in my happy life has been my meeting with you, dear Sergey Sergeevich.

I'm sure you're already aware of what it is that most interests me during your healing sessions. It's not just the search for a foundation, the attempt to make out the contours of the system or figure out the different phases along the path. The things that most interest me today are the approach and methods you use in working with people in every part of the auditorium. I think I know that this is also part of the path to cognition although, once again, the prescribed meaning of words doesn't get to the real sense.

Being in communication with you is like being in an enormous field, or rather an undulating, overflowing ocean of possibilities:

- The universe, God, the Good Lord, the earth;
- The system of the celestial bodies and their interaction;
- Space, time, infinity;
- The organism as the principle of the organization of the cells (in contrast to something mechanical, for example).

... And then there's your music. I clearly remember the day and the hour when my "soul" finally opened up to a higher level of music. For many, many years now, music has been a rarefied experience for me, higher than any other form of art, or any means by which human beings or society express themselves, their aspirations and their understanding of things. Music seems greater even than language. And what is more, music is more accessible, that is, can be heard everywhere. I gain something interesting, joyful and fruitful from every one of these aspects of my contact with you, dear Sergey Sergeevich.

Am I having a discussion with you? Like as not, no. For in a discussion each person has to state their own point of view. But why? I am trying to feel things, to sound out your view.

The world is constructed quite differently from how we imagine it, and how we were taught about it. All our attempts to convey this, to explain things and get an overall idea of the world, turn out to be vehicles for our own personal or human powers of description. The wisdom of humanity, of its finest intellects, of those who have been initiated and called, has been gathered up in the treasure of such descriptions. But the path to cognition continues. It is unavoidable, it is man's destiny. Only human beings are endowed with reason – a higher form of consciousness that is made accessible to us by the spirit in all its many manifestations.

You, dear Sergey Sergeevich, the chosen doctor-healer, reveal to us what it is that each of us in essence is striving towards; you help us and give us strength whilst on this path. Allow me once more to sincerely rejoice at the fact that you are here, to thank you and all your works, and ask your permission to remain with you on the path of cognition, on the path to health and joy.'

*July 1999, St Petersburg*
*(According to physical observations made in October 2001, the patient's condition was normal)*

**From case history 1015742 (born July 1979)**
'I'm now on my 16th treatment programme.

My mum first brought me to you, when I was still at school. Now our treatment hall feels like home to me. I've always been struck, and still am, by how much warmth and understanding people show for each other here. When you look in the eyes of the person sitting next to you, or simply someone as they pass you by, you notice they are radiant with the joy of taking part in things. At times you can almost catch a little spark, a spark of something vast and incomprehensible. And in these moments you understand that the people who come here are heroes of a kind. They're heroes because, despite the difficult lives we live, they have held on to their faith – faith in themselves, the strength they have in their future. They love life and are ready to fight for it.

If you want to talk about my results, then as far as the physical problems are concerned: chronic allergic rhinitis has reduced by 80 per cent; tracheobronchitis with asthmatic syndrome has completely gone; the herpes hasn't yet gone completely, but appears less often; my stomach and digestive tract are working normally; the eczema went after the 3rd treatment programme, ... but, in any case, the major success has not been a physical but a spiritual one.

I hadn't even got through all of the first treatment programme (around eight sessions) when it seemed as though something clicked inside and turned me in a different direction. I even began to think differently. I started thinking more carefully about the things I did; I was less irritable and now I don't have a go at people for no particular reason.

Sergey Sergeevich, I'm treating people much better and I'm more patient. I take a look at the way people around me are behaving, and if they seem to be unhappy about something then I wonder whether maybe I have done something to provoke it. Whereas before, I'd just think this was the bad side of people's character and it was their problem.

Before I started coming to sessions, my relationship with my mum was far from ideal. We come to your sessions together now, doctor. It's as though we flow into one another and can understanding what is happening to each of us without saying a word. When we do have arguments, I ask myself: "We know why we are doing this. Then why do we do it?" And honestly, why do we do this? What point is there in winding ourselves up, our family and everybody around us?

Life gets so much easier, simpler, when there are no rows, swearing and endless going on about stupid things.

Dear doctor, thank you, thank you for being here, for being with us and helping us. In turn, we, your patients, will try to repay you with warmth, love and respect.'

*(In October 2001 still feeling well)*

*From case history 1013502 (born 1973)*
'It will soon be three years since the moment when I first crossed the threshold of our temple. At first I came for Dr Konovalov's healing sessions; now I just come for the sessions themselves, which are our sessions – a point of contact, instruction and finding oneself.

When I came to you, I thought at the time that it was with only one problem – chronic adnexitis, caused by severe inflammation of my ovaries.

I simply didn't give any thought to my other ailments, because I'd already got used to living with them and had become reconciled to the fact that they were chronic. They didn't hurt that much, so it was OK. It was only gradually, as I began to get some relief, that I began to understand that everyone in our temple is given the chance to gain their health in the full sense of the word; I'd already been lucky enough to get the chance to come to our sessions and I had to make full use of this unique chance. ...

I believe that, bit by bit, we will succeed in overcoming our remaining problems. Lately my faith that my body is capable of coping with disease has grown stronger. If before I relied totally on you, Sergey Sergeevich, and clutched at you like a drowning person does at a straw – worn out by insomnia as a result of extreme emotional agitation, when I had to write you notes begging for help, to which you always responded and never demanded a reply – then today, even if my sleep is bad again, I make an effort to calm myself. I try, as much as possible, to relax during the healing sessions and chase away bad thoughts and try and think about good, pleasant things. Then gradually my sleep once again gets a bit better. My self-confidence is awakening in me and in the strength of my body and I'm no longer afraid when there's a break between treatment programmes.

Sergey Sergeevich, you say that some patients look upon you as some kind of pill that will take the pain away and relieve their suffering. This is probably due, in part, to their own lack of confidence, both in themselves and in their body's potential. At first I thought "You will help me", but now I say to myself, "You and I together will help me."

When I first began the treatment programmes, I thought that gradually, on account of the influence of the energy of creation, my sensitive-body system would be restored, my cells would revive, my body's defence mechanisms would be activated, the pain would go, and sooner or later I would be completely well again. I didn't yet know that the road to health was not simply a matter of sitting comfortably in a chair, trying to concentrate, listening to the doctor's recommendations and soaking up the energy. I didn't even realize that I had now embarked on probably the most important path in my life just by coming to our sessions.

You have spoken to us, during sessions, about the necessity of working on our inner selves, about how it's impossible to be physically healthy without going through a spiritual transformation. Listening to you, the idea of the mutual interchange and influence existing between the body and mind kept coming into my mind. I first started thinking about the need to change my life and the way I think some time ago. I'd analyse my day-to-day behaviour, how I related to the people around me but, of course, this was all very much on the mental level. Was there something that I radically needed to change in myself? After all, I hadn't done anyone any harm, nor did I harbour unkind thoughts. But yet, I was always rushing around, getting wound up and irritable over trivial things. And when I got tired I'd shout and get angry with myself and with others because my life was bound up in so many worries and problems. I never even stopped to think that, susceptible and impressionable as I was, always craving something new and trying as hard as I could to get on in life, that this in itself was feeding my stress levels.

The realization that I needed to re-examine and change things in myself still didn't signify that I'd actually begun to change. To abandon a well-practised even if unsuitable lifestyle isn't easy, nor is it easy to change one's entrenched attitudes and convictions. Now I think, "Good God, I'm still only about 26. You'd think that a young woman of my age would be adaptable and open to change." But as it turned out, it isn't easy to reappraise the way you live and how you think, even at such a relatively young age.

If I'm not mistaken, some of your patients have written that, as they made their way along the path to transformation, they literally had to break and remake themselves. I haven't yet had to do this. Entering on the path of inner re-evaluation, as it seems to me now, came naturally, harmoniously, as part of our healing sessions. Little by little my attitudes towards people and the world around me began to change. An inner sense of harmony took root in me, the desire to do good. I gained insight into my relationships with those close to me. My way of thinking changed, as did my priorities, and, with them, the way I lived.

I wrote something to this effect on a questionnaire a year or so ago, when I wrote to you: "Doctor, I feel as though I've started on the path to transformation." Nevertheless, at the time, I was only just opening the door to the temple, as the first step on the path to the truth which I am now following . ...

Dear Sergey Sergeevich, whenever I think of my path to transformation I often recall what you said: "I don't understand why some patients never get well." A lot of things started from that. I'd look at you sitting there on the stage in your chair and I thought: "Lord, you give us all this strength to do both the possible and impossible in recovering, you give of yourself without rest, you've dedicated your life to the healing of our wounded spirits and our sick bodies!"

You literally beg us to look inside ourselves, you find new ways and words and music with which to get through to those of us who are deaf and blind. And I felt ashamed. Ashamed that I indulge myself in everything and that, once I've left the sessions, I plunge back into my habitual life and don't take care, don't conserve the energy that I've soaked up in the temple.

And then the desire to try and change myself was suddenly aroused in me, not for my own sake but for yours, in order not to disappoint you, so that I could justify your trust and the trust of the universe which had brought me to the temple, and so that I could become worthy of this honour.

My warmest thanks and respect for what you have done for me. It's something I could never have done for myself. ... You are an amazing person and I am happy that fate has given me the chance to find out about you.'

*20 July 1999, St Petersburg*
*(In October 2001 condition still good)*

### From case history 1011754 (born 1943)

'I'm attending my 29th treatment programme.

My diagnoses are: aortal insufficiency; stage 1 circulatory insufficiency; osteochondrosis of the neck and chest region of the spinal column; lymphodenopathy of the armpits; diffused fibroadenomatosis of the mammary glands; neuritis on the base of transverse flat-feet; deformed arthrosis in the joints of the hands and feet; dilation of varicose veins.

I've been coming to healing sessions for more than four years. I was very sick in body and soul when I first came to you and had a mass of unresolved problems and questions. I felt like an animal that had been hounded into a corner. The doctors, as one, insisted on an operation to replace the aortic valve. I had problems with my son, problems at work and with how I was going to feed the family at this difficult time. You have an excellent opportunity of comparing the questionnaires I filled in then and now. You'll see that the contents and the handwriting indicate the extent to which a person can change.

Everything is improving today: both people's health and their mental condition. And this has happened to me too. I owe much of this to you, of course, to the other people who attend your temple, and to the living energy which I sensed from the very first moment I entered it. It's true that no single healing session is like another. Sometimes I just can't relax or concentrate during the session. It's important, of course, to get to the hall a bit early, make yourself forget everything and let go of your problems.

Thank God that your books have come out. Reading them over and over again, you discover something new for yourself every time. How difficult it must have been for you to write these books, selecting from a huge intake of knowledge and information the things that were essential for our treatment and working out how best to help us understand it. In your books you not only cite examples of recovery, but also quote from patients' questionnaires. Many of the things patients say concur with my own thoughts. In short: you are constantly with each and every one of us, in sickness, in grief, in joy, and in all our problems – both the large and the small.

I long since noticed that the questionnaires do, of course, provide a way, a means of direct contact with you. But I've been making contact, talking with you and soliciting your advice for a long time now without using the questionnaire. If I feel something, then you listen to me. I get the answers to my questions and to my thoughts in the hall, during healing sessions, and also in my everyday life. And now there's yet another opportunity for discussing things with you – through the books.

What you write about the structure of the universe and man's place in it is very interesting to me and it makes sense. As soon as I started reading things about myself I began to be aware of the union of man with the universe.

Thank you so much for your books and your beautiful music. Over the last four years, no two healing sessions have been the same. I miss them terribly during the break between treatment programmes and return to the hall each time with great hope and joy. ...

Four years of treatment have passed by. I've become much calmer. I think about the past with sadness but resignation. God has not let me down and I am grateful to him. He has given me the chance to love. I have two wonderful children, and now an enchanting grandson. ...

My thanks to you and to the energy of creation for our physical and spiritual renewal.'

*19 October 1999*

*From case history 1017690*
'My 13th treatment programme is coming to an end. In my heart I want to write only about what's good, because as things have turned out there's nothing bad. During my childhood I was lavished with love and have been ever since. So I've been lucky. I have a wonderful husband, a beautiful daughter and granddaughter, and a good son-in-law. All my illnesses are going away:

- I've lost 33 kilos [72 lbs; 5 stone]. I now weigh 70 kilos [154 lbs; 11 stone]. The veins on my legs have gone down, my head doesn't ache, I sleep through till morning, and for nearly a year I haven't taken any pills for high blood pressure or high blood sugar. Nothing hurts!
- In the morning I wake up and make time for myself. I do everything I've planned for the day with huge pleasure and take joy in every single minute of my life.
- My husband is gradually getting better. His bronchial asthma has gone. At work they were talking of sending him away to a sanatorium. He said to me: "How can I go if I'm well and nothing hurts any more?" You need to feel really well to say this. And this makes me very happy.
- My granddaughter calls me from another town and says: "I wasn't off sick once from school all last year, Gran." And I say to her: "Well done, you're doing everything just as Sergey Sergeevich says."

- A year ago, I took the books and leaflets to my older sister. She called me just recently and said that her niece had lost 19 kilos [41 lbs; 2 stone 9 lbs], her sister's husband had stopped drinking strong liquour and was doing everything around the house – he even had dinner ready when she got home from work – and that there wasn't a single dirty thing in the house – everything had been washed and ironed.

I live my life as a fairytale and try to do good to everyone. And all of this is because Sergey Sergeevich Konovalov, the kindest and wisest of men, came into my life – a Doctor with a capital D.

I kneel in gratitude before you. Thank you, on behalf of all of us.'

*11 April 2001, St Petersburg*

# GLOSSARY OF
# MEDICAL TERMS

*The following list of medical terms used by patients in their letters to Dr Konovalov is by no means exhaustive. The more commonly known medical complaints are not included here, the objective being to explain the less well known terminology with which the lay reader may not be familiar. In all cases, readers seeking more detailed, professional medical explanations of the terminology in this book are advised to consult a medical dictionary. It should be pointed out that in Russia it is normal practice to give patients their diagnoses using the correct medical terminology rather than the more commonly used terms by which conditions are known in the West.*

| | |
|---|---|
| adenoma | a benign tumour which can occasionally mutate and become cancerous. In women, a **fibroadenoma** commonly occurs in the uterus. |
| adnexitis | inflammation of the adnexa, the appendages or conjoined parts of the uterus, such as the uterine tubes and ovaries. |
| aetiology (etiology) | the cause or causes of a particular disease under clinical investigation. |
| aneurysm (aneurism) | enlargement or 'ballooning out' of a portion of an artery or blood vessel caused by the weakening of its wall. The most common type of aneurysm occurs in the **aorta**. |
| aortic valve | the valve which controls the flow of blood in and out of the **aorta**, one of the body's major arteries, which carries oxygenated blood from the left ventricle of the heart to the rest of the body. |
| arrhythmia | a disturbance – either intermittent or continuous – to the electrical impulses controlling the normal rhythm of the heart beat. This condition causes shortness of breath and chest pain and in extreme cases can lead to heart attack. *See also* **tachycardia**. |
| arteriosclerosis | any of a number of conditions caused by the gradual hardening of arteries, which particularly afflict the elderly and which in turn affect the efficient flow of the blood along them. |
| arteritis | inflammation of the wall of an artery, caused by any of several factors, including a malfunction in the auto-immune system, an allergy, or a toxic response to certain chemicals. |

arthrosis
degenerative joint disease, a non-inflammatory form of arthritis.

astrocytoma
a tumour of the central nervous system, the cells of which are composed of astrocytes. Its most common form is in a primary brain tumour.

auto-immune thyroiditis
any of a variety of types of **thyroiditis**, an inflammation that occurs when a person's own antibodies attack the gland and cause **hypothyroidism**. The disease is particularly common in elderly women and can become chronic. It is also known as **Hashimoto's Disease**.

bicillin
the trademark name of a commercially produced form of penicillin.

bilateral fibroma
a benign tumour affecting opposite or symmetrical sides of an internal organ or a part of the body, commonly in fibromas of the breast.

bronchial asthma
a respiratory condition caused by the narrowing of the pulmonary bronchi, where the patient has difficult taking in air through the bronchial tubes which connect the windpipe to the lungs. This is often provoked by an allergic reaction to certain flower scents and pollen, pet hair, chemicals and so on.

calcinosis
any of a variety of conditions where calcium salts are deposited in tissue, muscle or some internal organs.

callus
a hardened area of skin or tissue, often found on the elbows, palms of the hands and soles of the feet, the fingers and toes and often caused by repeated friction or pressure. Its causes are often occupational.

calyx
a cup-shaped structure or cavity forming part of an organ, notably the kidney. Plural **calices**.

carotid stenosis
the narrowing of, or a blockage to, the carotid artery of the neck or its branches which supply blood to the brain. The condition is often linked to heart disease or diabetes. The restriction to the flow of blood that the condition causes, can provoke fainting and collapse; in elderly people it can bring on a stroke.

cholecystitis
inflammation of the gall bladder, usually caused by an infection (such as in cases of typhoid) or a stone blocking the cystic duct.

chondrosis
the formation of cartilaginous tissue in the spine and other joints. The condition, most commonly brought on by the aging process, is degenerative and manifests itself in the loss of elasticity in the tissues between joints and the discs of the spine. **Osteochondrosis** is another form of this condition.

coccyx
the triangular shaped group of fused vertebrae (back bones) located at the base of the spinal column.

colitis
inflammation of the lining of the colon of part of the large intestine.

colposcopy
an internal examination of the vagina and neck of the womb by means of a **colposcope**.

commissure
any band of tissue linking the two corresponding parts or sides of an organ, most commonly found in the central nervous system, such as between the two sides of the brain.

| | |
|---|---|
| cusp | a small triangular flap or fold forming part of a valve of the heart. |
| cystitis | a condition frequently affecting women, where the bladder becomes infected and inflamed, causing frequent and painful urination. |
| D & C | popular abbreviation for **dilation and curettage**. A surgical procedure whereby the cervix of the uterus is stretched or dilated in order to allow the **curettage** (scraping) of the lining of the uterus with a **curette** in order to gather tissue samples. The procedure is commonly used in the diagnosis and treatment of various gynaecological conditions affecting the uterus, such as heavy periods or post-menopausal vaginal bleeding. It is also used to terminate pregnancy in the early stages. |
| diffuse glomerulonephritis | a form of **nephritis**, where there is widespread inflammation of the **glomeruli** of the kidneys, which can become severe or chronic. |
| disbacteriosis | condition caused by disturbance to the natural balance of bacteria in the digestive system and intestines. It often occurs when a patient has been put on a course of powerful antibiotics. It can also be provoked by food poisoning. |
| disseminated encephalitis | a form of inflammation of the brain and or spinal chord, which often develops when a patient is recovering from an acute viral infection such as measles. In the past it was a complication that often occurred after vaccination against smallpox or rabies. |
| dropping | *see* **prolapse** |
| dystrophy | the progressive wasting of the muscles or tissues of the body which occurs in a number of medical conditions, notably muscular dystrophy, which is hereditary. |
| electrocardiogram *or* **ECG** (abbrev.) | an electronic instrument used to measure and record a patient's heartbeat, and commonly used in the diagnosis of a range of heart conditions. |
| encephalitis | any of several types of inflammation of the brain and/or the spinal cord, caused by either a viral or other infection, or the action of a parasite. |
| endarteritis | severe inflammation of the inside wall of an artery which constricts the flow of blood through it. The term **progressive endarteritis** is used to describe the condition when it is in an advanced or more severe state. |
| endometriosis | a condition where tissue from the **endometrium** or mucous membrane lining of the womb is found outside this area, particularly in the ovaries. |
| endometrium | *see* **endometriosis** |
| endoscopy | an internal medical examination of the hollow organs of the body, such as the stomach and bowel, by means of a long thin surgical instrument known as an **endoscope**. |
| enteritis | inflammation of the mucous membrane of the small intestine, which frequently causes diarrhoea. |

| | |
|---|---|
| enterocolitis | inflammation of the mucous membrane of the small intestine and colon, accompanied by excessive loss of fluid (such as in cases of cholera) and sometimes septicaemia. |
| extrasystole/~ia | a premature beat or contraction of the heart which interferes with normal cardiac rhythm. |
| exudative pleurisy | a form of pleurisy marked by the presence of fluid in the pleural space and the discharge of sputum. |
| fibroadenoma/~tosis | a benign tumour composed of fibrous tissue, typically found in the female breast. |
| fibroid | a benign, fibrous tumour. A form of **fibroma** or **myoma**, it occurs especially in women, often in the wall of the uterus. It can cause increased bleeding during menstruation and can severely affect fertility. If the fibroid becomes too large or painful this may necessitate a hysterectomy. |
| fibroma | a benign tumour composed of fibrous connective tissue, which on clinical examination may be found to be malignant. |
| fibromyoma | a fibrous or muscular form of the benign tumour known as a **myoma** which in women often occurs in the wall of the uterus. In cases of **leiomyoma** the tumour can become malignant. |
| fissure | a general medical term for a groove, fold or cleft in an organ of the body, usually the brain. |
| frontal cortex | the outer layer of the brain, located immediately behind the forehead. |
| gastritis | inflammation of the lining of the stomach causing pain which in severe cases can cause vomiting. |
| glaucoma | any of several degenerative diseases of the eye, characterized by opacity (clouding) of the lens of the eye, which is brought on by increasingly high pressure on it. Treatment is aimed at reducing the pressure by applying drops to the eye on a regular basis. But in acute and chronic cases, surgery may be necessary in order to relieve this by draining away some of the fluid in the eye. If the condition is not treated it causes progressive impairment of vision and can, in some cases, lead to total blindness. |
| glomerulonephritis | a form of **nephritis** characterized by inflammation of the **glomeruli** (internal tubes) of the kidney. |
| haemorrhoid ganglions | knots or masses of connective tissue or cystic swellings occurring in the interior veins of the anus and often causing them to protrude outside the sphincter muscle controlling it. |
| hydronephrosis | a cyst-like formation on the renal pelvis (the funnel shaped structure at the end of the ureter) or in the calices of the kidney caused by a blockage in the ureter which impedes urine flow. Pressure from the build up of this fluid can damage the kidney. |
| hypertension | a term for excessively high blood pressure. |
| hypothyroidism | a condition in which the thyroid gland produces less hormone than normal, resulting in a reduced rate of metabolism and in severe cases cretinism (if congenital) or myxoedema (if acquired). |

| | |
|---|---|
| iliac bone | a bone comprising part of the ilium, or uppermost bone of the pelvis. |
| induration | the abnormal hardening of soft tissue or an organ, caused by inflammation or as part of the aging process. In particular this occurs in the brain and spinal cord – leading to progressive paralysis, commonly in the form of **multiple sclerosis**. It also occurs in the lungs, liver and kidneys. The conditions **arteriosclerosis** and **sclerosis** are caused by indurations in the walls of the arteries. |
| infarct/~ion | the failure of an organ or the creation of an area of dead tissue caused by the cutting off of the blood supply to it by a blockage (embolus) or blood clot. The term **myocardial infarct/~ion** is used to describe the failure of an area of muscle in the heart caused by a blockage in an artery leading to the heart. |
| intercostal neuralgia | a sharp, intermittent pain occurring between the ribs. |
| ischemia (ischaemia) of the heart/ischemic | coronary heart disease, caused by the restriction of the blood supply to the heart. |
| isthmus (of the thyroid gland) | a narrow channel or band of tissue connecting two larger parts of an organ. |
| lesions | damage or change to the texture of the skin or an organ caused by an injury or disease. |
| leukocytosis | any of several conditions characterized by an increase in the number of white blood cells (leucocytes) in the body. The condition is usually accompanied by haemorrhage, fever and inflammation or infection of various parts of the body. |
| lumbar-sacral area | that area of the lower back between the ribcage and hips. |
| lymphadenitis | inflammation of the lymph glands or nodes caused by an infection elsewhere in the body. |
| lymphadenopathy | disease of the lymph nodes. |
| macular dystrophy *also known as* macular corneal dystrophy | a progressive degenerative condition of the cornea of the eye brought on by the presence in the eye of a **macula** – a spot or scar on the retina. |
| mastopathy/mastopatia | any of several diseased conditions of the breasts, predominantly in women. |
| mediastinum | a membranous area, dividing the two sides of an organ, notably the pleural tissue that separates the two sides of the lungs. |
| metastasis | the spread of diseased cells leading to the formation of secondary tumours away from the primary site of a disease, particularly cancer. |
| metatarsus | one of five long bones in the middle of the foot, above the toes. |
| mitral valve/ | a valve composed of two membranous flaps or **cusps** |
| mitral insufficiency | located between the left ventricle and the left atrium of the heart. **Insufficiency** occurs when the valve ceases to function correctly. |

| | |
|---|---|
| MRI scan | abbreviation for **magnetic resonance imaging**, a non-surgical, non-invasive technique for scanning the internal organs and tissues of the body, obtained by positioning the patient inside a body scanner containing an electro-magnet, which provides an image which can be viewed on a computer screen. |
| myocarditis | inflammation of the heart muscle. |
| myoma | a benign tumour made up of muscle tissue. A **leiomyoma** is a benign form, occurring in a smooth muscle, notably the uterus (see also **fibroid**). The leimomyoma can occasionally become malignant, as a **leimosarcoma**, occurring in the uterus as well as the stomach, bowel and bladder. |
| myopia | short-sightedness. |
| myositis | a degenerative disease involving inflammation of any of the voluntary muscles (i.e. those muscles controlled by the human will), of which **polymyositis** is the most common form. |
| myxoedema | a syndrome caused by under-activity of the thyroid in adults, involving mental slowness, intolerance of cold, coarsening of the skin, and other symptoms. Also, a firm wax-like subcutaneous swelling associated with this. |
| nasopharynx | the section of the palate located above and behind the soft palate of the mouth. |
| nephritis | inflammation of the kidneys. Also known as **Bright's Disease**. |
| nephroptosis | abnormal mobility of the kidney, usually caused by its displacement downwards, towards the pelvis. |
| neuralgia | the occurrence of intense, intermittent pain along a nerve pathway. |
| neuritis | inflammation of a nerve or several nerves resulting in impairment of the functioning of the area of the body affected. |
| neurodermitis | a skin condition, characterized by isolated scaly patches or lesions, caused by repeated rubbing or scratching of the neck, lower leg, face, hands and feet. It often accompanies cases of eczema. |
| non-toxic goitre | a swelling in the neck caused by enlargement of the thyroid gland, but not associated with hyperthyroidism and the production of excess hormones; the fluid produced is thus not infectious or poisonous. |
| nitro-glycerine | a viscous yellow liquid made from glycerol combined with nitric and sulphuric acids which is used in medicine to dilate the walls of the blood vessels when the flow of blood is constricted. |
| obstructive bronchitis | a general term for a form of bronchitis where the upper and/or lower bronchi or air passages to the lungs are chronically obstructed, causing the patient to have difficulty breathing. |
| optic nerve | a nerve running from the skull (cranium) to the retina at the back of the eye, along which the impulses controlling sight are transmitted to the brain. |

| | |
|---|---|
| osteochondrosis<br>*also known as*<br>osteochondritis | a painful degenerative disease of the spine and the joints, caused by inflammation of the bone and the deposition of bony tissue and/or fragments of bone in the joint. It often occurs in children, affecting the growth of cartilage in their joints. |
| osteoporosis | a condition of the bones, whereby they become brittle and break easily. It particularly affects the elderly and is sometimes triggered by hormonal changes in the body after the onset of the menopause. In rarer cases among young people it can be caused by bodily deficiencies in calcium and vitamin D. |
| pancreatitis | inflammation of the pancreas, the organ which supplies digestive enzymes to the gut and controls the release of insulin into the bloodstream. It can be brought on by poor diet, heavy drinking or the presence of gallstones. |
| papilloma | a benign, wart-like growth or tumour, often caused by a virus, which most commonly occurs on the skin – of the face, breast and genital organs – inside the nose, and on the larynx and bladder. |
| paradontosis<br>(periodontosis) | inflammation and recession of the tissue surrounding a tooth which results in it becoming loose and even falling out. Although it often occurs in children and young adults, the condition can become severe and progressive in adults. |
| pericardium | the membranous sac which surrounds and protects the heart. |
| pituitary adenoma | an **adenoma** found in the pituitary gland at the base of the brain which secretes essential hormones into the body. |
| pleurisy | inflammation of the pleura or membranes that enclose the lungs, accompanied by fever and pain when breathing or coughing. **Exudative pleurisy** is a form of pleurisy accompanied by the coughing up of sputum. |
| polyp | a growth located in the mucous membrane of a body surface and which protrudes outwards. These are most commonly found inside the nose, the mouth, the stomach, intestines and cervix. |
| prolapse | the dropping or downward displacement of an internal organ, most commonly of the womb or rectum. |
| prolymphocytic lymphoma | a cancerous condition affecting the lymph nodes and/or lymphoid tissue, caused by the presence of a malignant tumour. **Hodgkin's Disease** is a form of lymphoma. **Lymphocytic** and **prolymphocytic** lymphomas are much rarer, and are forms of leukaemia. |
| prostate | in men, the gland surround the neck of the bladder and urethra which releases one of the constituent fluids of semen. |
| pseudotuberculosis | a general term for any of several diseases of the lungs that mimic the symptoms of tuberculosis, but which are caused by micro-organisms rather than the tubercle bacillus. |
| pyelonephritis | inflammation of the kidney and the renal pelvis– the funnel shaped structure located at the end of the ureter – caused by a bacterial infection. |

radiculalgia — an ache or pain in the spinal root of a nerve. *See also* **radiculitis**.

radiculitis — inflammation of one or more nerve roots, especially those located in the back between the spinal chord and the intravertebral canal.

reactive arthritis — a form of arthritis triggered in patients already suffering from rheumatism.

renal insufficiency — failure or dysfunction of the kidneys leading to problems in the production and excretion of urine.

rheumathoid polyarthritis — a symmetrical form of inflammation of several joints, usually resembling the symptoms of rheumatism.

rhinitis — inflammation of the inner mucous membrane of the nose, which can be caused by hay fever or the common cold.

scoliosis — abnormal, lateral curvature of the spine. The condition is often congenital but can also be caused by severe injury to or disease of the vertebrae.

seborrhoea — a malfunction of the sebaceous glands causing the excessive release of the oily substance, sebum which lubricates the skin and scalp.

spastic colitis — inflammation of the colon characterized by spasms of pain and diarrhoea, more commonly known as **Irritable Bowel Syndrome**.

spirogram — a graph showing the record of breathing movements that have been recorded by a **spirograph**.

spurs — bony projections or protrusions on the **calcaneus** or heel bone, which cause pain when walking.

stenocardia / stenocardic pain *also known as* angina pectoris — any of a variety of diseases or conditions caused by contraction and pain in the chest and arms, brought on by the narrowing of the arteries in coronary disease. More commonly known as **angina pectoris**, the condition can be exacerbated by physical exertion, anxiety or stress.

stomatitis — inflammation of the mucous membranes inside the mouth.

streptococcal infection — in infection caused by the *Streptococcus* bacterium, frequently affecting the throat and lungs, notably in diseases such as pneumonia and scarlet fever.

subclavian nodes of the mediastinum — a bulge or swelling in the lymph nodes located under the collarbone (or clavicle), which serve the mediastinum. *See also* **mediastinum**.

syringomyelia — a progressive disease affecting the central spinal cord, whereby fluid collects in cavities, mainly in the cervical region of the cord, causing the weakening and wasting away of the arms and/or legs and with it the loss of sensitivity to pain, heat and cold.

systemic disease — a disease affecting the whole body rather than a particular organ or area.

systemic vasculitis — *see* **Takayasu's Disease**

| | |
|---|---|
| systolic form | with reference to the heart rate, the regular contraction of the heart, usually at intervals of 0.3 seconds, as blood is pumped around the arteries. In cases of **arrhythmia** the systolic contractions become irregular. |
| tachycardia | a form of **arrhythmia** causing an abnormally rapid heart rate, usually over 100 beats per minute. |
| Takayasu's Disease | a form of **arteritis** (inflammation of the arteries), also known as **systemic vasculitis**, this progressive disease is characterized by the formation of granulation or lesions in the arteries, especially the aorta, leading to the loss of a pulse in both arms. |
| tracheitis | inflammation of the trachea, the cartilaginous tube or windpipe which during breathing conveys air down through the larynx into the lungs. |
| tracheobronchitis | an infectious or viral chest condition characterized by inflammation of the bronchi and trachea. |
| trachoma | painful and highly contagious inflammation of the cornea and conjunctiva of the eye which is caused by the virus *Chlamydia trachomatis*. |
| tricuspid valve | a valve of the heart comprised of three triangular sections or cusps. |
| tuberculous aetiology | the diagnosis of a disease, caused by the bacillus *Mycobacterium tuberculosis*, bearing the characteristics of tuberculosis. |
| umbilical hernia | protrusion of the wall of the abdomen located at the site of the umbilicus or navel. |
| urographic examination | the radiographic examination of the urinary tract using an opaque fluid, injected intravenously, which is later excreted in the urine. |
| vagus | one of ten pairs of nerves in the cranium or skull, which supply the heart, lungs and viscera. |
| vascular dystonia | an abnormality or disorder affecting the muscle tone of the blood vessels which causes extreme tiredness and weakness in the sufferer. |
| vasomotor rhinitis/ ~rhino-sinusitis | a severe form of rhinitis, where the membrane of the nose becomes thickened and secretes an excess of fluid. |
| vesicular breath/~ing | the intake of breath through the pulmonary vesicles of the lung. |
| yeast colpitis | a common condition in women, characterized by inflammation of the bladder, and a sensation of soreness or burning in the vagina. Also known as **vaginitis**, the condition is caused by a yeast-like viral infection and arises when the delicate balance of micro organisms and hormones (particularly oestrogen) in the vagina is disturbed. |